# HABSBURG PERU

# Liverpool Latin American Studies

Liverpool Latin American Studies, New Series 2

# Habsburg Peru
## *Images, Imagination and Memory*

Peter T. Bradley
and
David Cahill

LIVERPOOL UNIVERSITY PRESS

First published 2000 by
LIVERPOOL UNIVERSITY PRESS
4 Cambridge Street
Liverpool, L69 7ZU

*British Library Cataloguing-in-Publication Data*
A British Library CIP record is available

ISBN 0-85323-914-2 *paper*

Typeset by Carnegie Publishing, Chatsworth Rd, Lancaster
Printed and bound in the European Union by
Bell and Bain Ltd, Glasgow

# For John Fisher,
# whose idea it was

# Contents

# Preface

The reception of the 'discovery', conquest and colonisation of Spanish America spawned a rich imaginative literature, in which prosaic blow-by-blow accounts of particular campaigns by chroniclers of the Indies and official 'press releases' were mixed with the fanciful reports of real and imaginary travellers, both of Iberian and northern European origin. More than this, however, from the first words of Columbus the supposedly factual reporting of the 'new' would stretch beyond the bounds of tolerance even the imagination of Europeans familiar with illustrations and representations from the sort of imaginative Early Modern bestiary to be seen in the canvases of Hieronymus Bosch and his contemporaries, or bred on myths of unparalleled wealth, the travels of Marco Polo, and novels of chivalry whose authors' imagination rendered plausible seemingly impossible events. Each would find their complement, if not their rival in marvel and monstrosity, within the environment of the New World. Foremost among the 'new' novelists of the late twentieth century, Gabriel García Márquez has often exploited the sometimes unfathomable dilemma of those interpreters of Spanish America baffled by its seemingly boundless reality. As a writer, he comments that 'mi problema más importante era destruir la línea de demarcación que separa lo que parece real de lo que parece fantástico, porque en el mundo que trataba de evocar, esa barrera no existía'.[1] Although in his case it is deliberate rather than accidental, it is hardly surprising that he should add, 'no hay autores menos creíbles y al mismo tiempo apegados a la realidad que los cronistas de Indias, porque el problema con que tuvieron que luchar era el de hacer creíble una realidad que iba más lejos que la imaginación'.

Making sense of the literature and its transmission – whether geographical and historical treatises, tall tales, travellers' journals, or surviving ephemera representing both the intellectual world and its more shadowy literary 'underworld' – is a complex question. In part it represents one indication of the multiple ways in which the Americas fructified the European imagination(s), the intellectual counterpart of the manifold transfer of flora, fauna and epidemiology known generically as the 'Columbian

---

[1] Cited in José Domingo, 'Entrevistas. Gabriel García Márquez', *Insula*, 259 (1968), p. 6.

Exchange'.[2] This transfer of ideas and knowledge systems was also reciprocal, and abiding, in that conquest of the New World inaugurated a contest for cultural space that is still working itself out. European reception of the reported marvels of the Americas is not merely a matter of antiquarian interest, however, for the imaginative 'spin' placed on such reports by European writers ineluctably influenced later writers, up to and including our own times, for instance the eighteenth-century vogue for narratives of travel both actual and imagined. These (in this case English) writings were consulted by Robertson, Prescott and their ilk, who provided those 'grand narratives' whose traces are sometimes still detectable in the modern historiography on Latin America.[3] This was the English counterpart of the ways in which Spanish chronicles materially affect all works on colonial Spanish American history, their tropes, *topoi*, prejudices and overarching classical paradigm quite as much as their factual and descriptive content. However, European imagination – in the case of the British, mainly 'arm-chair' imagination – met something other than its mirror image in the case of Native American imaginations, not least because the latter comprised rather more than just the responses of the subjugated to the conquering culture. Their 'known world'[4] had suddenly expanded prodigiously, and they scrambled to make sense of this new starburst of knowledge and quite where and how they might fit into it. The process of encounter was not only adaptive but creative. The autochthonous response rarely failed to modify in form or content that which was culturally transmitted: 'whatever is received is received according to the manner of the receiver'.[5]

[2] The term coined by Alfred W. Crosby, *The Columbian Exchange. Biological and Cultural Consequences of 1492* (Westport, Conn.: Greenwood Press, 1972).

[3] The concept of 'grand narrative' or 'metanarrative' or 'meganarrative' refers to Lyotard's concept of *grands récits*: see Jean-François Lyotard, *The Postmodern Condition: A Report on Knowledge* (trans. G. Bennington and B. Massumi, Manchester: Manchester UP, 1988 [1979]). There is obviously some correspondence between Lyotard's concept and Hayden White's study of historical narrative by way of rhetoric: see White, *Metahistory: The Historical Imagination in Nineteenth-Century Europe* (Baltimore: Johns Hopkins UP, 1973). White's approach to historical texts has come under considerable fire in recent years, criticism distilled in Richard Evans, *In Defence of History* (London: Granta, 1997), passim; note Evans' comment (p. 264, n. 43) that White's work subsequent to 1973 'contains almost no references at all to history as it has been researched and written in the twentieth century'! With regard to Lyotard's 'death of the metanarrative', Terry Eagleton, *The Illusions of Postmodernism* (Oxford: Blackwell, 1996), p. 34, notes Peter Osborne's mordant remark that 'the narrative of the death of metanarrative is itself grander than most of the narratives it would consign to oblivion'.

[4] The allusion is to the classical notion of the *oikoumene* or *oecumene*, meaning the known or inhabited world as seen from the perspective of a particular civilisation.

[5] Peter Burke, *Varieties of Cultural History* (Cambridge and Oxford: Polity Press, 1997), p. 196, in dealing with 'reception theorists' such as Michel de Certeau, translates thus the logical position of medieval scholastic philosophers ('Quidquid recipitur, ad modum recipientis recipitur'): *plus ça change!*

Imagination is of the essence of historical studies. Whatever approach a historian takes in addressing the past involves an act of imagining. More recently, historians have drawn on another and more problematic sort of 'imagining' which derives from French post-structuralism, associated above all with the names of Jacques Lacan and Julia Kristeva. It should also be seen as partly a response to Foucault's criticism of historians' supposedly impoverished idea of the 'real'.[6] However, the gap between that construction and the use which historians have made of it is so radical as to be more of a cannibalisation than a borrowing. Historians have stripped it of much of its original context as well as content. For example, in its original Lacanian formulation, the 'imaginary' forms part of an interlocking triad with the 'real' and 'the symbolic order'; historians have kept the 'real' and the 'imaginary' but severed the (supposedly symbiotic) 'symbolic order'.[7] One necessary distinction continues to be made, however, and that is the distinction and distance between the 'real' and 'reality', the latter being the interpretation which individuals and groups make of the 'real'.[8] These seemingly innocuous terms, then, come charged with a philosophical context rarely obvious in their application to concrete historical situations. It has been argued that, extricated from its jargon and tortuous syntax, this type of imagining (*l'imaginaire*) can be seen as contributing to the

---

[6] Ibid., p. 197, noting that the study of the 'collective imagination' is largely either an offshoot or an integral part of *Annalistes'* long-standing interest in the history of (collective) mentalities.

[7] On Lacan, see in particular Malcolm Bowie, *Lacan* (London: Fontana, 1991), pp. 88–120, who refers (p. 102) to Lacan's 'ability to invent the concept [of the "Real"] from moment to moment', while also noting (p. 109) that at one point 'the always uneasy relationships between Symbolic, Imaginary and Real reach a point of grotesque incoherence' – caveat emptor. See also Toril Moi, *Sexual/Textual Politics: Feminist Literary Theory* (New York and London: Routledge, 1985), pp. 99–101; Raman Selden and Peter Widdowson, *A Reader's Guide to Contemporary Literary Theory* (3rd edn, London: Harvester, 1993), pp. 139–140. Lacan's psychoanalytical notion of the imaginary is explicitly renounced by Cornelius Castoriadis, *The Imaginary Institution of Society* (Cambridge and Oxford: Polity Press, 1987 [1975]), pp. 117–119, who elaborates his own 'social imaginary', which 'is not an *image* of [something]. It is unceasing and essentially undetermined (social-historical and physical) creation of figures/forms/images ...'. See also Castoriadis, *World in Fragments: Writings on Politics, Society, Psychoanalysis, and the Imagination* (Stanford: Stanford UP, 1997). Peter Burke, *History and Social Theory* (Cambridge and Oxford, Polity Press, 1992), p. 120, mentions also the influence of Foucault, Althusser and Godelier in relation to the concept of *l'imaginaire*.

[8] The term appears to have been introduced into Latin American historiography by Serge Gruzinski, *La colonisation de l'imaginaire: Sociétés indigènes et occidentalisation dans le Mexique espagnol, XVIe – XVIIIe siècle* (Paris: Gallimard, 1988), translated into English as *The Conquest of Mexico: The Incorporation of Indian Societies into the Western World, 16th–18th Centuries* (trans. Eileen Corrigan, Cambridge and Oxford: Polity Press, 1993). He does not explain the extent to which his use of the concept depends on that of Lacan, Kristeva, Castoriadis and others, save for remarking (n. 1 of introduction) a distinction between 'real' and 'reality': 'Reality is the way we perceive and interpret the real. Each group, each culture produces its own reality through contact with the real'.

historical outcomes of any given society quite as much as ideas or actions, wars or great statesmen. The 'imaginary' is thus not just a mirror-image of the 'real'. The 'real' includes the reality of what is being imagined and is correspondingly partly shaped by it. Here, then, we find ourselves in the familiar territory of the relationship of ideas to historical events and processes, though this notion of ideas is now amplified to include wider, less formal perspectives. It seems remarkably close to the *Annales* concept of 'mentalities', though perhaps more dynamic and creative than the kind of group world-view implied by this term. Insofar as this 'imagining' affects the historical formation of a society, it probably occurs at several removes and in unexpected, creative ways. It is protean, in that the imaginings of groups and individuals react with those of others, mutually enriching each in the process; and thereby creating new *imaginaires*. And what is imagined affects the course of history quite as much as actions; the two are thus inseparable in historical causation. English writings about Peru, of diverse origin, shape and guide the aspirations of many generations of those who unquestionably founded their materialistic proposals for plunder, commerce and settlement upon such literature.

In its original formulation, there was a close connexion between utopian projects and the imaginary.[9] The imaginary dissolves or 'homogenises' the contradictions and differences inherent in society.[10] While ostensibly passive, it implies a sharp critique of the prevailing social order combined with the creation of alternatives to that order. In times of accelerated change and (often related) social and cultural crisis, it can provide the ideological seedbed for rebellion or revolution. The generic class of radical political uprisings known as revitalisation movements derive much of their potency from their imaginary dimension.[11] In a colonial society under the stress of fast-moving change, the realms of memory and the imaginary often coincide, such that a return to, or revivification of, a supposed Golden Age can form the core of an alternative ideology.

Writing the history of such imaginings, however, is far from easy. Sources are not lacking, but memoirs, oral and judicial testimonies, literature, travel accounts and philosophies take us only part of the way. As the eighteenth-century wore on, the public sphere expanded and evolved, such that non-elite groups increasingly participated in civic and religious festive occasions. Somewhat more novel was the increasing presence in this am-

---

9 This appears innate to the studies on 'utopía andina' by Alberto Flores Galindo, *Buscando un inca: Identidad y utopía en los Andes* (Lima: Instituto de Apoyo Agrario, 1987), and Manuel Burga, *Nacimiento de una utopía: Muerte y resurrección de los incas* (Lima: Instituto de Apoyo Agrario, 1988). It is perhaps relevant that both Flores Galindo and Burga undertook their postgraduate studies in Paris.

10 Moi, op. cit., p. 122, who refers to 'the homogenising space of the Imaginary'.

11 See, e.g., Anthony Wallace, 'Revitalisation Movements', *American Anthropologist*, vol. 58, 1956, pp. 264–281; Michael Adas, *Prophets of Rebellion: Millenarian Protest Movements against the European Colonial Order* (Cambridge: Cambridge UP, 1987 [1979]).

plified public sphere of new outlets for the expression of public opinion, which had hitherto not existed in the modern sense of the term.[12] The plazas of Europe were now full, a phenomenon reproduced in Spanish America, which in any case already had a tradition of ceremonial public space, as early-contact reports of the teeming plazas of Tenochtitlan and Cuzco attest. This transformed public sphere was political, a separate critical realm unconnected with Church or State. Such public forums provided virtual theatres for the public display of individual and group *imaginaires*, on the one hand, and increasingly less marginal spaces in which critiques of the status quo were relatively unchecked – 'the sphere of private persons come together as a public'.[13] As we shall see in England, the theatre proper at times could gather and express widespread public conceptions, whilst promoting rowdy debate of opinions that reflected popular sentiment, especially when allied to patriotic motives. We have abundant evidence in the form of written accounts or iconological representations of popular and elite cultures and religions, but equivalent data for the emerging critical opinion of the taverns, coffee-houses and salons of the time is usually fragmentary. This is above all true where it concerns non-European peoples, whence the traces are customarily refracted through colonial lenses. Even in those cases for which abundant sources are at hand, approaching past imaginings is an exercise fraught by uncertainty and confusion, partly a reflection of the quality of the sources. In seeking to recover past *imaginaires*, the historian looks through a glass, darkly indeed.

The two case studies presented herein represent two distinct types of imagining by two diametrically different groups: literate, and in some cases erudite Europeans, and a vanquished native nobility. The former endeavoured to make sense of Spain's (and Portugal's) 'marvellous possessions'[14] in the New World with the limited conceptual tools at their disposal, the latter to construct a colonial identity based on their shared ancestral memory while incorporating elements from the even more wondrous Hispanic culture that had overwhelmed them. To some degree, of course, these inquisitive Britons and remnant Incas were attempting to imagine each other, the former 'orientalising' the latter, who in turn 'occidentalised' Europeans, British as well as Spanish.[15] There were, of

---

[12] The concept derives from Jürgen Habermas, *The Structural Transformation of the Public Sphere: An Enquiry into a Category of Bourgeois Society* (trans. Thomas Burger and Frederick Lawrence, Cambridge and Oxford: Polity Press, 1989 [1978]). There is a brief but excellent discussion of it in Roger Chartier, *The Cultural Origins of the French Revolution* (trans. Lydia G. Cochrane, Durham and London: Duke UP, 1991), pp. 20–37.

[13] Chartier, p. 20, quoting Habermas.

[14] The phrase is taken from Stephen Greenblatt, *Marvelous Possessions: The Wonder of the New World* (Oxford: Clarendon Press, 1991).

[15] The reference is to Edward Said, *Orientalism: Western Conceptions of the Orient* (London: Routledge and Keegan Paul, 1978). Said, and those who follow his line, appears significantly to underestimate the degree of the contrary current of prejudice and incomprehension, of the often bizarre views of the Western Other held by their non-Western homologues.

course, multiple misunderstandings and misinterpretations. Yet for the Spanish such distortions were a matter of government and religion, rectifiable in the fullness of time, whether by evangelisation or the relentless application of civil and canon law. For British and other dispassionate European observers, the expressed views of conquerors and conquered, and the gulf of understanding that separated them, in some cases further transfigured by the no less fertile stimulus of their own direct observation, were all grist to the mill of their imagination. By contrast, the remnant Inca nobility could not wait. It was urgent, to their very survival as a group, that they convince the crown both of their 'nobleness' and of their utility to the colonial regime then in process of construction. The conquest *ipso facto* had rendered them an anachronism. No longer attached to the state power that had been their lifeblood and their raison d'être, they sought to recover those traces of their erstwhile political, social and ritual roles that might be parlayed into a share in the operation of the colonial system. In doing so, they appropriated parts of Spanish culture that were useful to, indeed necessary for, securing official acceptance of their pretensions.

Peter T. Bradley
University of Newcastle upon Tyne

David Cahill
University of New South Wales

PART I

*Peru in English:*
*The Early History of the*
*English Fascination with Peru*

Peter T. Bradley

# CHAPTER ONE

# Introduction [1]

For many a long day in the past, in the multiple guises of seamen, merchants, explorers, overland travellers, settlers, geographers and scientists, the English were captivated by South America. By comparison with lands to the north of that continent and with Africa or Asia, where they were to carve out their own spheres of imperial dominance, their numbers were relatively small. But for over three hundred years during the age of sail, the most remote of Spain's New World possessions, originally the Viceroyalty of Peru, nourished their imagination and whet their appetite for overseas enterprises, and above all profit, in a distant land. In particular, enhanced by its very remoteness and endowed with what were perceived to be strange and wondrous attributes, the lure of Peru seemed capable of satisfying the wildest dreams that the imagination could forge. Consequently, when at the end of the sixteenth century Walter Ralegh chose the words to describe the fabulous assets of the kingdom of El Dorado that he desperately sought in Guiana, for purposes of comparison he selected a name that was instantly recognisable to his fellow Englishmen and by which its wealth could be measured. He wrote of Guiana, 'it hath more abundance of Golde then [sic] any part of Peru, and as many or more great Cities then euer Peru had when it florished most'.[2] In fact, what was set down as the reality of Peru by English writers constituted a composite based on personal observation and written texts, in themselves already suffused with ingredients which surpassed the limits of the imagination, but always interpreted by a gaze through the transmuting lens of myths and beliefs both of New and Old World origin. Moreover, it was a foreign reality frequently further contrived in hopeful expectation of its ability to overcome personal adversity and hardship in England and fulfil personal aspirations for betterment.

In contrast, today the popular concept of the Republic of Peru is very

[1] I am grateful to the British Academy for a grant which enabled me to undertake research on foreigners in the Viceroyalty of Peru, including the English.

[2] Robert H. Schomburgk (ed.), *The Discovery of the Large, Rich and Beautiful Empire of Guiana* (Hakluyt Society, 1st series, vol. 3, London: 1848), p. 13. There is a recent edition by Neil L. Whitehead (Manchester: Manchester UP, 1997).

different, seen through the stunning impact of television images instantly transmitted globally by satellite, which shock by displaying actual scenes of life and death that reveal the economic, social and political realities of the so-called 'Third World'. Most recently, in 1997, this was achieved by world-wide coverage of the siege at the residence of the Japanese Ambassador in Lima, which resulted in the killing of the perpetrators belonging to the Movimiento Revolucionario Túpac Amaru, and a year later with the reporting of the devastation caused by 'El Niño', one of the most damaging occurrences of this periodic phenomenon, in terms of human and material cost. However, it was especially during the 1980s, on the one hand in the barbarous context of revolutionary and state violence associated with the actions of *Sendero Luminoso*, which it is reported killed some 27,000 Peruvians, and on the other a chronic epidemic of cholera, that endless series of seemingly ever-worsening statistics recorded higher levels of inflation, foreign debt and unemployment, accompanied by lower indices of per capita income and GDP. These relegate contemporary Peru to a lowly position not only in the world environment, but in comparison with most other kindred Latin American states. In sharp contrast, European languages of today still have buried within them, though not always in the most recondite and unvisited corners, the phrases which are a legacy of that previous age. In French one may still encounter *ce n'est pas le Pérou, gagner le Pérou, un vrai* or *petit Pérou*. Portuguese dictionaries invariably record Potosí as signifying a *grande fonte de riquezas* or *tesouro*, whilst the Spanish language naturally recalls the treasures that were once synonymous with the name, in phrases such as *valer un Perú, valer un Potosí* and *vivir en Jauja*. Roget too, in the ever-popular thesaurus of English words and phrases, under the heading 'wealth' and alongside 'mint of money' and 'mine of wealth', includes both El Dorado and Potosí, although the latter has been dropped from recent paperback editions.[3] Moreover, the heraldic arms of the present Republic of Peru are a further reminder of those past riches, for beneath the vicuña and the cinchona tree signifying animal and vegetable wealth, they depict a golden cornucopia pouring forth mineral treasures. English writers, both the merely curious and the shamelessly covetous, neglect neither.

The intention of this study is to record the accumulation and analyse the development and fundamental constituents of the body of information about Peru in writings in English, and in works translated into English,

[3] I am indebted to colleagues in the School of Modern Languages at the University of Newcastle for suggesting the following textual references to Peru: 'Point de bien! votre bonne mine est un Pérou: tournez-vous un peu que je vous considère encore' (P. C. de C. de Marivaux, *Fausses confidences*, 1737, Act I, Sc. 2), with its obvious play on the double meaning of the French word *mine*, as both 'mine' and 'appearance' or 'mien'; and 'Komm mit mir wann du kanst; ich wil dir etwas weisen / Darnach du nicht erst darffst biß in Peru hin reisen' (Martin Opitz, *Vielguet*, 1629) – 'come with me if you can; I will show you something for which you do not need to travel all the way to Peru'.

especially until the end of the seventeenth century. It scrutinises what people were reading about Peru. We can only presume that some of them and of those who could not read, may have been hearing and discussing similar information about Peru in ways that went unrecorded, formulating opinions that were not dissimilar. Attention will be paid in particular to those themes and opinions which shaped the earliest perceptions of the region in England from at least a century earlier and continued to do so for many years. Some of them were still underlying the motivations for maritime contacts in the eighteenth century, and even British commercial ambitions at least to the mid-nineteenth century, when rather than precious metals the objects of exploitation had become guano, nitrates, sugar and cotton, or investment in railways and financial institutions. Before we commence, we should remember that in the period covered by this study, until the early eighteenth century, Peru still comprised much of South America, save for Portuguese Brazil, being a vast administrative unit stretching from the Isthmus of Panama to Cape Horn, and from the South Sea or Pacific Ocean eastwards to the River Plate.

In general, as one would expect, the volume of publications which refer to Peru reflects the waxing and waning of English enthusiasm in general for exploration, discovery, transoceanic commerce and overseas enterprise in the New World. At its most active, it is expressed in the form of direct, personal contact and observation through participation in maritime expeditions to the South Sea. This is undoubtedly a characteristic of the closing decades both of the sixteenth and seventeenth centuries. The former is marked by a renewed and evolving fascination in the quest for a North-West passage to the East Indies, initiated by the expeditions of Martin Frobisher (1576–78) and John Davis (1585–87), by Walter Ralegh's earliest projects for English colonisation at Virginia in North America, commerce and privateering in the West Indies from the 1560s in the hands of John Hawkins and Francis Drake, and above all by Drake's entry into the South Sea during his circumnavigation of the globe (1577–80), a voyage which encapsulated within itself most English overseas interests and objectives of that age. Consequently, from the mid-1570s to the early years of the following century, we can record the writing of documents or pamphlets which constitute propaganda for discovery, trade and colonisation, for example by Humphrey Gilbert, Richard Grenville and Richard Hakluyt, as well as fuller though often still highly imaginative and sometimes eccentric accounts of Peru by writers of geographical treatises such as George Abbott and Robert Stafforde.[4] As their sources, these and others could call upon recent translations into English of the work of Spanish historians of the New World, such as Francisco López de Gómara, Bartolomé de las Casas, Agustín de Zárate and José de Acosta. However,

---

[4] See the 'List of Works and Documents in English Referring to Peru' in Appendix 1, for full bibliographical details of these and other authors cited throughout the text.

it is in Richard Hakluyt's expanded edition of his *Principal Navigations*, published between 1598 and 1600, that we find the most extensive compilation of information hitherto gathered directly by Englishmen or translated from foreign sources.

To some extent in the following century, the expedition of naval captain John Narborough to Valdivia in Chile (1669–71), fitted out at crown expense, may appear to be evidence of a genuine re-birth of English interest in the South Sea, following half a century in which Dutch attentions predominated.[5] In fact Narborough's journal, the product of meticulous observation and record with reference to the Argentinian coast of Patagonia and through the Straits of Magellan to southern Chile, was neglected and its publication delayed for over twenty years. Presumably, therefore, only a few felt the need for the practical information it contained, which was pertinent to the aspirations of any who might entertain commercial ventures in Chile, or perhaps even an English base there or on the Atlantic approaches. The journal was only published following the decade of the 1680s, in which Peru had once again been brought more vividly than ever to public attention by the exploits in the South Sea of buccaneers from the West Indies. The circulation of the narratives of their sometimes reckless and thrilling deeds, of a genre and appeal markedly different from the work of Narborough but which also in a few cases are supplemented with startling descriptive information, parallels the enthusiasm for Peru aroused by the age of Drake and his successors a century previously. On this later occasion, however, the tales would come to rest on more fertile soil and subsequently blossom in England into the vogue of travelogues real and imaginary, by writers such as Daniel Defoe, one of which, namely that of *Robinson Crusoe* (1719), could trace its origins at least in part to the accounts of buccaneering and privateering in Peruvian waters. At the same time in the late seventeenth century, buccaneering adventures were accompanied by a greater attention to Peru in geographical works, and by translations from foreign sources such as Acarete du Biscay, François Froger, the Inca Garcilaso de la Vega and Pedro Cieza de León, although the latter not until 1709.

In contrast to the swell of editorial activity at the end of each century, one must surmise that prior to the 1570s, what was known in England about Peru was derived largely either from works written originally in Spanish and other European languages, or else from elusive oral sources difficult for the historian to track down. Undoubtedy the well-documented

---

[5] For recent accounts of voyages to Peru and their repercussions, see Peter T. Bradley, *The Lure of Peru: Maritime Intrusion into the South Sea, 1598–1701* (London: Macmillan, 1989), *Navegantes británicos* (Colección Mar y América, 13, Madrid: MAPFRE, 1992), pp. 197–318, and 'Historia marítimo-militar del Virreinato del Perú, siglos XVI–XVII', in Teodoro Hampe Martínez and Peter T. Bradley, *Compendio histórico del Perú* (6 vols, Lima: Milla Batres, 1993), vol. 2, pp. 385–510.

presence of English sailors and resident merchants in the ports of Andalusia created the opportunity for the gathering of news, the swapping of seamen's yarns and observation of galleons returning laden with American goods and bullion.[6] The only exceptions in terms of written texts in English seem to be the brief references made in the translations of Martín Fernández de Enciso and Peter Martyr by Roger Barlow and Richard Eden respectively, as well as the English edition of André Thevet's account of the French colony in Brazil.

What appeared in print during the early decades of the seventeenth century may justifiably be classified as a lingering legacy both of the magnified curiosity aroused by Drake, and the hitherto only imagined prospects of gain now converted stunningly into reality by his return with plunder from the South Sea. This is certainly the case of the tardy publication of two works, namely the account of Drake's own circumnavigation, in part attributed to Francis Fletcher, and Richard Hawkins's *Observations*, a brimming report of personal memories, comments on nautical topics and of course the events of his voyage to Peru (1593–94). In the sense that they shared similar motives, it is also true of the translation of the journals of the first Dutchmen to glimpse the coasts of Peru, whether published as individual volumes or as abridged by Samuel Purchas, the inheritor and continuator of Hakluyt's work of compilation. Purchas also perpetuates the enterprises of the Elizabethan age of privateering with his compilation of documents relating to voyages by the successors of Drake such as Thomas Cavendish, to which are added brief contributions drawn from Spanish chroniclers like Francisco Xerez, Cristóbal de Mena, Pedro Sancho de la Hoz and Pedro Ordóñez de Cevallos.

The only other distinctly identifiable period in the production of English works rendering some account of Peru, is that which broadly speaking coincides with the protectorate of Oliver Cromwell (1653–58). It embraces both the seizure of Jamaica (1655), as a compensation for the failure of more ambitious aims, and a bitter legacy of popular feelings of animosity towards Spain. In a blatant and resonant crescendo of national prestige and aggrandisement overseas, a renewed interest in the Spanish New World, including Peru, was expressed in several volumes of geography. In the case of George Gardyner, Ferdinando Gorges and the writer known as N.N., they betrayed the markedly anti-Spanish sentiments that characterised the period. These also came to the fore at the same time in a more public and dramatic form in the work of William Davenant, giving vent to the politics of imperial conflict through expressions of anti-Catholicism and attacks on Spanish cruelty towards the native population of the New World.

Before moving on to the texts themselves and the evidence in support

---

[6] On the English in Andalusia, see Gordon Connell-Smith, *Forerunners of Drake: A Study of English Trade with Spain in the Early Tudor Period* (London: Longmans, 1954).

of these introductory remarks, we should briefly investigate this question of the motivations of those who wrote about Peru. Furthermore, we should remember that not only those who composed works, but also those who selected texts for translation and compilation, by the very choices they made and sometimes by the ways in which they presented those texts in English, betrayed their objectives and their preoccupations.

Those who travelled in the past to foreign lands may have done so for a variety of reasons – in a quest for adventure that hopefully would substitute domestic economic pressures with personal enrichment, to reveal and disseminate new facts or curiosities relating to strange peoples and their environment, on behalf of private entrepreneurs and sovereigns to gather information of practical benefit in the service of the commercial and political objectives of their nation, to enhance their personal prestige through exhibiting their knowledge of the unknown and wondrous, simply to entertain by publishing captivating accounts of their experiences and exploits, or more seriously for proselytisation.[7] The latter is not relevant in the case of those Englishmen who sailed for Peru, although their own anti-Catholic beliefs certainly coloured their response to what they saw and how they recorded it.

William Dampier and Lionel Wafer at the end of the seventeenth century probably come closest to embodying, at one and the same time, several of these designs, which were subsequently to typify more generally the more enlightened voyagers of the following century. Rather than simply recording the day to day occurrences of their bucaneering enterprises, they displayed an inquisitive perspective of the natural environment. Dampier, for example, wrote descriptive and comparative analyses of the flora and fauna of the coasts and of islands such as the Galapagos, a precursor of the scientists who would follow him. Wafer, furthermore, prepared critical assessments of the feasibility of English settlement in a variety of different locations. Richard Hawkins, too, critically cast a curious gaze over the new world around him, but in particular was drawn to all novelties pertaining to the maritime environment and to ships. Narborough certainly addressed topics of concern to those who had commercial projects, or even a settled outpost in mind. Like his fellow compatriots, Fletcher, Winter, Pretty, Jane, Knivet, Cavendish, Carder and others, and like the Dutch who followed them en route to Peru, Narborough also recognised the import-ance to men of the sea of accurately chronicling the seasonal hazards and constant perils to health of a voyage with such a distant destination, assessing the viability of overcoming them both on the outward and the return voyage. Hence, features of the maritime approaches to Peru – the River Plate, the coasts of Patagonia, the Straits of Magellan, and the islands

---

[7] These issues are discussed at greater length in J. Edgardo Rivera Martínez, *El Perú en la literatura de viaje europea de los siglos XVI, XVII y XVIII* (Lima: San Marcos UP, 1963), and in Estuardo Núñez *Viajes y viajeros extranjeros por el Perú* (Lima: 1989) and *El Perú visto por viajeros* (2 vols, Lima: Peisa, 1973).

and coasts of southern Chile, all become familiar landmarks to English readers, at least in name if not always with their accurate location. Furthermore, although the significance was not at once immediately understood, writers of journals contributed importantly to the work of geographical discovery, pertaining to the passage of Cape Horn, the appropriation of the Falkland Islands (or Malvinas) as an English base, the correct outline of the Chilean coast, and the alleged existence of a *Terra Australis Incognita* or southern continent.

Similarly, when English descriptions were derived from eyewitness experience, once in the South Sea the focus of observation was primarily from the sea and the eye of the observer was that of a mariner. The result is that we learn much of coastal landscapes and their settlement in terms of the requirements, preoccupations and tastes of transoceanic voyagers from far-off lands. A strong nautical flavour, conveyed through the attention given to the recording of anchorages, points of disembarkation, secure harbours, tides, climate, sources of fresh food and other matters pertaining to navigation, is particularly noticeable in the writings of men such as Richard Hawkins, Thomas Fuller (in Hakluyt), and John Ellis (in Purchas). Wherever the human environment becomes the focus of attention, above all it is to register the response of the local population to the arrival of interlopers in what was, after all, a supposedly closed and often alien Spanish world, their willingness to barter for provisions, and their defensive capabilities with which to resist what they might consider to be an unwelcome landing. Consequently, although Ellis is an exception, by and large the English reader had to rely on translations of foreign sources for information about the land and people of the interior of Peru, hence the value of the information provided by Lopes Vaz, Acarete du Biscay and the works of Spanish chroniclers. It was the latter, of course, to whom English readers also turned, even before their translation, in order to glean the essential facts concerning the Spanish conquest of Peru and its later political, social and commercial administration.

But whatever the category of the works available to English readers, whether it be geography, travel journal, multi–volume collection, short pamphlet, theatrical work or translated chronicle, the one overriding theme and eternal source of wonder, told and re-told with reference to the same corroborating testimony, was that of the mineral wealth of Peru, fabulous both in its profusion as well as the luxuriance and exquisite artistry of the objects into which it was fashioned. The essential ingredients were the silver, gold and precious artefacts gathered by the Inca Atahualpa to achieve his ransom, the shimmering wealth of Cuzco's Temple of the Sun, the inordinate richness of the mines of Potosí, the seemingly unending and undiminishing exports of silver to Spain, and the sparkling golden sands and rivers of Chile. The whole was nothing less than an irresistibly tantalising blend of myth and fact. After all, Drake's booty, in large part garnered from a Peruvian galleon, appeared to have proved that the stories the

English had heard and read were true, and despite the fact that none of his compatriots was to gather such a bountiful windfall of gold and silver for more than a century, rare was the English voice that claimed that Potosí, or indeed Peru itself, was in decline even late in the seventeenth century. Peru, in short, had become the basis of a reality clothed in the proportions of a legend.

Hence, to a certain extent Estuardo Núñez is correct in his affirmation that Peru 'era la leyenda y el mito del Dorado mítico', 'una poesía histórica'. In contrast, Chile 'era la realidad de atractivo geográfico, el paso obligado para los mares del sur ... la recalada forzosa de los navegantes', 'una verdad geográfica'.[8] Certainly, throughout the entire period under discussion, the first English visitors, the Dutchmen Olivier van Noort and Joris van Spilbergen, writers of geographies such as Samuel Clarke and George Gardyner, Narborough and the buccaneers in the 1680s, all delight in and handsomely praise the fertility of Chilean soil, citing evidence of the welcome abundance and variety of its produce. One can readily appreciate their warm and enthusiastic memory of those islands in the south, such as Juan Fernández, which offered a safe, uninhabited refuge and the chance to recover from the devastating effects of illness after a long and perilous passage into the South Sea, during which they were frequently starved of normally acceptable foodstuffs.

But more than this, on reading English accounts of Chile, one cannot help but be tempted to draw comparisons with the descriptions drafted by Columbus in the West Indies during his first voyage, to convey his impressions of landscapes to which, for a time at least, he ascribed the traits of an unspoilt paradise. Everything there is reduced to lushness, greenness, fertility, abundance and sometimes wonder.[9] After all, for centuries European travellers to distant lands, for example Asia, either claimed to have seen or heard tales of what they interpreted as the earthly paradise, portrayed at the feet of God in the easterly-oriented medieval *mappaemundi*. Some had doubtlessly read the descriptions of Sir John Mandeville. It was not unexpected, then, that America should become the new and perhaps most fecund repository of all such beliefs, beginning with Columbus's identification of Paria as the terrestrial paradise during his third voyage. A century later, Walter Ralegh was consumed by the conviction that it lay in Guiana, claiming that along the banks of the Orinoco he looked upon 'the most beautiful country that ever mine eyes beheld'.[10]

In likewise manner, the words of Grenville and Hakluyt who knew it only by hearsay, or of Wafer and Narborough who were able to rely on

8 Núñez, *Viajes y viajeros*, p. 25.

9 Beatriz Pastor Bodmer, *The Armature of Conquest: Spanish Accounts of the Discovery of America, 1492–1589* (Stanford: Stanford UP, 1992), pp. 9–49, examines Columbus and the discourse of mythification.

10 Schomburgk, *Guiana*, p. 57.

their own eyes, at times invest the reality of Chile with the attributes of a marvellously fertile, virgin land, shorn of blemishes, beyond the effectively settled frontiers of Spanish domination, a land indeed where Spanish domination was not only resented but resolutely resisted by its indigenous population. From the very earliest of English writings, Chile was also conceived of as a region in which Englishmen might encounter a welcoming and hospitable habitation, in which to settle and from which to trade. Moreover, again from the Elizabethan age onwards, and with barely any let, hindrance or doubt ever being expressed, Chile became imbued with the gifts of a region fabulously endowed with ubiquitous sources of gold. The European concept of paradise, of course, was often one that was extravagantly invested with all such manner of natural resources. Long before Englishmen journeyed to it, as well as at the first hearing and reading of it, the Spanish New World and the Viceroyalty of Peru in particular, was already proved to conform to this likeness in reports of its mineral wealth. Most English writers, from the time of Hakluyt, would habitually place side by side with the immense silver treasure of Potosí, their wondrous imagination of Chile as a golden land, and they continued to do so long after the brief gold cycle of the sixteenth century had faded. Indeed, in some cases they persisted in doing so until the disclosure of nitrate deposits in its deserts during the nineteenth century, attracted a different generation of seekers and exploiters.

Nevertheless, the truth is that although the marvellous, bizarre and the exceptional often captured the gaze of the onlooker, many English writers from very different backgrounds do endeavour to convey their perceived reality of many of the coasts and islands of the Viceroyalty of Peru, both in the South Sea and the southern Atlantic Ocean, and do gather a significant quantity of accurate data. Although doubtlessly more barren and, therefore, more alien than central Chile to eyes accustomed to green fields, gently-flowing and generally peaceful rivers, rolling hills and shady woods, the coastal landscapes of what is now the Republic of Peru, with the diverse activities, customs and lifestyles of its people, are at times faithfully transcribed, alongside the seemingly imaginary reality of mineral treasures. But what unites virtually all writers, in the context both of Peru and Chile, is common motivations, common dreams, and above all that sense of bewilderment and amazement in face of the hitherto unknown and seemingly inexplicable.

As a consequence, therefore, the 'real' can be deformed or its traits amplified in this quest for explanation and believability. For in common with Spanish chroniclers, and even with novelists of today like García Márquez and Alejo Carpentier who can make an asset out of such ambiguity, English observers strive to define the frontiers between the 'real' and the 'imaginary', forever easily tempted to assent to an imagined reality that is so different from, and in most cases so much better than the one they know, or may be seeking to escape. Taken to its ultimate extreme, in the words of several of our commentators, the vision of the 'new' quite literally assumes a stature that is akin to that of an earthly paradise. Elsewhere, giants, cannibals and fighting women, along with otherwise peculiar and savage peoples roam the earth. Whilst strange, if not always fierce and man-eating beasts live on, in company with the ever enchanting but ever elusive dreams of wealth. They are all richly kindled by legends of classical and medieval origin, further ignited by popular tales remembered from novels of chivalry, and apparently verified by the testimony of eyewitnesses like Thevet, Knivet, Carder and Wafer. Carpentier's final words in his prologue to *El reino de este mundo* may be asked of many of those who write in English and not just Spanish. '¿Pero qué es la historia de América toda sino una crónica de lo real-maravilloso?'

Finally by way of introduction, we should add a few words on allusions to the native population of Peru. In fact, English writers seldom seem to have been moved personally to delve deeply into the Indian heritage of the land, or explore the lifestyle of indigenous peoples. The exceptions might be Ellis or Wafer, whenever they recorded their personal confrontation with relics or monuments of that past age. As a result, the first references we shall see in English are an uncritical acceptance of those encountered in translations of the earliest Spanish chroniclers, such as López de Gómara who had never been in the Indies. They are images deeply rooted in European beliefs, which assigned a lowly condition to peoples who did not conform to the civil order of society, nor its Christian dogma, now utilised to render the population of the New World understandable within that hierarchy. Consequently, in general they are unfavourable images of ungodly, brutal savages lacking the basic attributes of humanity, intended furthermore to provide justification for the Spanish conquest. Gómara's sickening account of Aztec sacrifice and subsequent cannibalistic acts, whose effusively spilled human blood no doubt tainted not just English mental images of all Amerindians, was hard to eradicate, all the more so for the fact that it conformed to pre-conceived notions of such societies. The true lives, history, achievements and grandeur of the peoples of pre-Spanish Peru, went unrecognised and unappreciated, which is hardly surprising when late in the twentieth century the unjustly downtrodden remnants of that civilisation are still so frequently misunderstood and neglected. Hence, Indian Peru was only more fairly and more sympathetically placed before the English reader for the first time, in the translations of José de Acosta and the Inca Garcilaso de la Vega in the seventeenth century. At the very least, that experience must have been somewhat disconcerting for those accustomed to more one-sided descriptions. However, even when the work of Las Casas was repeatedly published or mentioned in England, or when geographers and ecclesiastics such as Fletcher and Abbott remind us at what cost to the Indian population Spanish wealth was obtained, one should still wonder and question whether the motives really derive from sympathetic personal contemplation, an unbiased appreciation of the past attainments of the Indian race, or from a sincere concern for their present plight as a result of alleged Spanish cruelty. The reality was that like many Spanish allegations of native barbarism used to throw an ignominious mantle over their own barbarity (although quite unlike the opinions of Las Casas), expressions of English horror in face of Spanish ill-treatment of indigenous peoples were founded less on sympathy and moral indignation than on finding grounds for English proposals to intervene in Peru.

Nevertheless, in the case of the coasts of the Viceroyalty of Peru from the southern Atlantic to Panama, the English to a certain degree were freer to record spontaneously their response to the native populations. This sometimes does lead to an ambiguity of representation, for example in the writing of Richard Hawkins, born of a conflict between what they had previously imagined of the indigenous population whom they later met and what they actually saw. The natural and acquired skills of those people, with their knowledge of and respect for the environment, uneasily sat alongside traits that were deemed to warrant the claim that they were uncivil. On the other hand, in contrast to those who transcribed their impressions of North America, the English observers of Peru were untrammelled by the need to temper the ever-popular taste for tales of Indian savagery, cannibalism, extraordinary practices and beliefs, that ran counter to the aims of those writers of English propaganda whose purpose was to encourage investment and settlement in what needed to be not only a bountiful but also a peaceful and hospitable world in Virginia.[11]

Nevertheless, reservations must remain about questionable motives, particularly in the instances where Hawkins, Narborough, Wafer and Dutchmen such as van Noort and Spilbergen, are united in the dream of exploiting Indian animosity and hatred towards the Spanish, by forming an alliance with them against their oppressors.[12] As we shall see, these issues certainly gained a greater resonance and much popular enthusiasm when graphically staged through the work of Davenant and Dryden. The Indian world as a thrilling spectacle of the strange and wonderful still remains as a backcloth in their work, though perhaps with less effect than fifty years earlier. What predominates in the mid-seventeenth century,

[11] For an excellent study of this topic with regard to North America, see Loren E. Pennington, 'The Amerindian in English Promotional Literature (1575–1625)', in *The Westward Enterprise. English Activities in Ireland, the Atlantic and America (1480–1650)*, ed. Kenneth R. Andrews, Nicholas P. Canny, and Paul E. H. Hair (Liverpool: Liverpool UP, 1978), pp. 175–94.

[12] Pennington, 'The Amerindian', pp. 185–187, has drawn attention to the fact that Walter Ralegh's *Discoverie of Guiana* (1596) preceded them in an 'optimistic portrayal' of the natives of South America, with whom he proposed an alliance both for the discovery of El Dorado and the subsequent conquest of Peru, provided that they accepted Christianity. In this case, precisely as in North America, Ralegh's projects depended upon the representation of a co-operative native population, as did the plans for settlement in Guiana and along the River Amazon of those who arrived at the beginning of the seventeenth century.

especially in Davenant, is the drawing of the indigenous population into the political and religious antagonisms between Spain and England. Obviously, in marked contrast with the learned disputations and debates in the Spain of Las Casas and Juan Ginés de Sepúlveda, the tenuous nature of English contacts with the Indians of Peru provided little inspiration for philosophical argument on the nature of their human condition or the question of their proper conversion to Christian beliefs. The only thoughts at a personal, individual and generally unexpressed level, may have been the tension between experience and the inherited assumptions concerning all peoples, including the natives of Peru, who apparently lacked the attributes of humanity.

CHAPTER TWO

# Historical Texts

As early as 1534, pamphlets had been produced in Italian, German and French which were translations of letters from Peru recording the early stages of the conquest – the departure of Francisco Pizarro from Panama, the progress of his march inland from Tumbes to Cajamarca, and the so-called 'ransom' of Atahualpa.[1] But the French document in particular added further details which would for centuries constitute the most irresistible of attractions for many who wrote of the region, since it extended its coverage of fabulous mineral wealth by listing that recently transported to Seville by Hernando Pizarro.

The lack of comment in England on such news is the best indication we have of the scant extent to which those events were known there, representative of a lack of interest at that time not simply in Peru but in the opening up of the New World generally. We can, however, with some certainty claim that early sources of knowledge about Peru, in their original Spanish language, were the histories of the New World and of Peru in particular, collected and consulted in prominent libraries in England, both private and institutional. These would eventually include Cieza de León, López de Gómara, Zárate, Xerez, Las Casas, Peter Martyr, Enciso, Herrera, Acosta, Oviedo and the Inca Garcilaso de la Vega.[2] However, in comparison with other European countries, translations into English were few in number, rather slow to appear, based on previous translations, usually French, and selective in their coverage, for example when used by Purchas.

In consecutive years, 1552 and 1553, two of the best-known Spanish

[1] Francisco Esteve Barba, *Historiografía indiana* (Madrid: Gredos, 1964), pp. 398–401. A sceptical view of the notion of a ransom agreement in the true sense is expressed by Silvio Zavala, 'Relecturas de noticias sobre botín de los conquistadores del Perú', *Revista de Historia de América*, vol. 97, 1984, pp. 7–22.

[2] As an introduction to this question of books in libraries and catalogues, see Colin Steele, *English Interpreters of the Iberian New World. A Bibliographical Study* (Oxford: Dolphin, 1975), chap. V; Eva G. R. Taylor, *Tudor Geography, 1485–1583* (London: Methuen, 1930), Appendix II, 'Catalogue and Bibliography of Contemporary Libraries'. For a bibliographical study of the chronicles, see Peter T. Bradley, '*Crónicas de Indias*: Some Recent Editions', *Inter-American Review of Bibliography*, vol. 38, 1988, pp. 499–512.

chronicles of discovery and conquest were published. The first, *La historia de las Indias y conquista de México* by Francisco López de Gómara, awaited translation into English for a mere quarter of a century, at a time when the voyages of Martin Frobisher to the Arctic shores of North America had infected London with gold fever.[3] It included a comprehensive historical account of Spanish Peru, from Vasco Núñez de Balboa's first awareness of rumours about Peruvian gold and emeralds to the administration of Pedro de la Gasca (1547–50). English readers, therefore, were able to familiarise themselves with the major historical events, and were enthralled by tales such as the gathering from far and wide of the articles which constituted Atahualpa's 'ransom', or the triumphal entry of the bedazzled Spanish into a richly ornamented Cuzco, which would begin to lay the foundation of the viceroyalty's legendary mineral wealth. However, Gómara's description of the geography, natural history and inhabitants of Peru was brief and rudimentary, and as ever in early chronicles mingled a reality verging on fiction with the truly imaginary. A single section of the text served to convey the plain characteristics of a generally barren coast, compare fertile coastal oases with mountain valleys, note the production of typical crops like cotton, potatoes, maize and coca, and list birds and other animals. A taste for the unusual or remarkable emerged through the mention of Chilean rivers said to flow by day but not at night, the gurgling tar wells of Santa Elena to the west of Guayaquil, the giants of Puerto Viejo and Trujillo, a fountain whose water turned earth to stone, statistical accounts preserved by means of knotted strings (i.e. *quipus*), as well as an acknowledgement of the solid and ingeniously constructed stone buildings. In general, and especially in the part of the text referring to New Spain, the assessment of the Indian population was a critical and scornful one.

Some of the deficiencies of Gómara's work in respect of Peru were quickly remedied a year later in the original edition of the first part of Cieza de León's *Crónica del Perú*, drawing extensively on personal observation during travels through the New Kingdom of Granada and New Castile between 1535 and 1550. The result is an excellent, detailed record of mainly overland journeys in the northern kingdom, which includes cities such as Cartago, Cali, Popayán and Pasto that rarely feature in English writings, thence along the coast of the present Republic of Peru and once more inland to Cuzco. Cieza's coverage of the coast as far south as the latitude of Arequipa provides at the very least outline sketches and sometimes more extensive treatment of islands, notable landmarks, ports and the main characteristics of each of the fertile valleys. Typical is the mention of the Island of Gorgona, where the rain and thunder never cease,

---

[3] The bitterly learned lesson that the 200 tons of shining black rock transported to England from the Arctic were no more than fool's gold, did nothing to dampen enthusiasm for similar projects.

Guayaquil whose sarsaparilla roots could restore to good health bodies rotting from syphilis, the fort and silversmiths of Tumbes, the broad valley of Piura where several rivers meet, the indifferent port but fruitful soil of Trujillo, the graveyards of Santa, and the fresh water and wood available at Casma. But unusually for this period, Cieza includes practical navigational information on the sailing routes and sometimes difficult maritime conditions as far as Chile, especially with reference to the often tedious voyage between Panama and Callao.

The inclusion of inland towns in Cieza's work would, of course, for long continue to be a prime source of information to readers in England, since such regions would generally be inaccessible to their compatriots who came later to Peru. The same is true of accounts written by travellers from Holland and France who wrote of their experiences in Peru in the seventeenth century. These sections of his work are inevitably marked by the author's wonderment and awe in face of the architectural marvels and wealth of towns such as Cuzco and La Plata, but above all in reporting the seemingly inexhaustible supplies of silver from Porco (chap. CVIII) and Potosí (chap. CIX). The former is reputed to be the source of much of the silver used in the glittering decoration of Cuzco's Temple of the Sun, whilst descriptions of Potosí refer to refining techniques and production levels, claiming that 'in no part of the world was there found such a rich hill ... nor did any prince have such income or profit'. However, although collected in libraries in England in its original Spanish, the impact of Cieza's work was restricted and delayed, since it was not translated into English until 1709, and then in a version which abbreviated the geographical descriptions. Surprisingly, in view of English fascination with the area from the time of Drake, apparently even less well-known was Alonso de Ovalle's general history of Chile, only translated and published in an abridged form early in the eighteenth century, at a time of growing interest in the idea of creating a permanent settlement in the region.

Consequently, the first complete account of the discovery and conquest of Peru to be published in English in 1581, was that of Agustín de Zárate. The direction in which English curiosity was developing was at once apparent in the fact that the frontispiece of the translation bore an engraving which depicted 'the riche mines of Potosi'. Later, several pages describing the town and the discovery of its mines were added to the Spanish original. The basest ore, it is claimed, was capable of producing 480 ducats per hundredweight refined, 'which is the greatest riches, that ever hath been seen or written of' (90v). Zárate himself had already encouraged this kind of interest by his especially detailed accounting of the booty gathered as Atahualpa's 'ransom'. Elsewhere, his chronicle of Spanish deeds until the arrival of La Gasca generally follows the pattern of Gómara, to which he adds material relating to the geography, natural history and towns of Peru, based in part on personal observation. This is discernible, for example, in his estimates of population or in the description of Lima – its flour mills by the river, its varied agricultural produce, the construction of its houses, and its climate with the characteristic winter 'dew' (or *garúa*), reputed to be good for the treatment of headaches. A taste for the unusual is answered in Chile by a further reference to rivers which flow only by day, and the fact that the province is credited with being the home of Queen Gaboimilla, ruler of a large and rich province populated only by women.

Printed more frequently in English than in Spanish, for the first time in 1583 from a French translation, and in four completely different translations by the end of the seventeenth century, was the *Brevísima relación de la destrucción de las Indias* by Bartolomé de las Casas. The titles of two of these translations, *The Tears of the Indians* (1656) and *Popery Truly Display'd in its Bloody Colours* (1689), are evidence in themselves of the fact that this much-read text owed its popularity not so much to a sense of moral repulsion in face of Spanish cruelty, as to phases of anti-Spanish and anti-Catholic sentiment in England. As in the work of Davenant we shall discuss presently, by its being anti-Spanish at the outset the English reader or audience is readily induced to sympathise with a pro-Indian standpoint, at least on political or religious if not moral grounds. Furthermore, the reader infers that Spanish cruelty towards Amerindians is proof of barbaric behaviour towards other non-Catholics in Europe. Therefore, in violent contrast to the views expressed by López de Gómara of savage and idolatrous Indians, Las Casas produces a catalogue of bloody and infamous acts committed by Pizarro and his fellow Spaniards, such as the execution of Atahualpa, acts driven by the lust for gold. However, since Las Casas lacked personal experience of Peru, he was forced to rely in part on the words of the Franciscan Marcos de Niza. Apart from this, Peru itself is absent from the text, but the words of Las Casas gloomily overshadow many subsequent works in English whenever the encounter between Spaniards and Indians is recorded in that region.

José de Acosta's *Historia natural y moral de las Indias* (1591) certainly provided an English reader with a much more comprehensive view of Peru and particularly of its Indian peoples, but until modern times was translated only once, in 1604, from a French edition. Rather than a history of Indian or Spanish feats, this encyclopaedic work, in Book IV, studies at length all aspects of the discovery and exploitation of precious metals, with particular reference to the refining of silver by the use of mercury, and with statistics on levels of production attained at Potosí. But like Las Casas, Acosta provocatively states the repercussions for Indian peoples of their enforced employment in the operations by which such wealth is obtained, a pointer to his more balanced judgement of them. The remainder of the book is a list of other features of the natural world of Peru, describing the preparation of potatoes, the cultivation and properties of coca, the virtues of sarsaparilla from Guayaquil and of bezoar stones, the vineyards of Ica, the sugar of Nazca and Chicama, as well as animals such as chinchillas, guinea pigs, vicuñas and guanacos.

Acosta's moral history, in Book V, concentrates on the customs, religious beliefs and practices of the Incas, with sections, for example, on sacrifice and idolatry. Here the English reader would find evidence to confirm the alleged barbarous nature of Indians and the threat to Christianity of their pagan heathen beliefs, previously derived from other Spanish sources. Nevertheless, there is little doubt that Acosta's identification of Spanish excesses against native societies would appeal to these same readers for reasons of national rivalry and envy. However, having pointed to the serious defect of a lack of Christian belief, altogether more surprising would have been Book VI because of the novelty of its attribution of indicators of civility to Indian Peru, through an appreciation both of their practical achievements, as well as by demonstrating their capacity for reason and understanding. This is achieved by explanation of their methods of calculating time, examination of their laws, government and systems of labour, and by reference to their architectural and engineering achievements, use of *quipus* and employment of *chasquis*. This more favourable interpretation of Indian Peru coincides with what has been identified as a similar general trend, from about 1590, in the representation of Amerindians in English literature promoting colonisation in North America.[4] Just as in Spain, for the English reader too this challenged the pre-conceptions that once had categorised the indigenous population of the New World alongside those peoples who were most commonly termed 'savages'.

Coinciding with a period in which English interest in Peru had been re-kindled by the exploits of buccaneers, there came into print in 1688 the first complete, though not strictly literal, translation of Garcilaso's *Comentarios reales* (1609 and 1617), previously available only in the extracts selected by Purchas. Garcilaso's utilisation of the narratives of chroniclers such as those mentioned above, in combination with personal experience and traditions derived from his Indian and Spanish ancestry, enabled him to create a work of panoramic proportions and scope on both Indian and Spanish Peru.

The aim of enlightening a public often deliberately misinformed by Spanish chroniclers, somewhat belatedly gave to English readers by far the most sympathetic and extensive appreciation of the social, cultural and technical achievements of the indigenous race, placed into the context of the rich, varied and ever-fascinating natural environment of Peru. Judging, however, by the frequency of their subsequent citation, the most enduring and beguiling impressions gained from Garcilaso were those of the fabulous mineral wealth of Peru, measured by his extensive explanation of the distribution of Atahualpa's 'ransom', the output of the mines at Potosí, and most memorably of all by the scarcely credible descriptions of the Temple of the Sun at Cuzco. Its cloisters and inner sanctuaries with their decoration and cornice of gold and silver plates, and its garden whose flora

[4] Pennington, 'The Amerindian', pp. 185–86.

and fauna were unimaginably cast of the same precious materials, were some of the most popular images captured by English writers (Part I, Book 3, Chaps 20, 21 and 24). As for the history of Spanish Peru, Garcilaso extends the range of deeds and personalities beyond those recorded by earlier chroniclers, reflecting the turbulent nature of Spanish colonial society by including the conspiracy of Hernández Girón (1553–54) and the execution of Túpac Amaru (1572).

# CHAPTER THREE

# Accounts of Sea Voyages and Travel

The most valuable and the most numerous sources of information in English about Peru exist in the writings of those who travelled in the New World. Esteemed not only in their own right as first-hand records of visits to distant and exotic lands, they came to be prized by authors and compilers of works of history, geography and cartography, even of drama, and in the eighteenth century by the creators of the genre of fictional travel.

The earliest text in English to offer a complete view of America, north and south, was the translation of André Thevet's *Les Singularitez de la France Antarctique* (1557). As cosmographer to the French crown, he had accompanied the expedition of Durand de Villegagnon to a settlement near Rio de Janeiro in 1555. Based on a blend of observation and conjecture, it was particularly enlightening and exciting for its new English readers in respect of Brazil, with reports on the customs of its native population, including Amazons and cannibals. However, its author also drew attention to the various routes of access to Peru: by sea from the south through the Straits of Magellan, from Darien and the Isthmus of Panama in the north, and overland into the interior from the River Plate. The first of these routes, describing the coast to Cape Virgenes at the mouth of the Straits, gave wider currency to the legend of Patagonian giants up to twelve feet tall. The River Plate likewise was fancifully recorded as the site of encounters between Spaniards and Indians who were both giants and eaters of human flesh. Ever since Columbus, with a touch of regret, had commented that he had not yet found monsters during his first voyage, although he had received news of man-eaters, age-old European beliefs that amongst heathens there inhabited giants, warrior women, anthropophagi and wild men, were dragged along to take root with each advancing stage of Spanish exploration and conquest. There is no reason that Peru should be different, especially in its frontier or less well-known remoter zones. But the most typical note in Thevet is that relating to mineral wealth, for example 'greate pieces of fine and pure shining Golde, well polished and better than any other Golde in Perou' at Cuzco (112), as well as at the already 'famous and rich city of Platte, the countrey being very rich because of the fayre rivers and mynes of golde and silver' (113).

The remainder is merely a list of principal regions and places in Peru derived uncritically and without emendation from Spanish chroniclers, accompanied however with bare but intriguing descriptions derived from the same sources, such as that of the people of Cuzco who 'have their eares hanging down to their shoulders' (111v). In sum, it is sufficient to persuade Thevet to award Peru what must have been the ultimate accolade for men of his age, namely that 'ye will judge it to be another Europe' (114). True to his profession, therefore, Thevet not only re-circulates popular concepts of Peru current in the mid-sixteenth century, but for those who would dare to challenge Spain's exclusive enjoyment of them, identifies the directions from which any such action might be mounted. It is possible that the original French edition of his treatise figured amongst the foreign manuals with which Drake armed himself for his voyage to the South Sea.

Aside from the importance of the early publication date of Thevet, it is, however, from the reports and oral accounts of English seamen that one can justifiably expect some of the most accurate and vivid descriptions of parts of Peru. Necessarily close and painstaking observers of the distinctive features of coastlines, their vegetation and indications of human habitation, in their sometimes desperate search for a safe bay and a friendly reception in order to careen their ships, take aboard fresh provisions and restore their health, they are usually keen to identify places as accurately as the instruments and navigational skills of the time would allow. Some, in addition, display a remarkable interest in the peoples and natural environment of the new lands visited. Consequently, one could reasonably hope that the first English expedition to pass through the Straits of Magellan and enter the South Sea would furnish the material to fill a respectable volume. That may have been so, but in fact although partial and abbreviated accounts of Drake's voyage of circumnavigation (1577–80) were compiled by Hakluyt, neither Drake's personal diary nor any other complete version of the voyage appeared immediately, presumably for political reasons of secrecy. When it did, in 1628, its source was not exclusively the recollections of a seaman but the notes of Drake's chaplain, Francis Fletcher, and of others unspecified, compiled and edited by Drake's nephew and namesake.

For much of the time these constitute either a flat record of daily progress at sea, noting distances covered and logging latitudes, or the reporting of occurrences on land during, for example the coasting of the southern approaches to Peru from the River Plate to Cape Vírgenes, which would soon attract would-be emulators of Drake's venture. In contrast to the majority of these, who even as late as the second half of the eighteenth century perpetuated rumours of human rarities, although an encounter with the Patagonians left two of Drake's men dead, there is no temptation on Fletcher's part to magnify grossly the proportions, singularity or monstrosity of their attackers. For although 'they generally differ from the common sort of men, both in stature, bignes, and strength of body, as also in the hideousnesse of their voice', 'they are nothing so monstrous or giantlike as they were reported' (by Magellan) (60). He concludes, however, with a first allusion to Spanish behaviour towards these people that he will later apply to the indigenous population of Peru. 'But this is certaine, that the Spanish cruelties there used, haue made them more monstrous in minde and manners, then [sic] they are in body'.

In a similar vein, the day-to-day details of Drake's misleadingly rapid and relatively comfortable sixteen-day passage of the straits (Magellan took 37 days), arouses little excitement and warns of few dangers. Although winds were at times contrary and the cold 'nipping' (82):

> yet are the lowe and plaine groundes verie fruitful, the grasse greene and naturall; the hearbs, that are of very strange sorts, good and many; the trees, for the most part of them alwaies greene; the ayre of the temperature of our countrey; the water most pleasant; and the soile agreeing to any graine which we have growing in our countrie (77).

Hunger in the main seems to have been staved off by a diet of penguins and their eggs. 'It is not to be thought that the world hath brought forth a greater blessing, in one kinde of creature in so small a circuit, so necessarily and plentifully seruing the vse of man; they are a very good and wholesome victuall' (76). Tragically, the reality for generations of navigators subsequently lured to Peru would be markedly different from that recorded by Fletcher. Their passage through the southernmost regions would be one of perpetual hardship, frequent failure and in some cases death. Nevertheless, despite the undoubted hazards, Drake's voyage had established the preferred route of access to Peru by sea that would prevail long after the discovery of Cape Horn in 1616, largely due to the availability of sources of nourishment, albeit their seemingly unpalatable nature by modern standards. As we shall see presently, Hakluyt would soon be advocating the advantages that might accrue to England from a permanent occupation of the Straits of Magellan, with the implication of the ability to be able to control and exploit access to Peru.

As to the heart of the viceroyalty's coastline, roughly equivalent to that of the present day republic, the representation is a fair reflection of the reality:

> we found this part of Peru, all alongst to the height of Lima, which is 12 deg. South of the Line, to be mountainous and very barren, without water or wood, for the most part, except in certaine places, inhabited by the Spaniards, and few others, which are very fruitfull and commodious (93).

By contrast, a more bounteous earth had first been noted on the Chilean island of Mocha, declared 'to want no good thing for the use of man's life' (97), and compared to the Isle of Wight on the south coast of England. Mention of storehouses containing wines at Valparaíso confirmed the fertility of the land, a characteristic also of Arica which 'seemed to us to

stand in the most fruitfull soile that we saw all alongst these coasts ...
situate in the mouth of a most pleasant and fertile valley' (107). Here
again, we witness early accolades awarded to Chile, most probably com-
municated orally to Hakluyt, and henceforth confirmed and extended in
the works of those who followed him. However, in each of these cases, as
elsewhere, equal if not greater attention was given by Fletcher to Chilean
gold and Peruvian silver. Fine gold from Valdivia was found at Valparaíso,
'and a great crosse of gold beset with emeraulds, on which was nailed a
god of the same mettall' (101). Mocha was also 'thought to be wonderful
rich in gold' (97). All of which led to the extravagant assumption that
'hereabout, and also all along, and up into the countrey throughout the
Province of Cusko, the common ground, wheresoever it bee taken up, in
every hundred pound weight of earth, yeeldeth 25 s[hillings] of pure silver'
(107). Speculation and imagination apart, of course, in the plunder already
accumulated before approaching Lima, and then in the treasure found in
the galleon *Nuestra Señora de la Concepción* (once nicknamed *Cacafuego*
and which one wit is jokingly said to have altered to *Cacaplata*), these
Englishmen were able to hold in their hands copious tangible evidence of
the splendours of Peru that nourished such imaginings.

As to the natural environment, the curiosity and wonderment of these
first English observers of Peru was aroused by the common sight of a llama
at Morro Moreno:

> Their height and length was equall to a pretty cow ... Upon one of their
> backes did sit at one time three well growne and tall men, and one boy, no
> mans foot touching the ground, ... the beast nothing at all complaining of
> this burthen in the meane time. These sheepe have neckes like camels, their
> heads bearing a reasonable resemblance of another sheepe ... Their wooll
> is exceeding fine, their flesh good meate, their increase ordinarie, and besides
> they supply the roome of horses for burthen or travell (107).

Further contributions to these early perceptions of Peru, bearing in mind
that they are derived from the words of a Protestant preacher, doubtlessly
sprang from the deeply ingrained religious rivalries of the age. Mocha was
populated by native people driven from the mainland by 'the cruell and
most extreame dealing of the Spaniards' (97), a phrase which recalls the
earlier comments relating to the Patagonians. Sudden and painful evidence
of the depth of hatred felt by the native population came in the attack at
Mocha on an English landing party, on the understandable presumption
that they were Spanish. Drake himself was wounded. Nevertheless, despite
the affront, this early account of English encounters with native Americans
is at pains both to stress Drake's refusal to tolerate revenge, in contrast to
the behaviour of the Spanish, and insist on the inherently peaceful nature
of those people. An Indian in a canoe, therefore, is:

> verie gentle, of mild and humble nature ... In him we might see a most

liuely patterne of the harmlesse disposition of that people, and how grieuous a thing it is that they should by any meanes be so abused as all those are, whom the Spaniards haue any command or power ouer' (100).

Later at Coquimbo were sighted Spaniards accompanied by Indians 'running as dogs at their heeles, all naked, and in most miserable bondage' (101). This theme of Spanish cruelty towards the Indian population of Peru and towards all American regions subject to their domination was, of course, in England considered to have been shockingly proven by Las Casas's history. It would re-emerge as a common theme with political motives in the mid-seventeenth century in various forms of writing. Finally, on arrival at Callao, this vein of criticism erupts as a diatribe against 'the poisonous infection of Popery', in a land where 'there is no Citie, as Lima, Panama, Mexico, etc., ... wherein ... not onely whoredome, but the filthinesse of Sodome ... is not common without reproofe' (109).

As a result of the enforced delay in the publication of the foregoing account of Drake's voyage, that of another famous Englishman, Richard Hawkins, preceded it into print in 1622. From its opening pages it bears clear evidence that its author was a man passionately concerned for all matters related to the sea, with its observations on the construction, fitting out and management of ships, naval tactics, the organisation of dockyards, and problems pertaining to long voyages into tropical waters. Hawkins proposes remedies for scurvy (washing the ships down with vinegar, exercising daily, eating lemons and oranges, and reducing the consumption of salted meat and fish) and the sheathing of ships as a protection against ship worm. In Peruvian waters this interest is maintained through his comments on local ships and a favourable appreciation of the manner of their sailing. Even more than the customary descriptions of the Patagonian coast and its alleged giants, what has attracted much attention is his reported sighting and description on 2 February 1594, of a 'goodly champion country' (189–90), not marked on his charts and which he named Hawkins Maiden-land. It is now widely supposed to have been the Falkland Isles or Malvinas, despite his mistaken recording of 48°S as its latitude.

After passing into the South Sea, Hawkins's opinions habitually reinforce a favourable impression of the Chilean coasts of the Viceroyalty of Peru. Following his recounting of the legend that Indians slaked Pedro de Valdivia's thirst for gold by pouring it in molten form down his throat, the settlement named after him, and the region of Arauco are identified as the main suppliers of gold in the past, though now eclipsed by Coquimbo where deposits of copper had also been discovered.[1] Chiloé island is also

---

[1] Francisco Esteve Barba *Crónicas del reino de Chile* (Biblioteca de Autores Españoles, no. 131, Madrid: Atlas, 1960), p. 337, traces the source of the Valdivia legend to the chronicle of Pedro Mariño de Lobera, re-worked by the Jesuit Bartolomé de Escobar in 1554. The term Arauco, much used by English writers to identify the location of Chilean gold from the time of Hakluyt, appears in the poem of Alonso de Ercilla y Zúñiga, *La araucana* (Madrid:

reportedly 'rich in gold' (226). Indeed the very soil of Chile is mixed with gold, 'for the *botijas* (jars) in which the wine was ... had many sparkes of gold shining in them' (241). This resulted from the fact that 'it rayneth seldome, but every shower of rayne is a shower of gold unto them; for with the violence of the water falling from the mountains, it bringeth from them gold' (241).

As a recommendation to those who might pursue not merely plunder but other longer term objectives in Chile, Hawkins similarly praises the agreeableness of the land and climate. Valdivia is sited alongside a pleasant and navigable river in 'goodly, woody country' (226). The islands of Santa María and Mocha are fertile, the latter 'champion ground, well inhabited, and manured' (229), whilst those of Juan Fernández are 'plentiful of fish, and good for refreshing' (231), as many of those who came later to the South Sea would also discover. Finally, Coquimbo is considered to be 'the best harbor that I have seene in the South Sea, it is landlocked for all winds and capeable of many shippes' (239). With such favourable impressions as these of the southern frontier of the Viceroyalty, it is hardly unexpected that others, and not merely the English, would be attracted to them in search of wealth, commerce or perhaps even a place to settle. In short, it is 'one of the best countries that the sunne shineth on; for it is of a temperate clymate, and abounding in all things necessary for the use of man' (240).

Whilst still on the coast of Chile, at Mocha and to a lesser extent Arica, Hawkins demonstrates an inquisitive concern for the native population, something relatively rare amongst his fellow countrymen who headed for the South Sea. In sum, it is an ambivalent perspective. Inevitably, in keeping with the attitudes of the times, Hawkins is drawn with circumspection towards their supposed strangeness, but avoids a totally negative view by not focusing exclusively on barbarism and unchristian beliefs, and by recording what his eyes saw. The first stage of this, when still mindful of the attack suffered by Drake at Mocha, reveals him vigilant in the face of what he refers to as their 'treachery' and 'slyness', defects commonly ascribed by Europeans to those who did not conform to their norms of an ordered society. Nevertheless, motivated by the practical need for fresh supplies of food after his voyage, surely an awkward acceptance of what amounted to his dependence on the local population whatever his prejudgements of them might be, he warily established contact through a process of barter, but only after giving them 'three or four good lamskinnes (beatings)' (227–28) with a truncheon to demonstrate his intentions clearly. However, closer contact subsequently induced comments on the customs, homes, weapons and dress of the Indians of that region, including the view

1569). Although known in England, since a manuscript translation into prose of most of the first sixteen cantos was made about 1600, this was not published until the edition of Frank W. Pierce, *The Historie of Araucana* (Manchester: Manchester UP, 1964).

that they are 'the most valiant nation in all Chily', 'of good understanding, and agilitie, and of great strength' (229). Some attention is also directed to the reasons why they are 'mortall enemies to the Spaniards' (227), and have engaged in 'continuall and mortal warre' (230) with them for over forty years, ending with the conclusion that they are 'industrious and ingenious, of great strength, and invincible courage' (242).

After offering illustrative proof of such views in stories of Indian bravery and the mutilation of captives by the Spanish, Hawkins was given the opportunity to return to similar themes at Arica, where he seized a bark with a native crew bringing fish from Morro Moreno. Now there occurs both a broadening of the theme of Spanish cruelty in general, and the hint of a common sense of animosity against the Spanish, uniting the English and the native population:

> The Spaniards profit themselves of their labour and travell, and recompense them badly: they are in worse condition than their slaves, for to those they give sustenance, house-roome, and clothing, and teach them the knowledge of God; but the other they use as beastes, to doe their labour without wages, or care of their bodies or soules (254).

Consequently, Hawkins affirms, the Indians 'would by no meanes depart from us, but desired to goe with us to England, saying that the Indian and English were brothers; and in all places where wee came, they shewed themselves much affectionated unto us' (253–54). This thread which unites alleged Spanish cruelty towards the indigenous population, with the presumption that the natural corollary was at least an understanding and at best a military alliance between them and the English, indeed their defence and even their liberation in Davenant, is one which we shall see running through the entire fabric of English writing on Peru. More startling, however, than this outlandish but persistent proposition are two instances of native trust in English co-operation discussed by David Cahill in Chapter 9: namely the expectation of José Gabriel Túpac Amaru during his rebellion of 1780–81 that the English would come to his aid, and the popular prophecy foretelling the restoration of the Tahuantinsuyu, likewise under English protection.

Nevertheless, although Hawkins can observe and admire the fact that these individuals from Morro Moreno possess the great natural ability 'after the manner of spaniels', to 'dive and abide under water a long time, and swallow the water of the sea as if it were of a fresh river', as a result of his pre-conceptions they remain 'brutish' and 'altogether voyde of that which appertained to reasonable men' (254).

Even though he affirms that 'I disclaime from being a naturalist' (216), when the opportunity arises, Hawkins is attentive to animal life on land and at sea. As during Drake's voyage, llamas again provoked some fascination in Chile, but at Arica Hawkins chose to single out another of the local curiosities, now a common pet, the chinchilla, 'little beastes like unto a squirrel, but that hee is gray; his skinne is the most delicate, soft and curious furre that I have seene, and of much estimation ... in the Peru' (240).

Further to the north Hawkins returns to his roots as a navigator and seaman, identifying and describing coastal landmarks, bays and offshore islands. He singles out, for example, the Lobos Isles and Paita, later the haunt and target of buccaneer pillage respectively, the Island of Puná at the mouth of the River Guayas, whose water 'is medicinable for all aches of the bones, for the stone, and strangurie: ... because all the bankes and low lands adjoining to this river, are replenished with salsaperillia' (263); Punta Santa Elena – 'good anchoring, cleane ground, and reasonable succour' (ibid.); Capes Pasado and San Francisco, important landmarks for sailors; the Galápagos Islands – 'desert and bear no fruite' (264); and the bay of San Mateo – 'a goodly harbour and hath a great fresh river, which higheth fifteene or sixteene foote water' (267–8). Moreover, throughout the entire voyage along the South Sea coast, this interest in maritime matters is manifest in his discussion of the reasons for the greater navigability of Peruvian shipping which, he judged, could outsail his own. He describes too their low level of manning, some local customs of the sea, the prevailing winds and currents, and in some detail the three-day sea battle off Atacames with a Peruvian squadron commanded by Beltrán de Castro, which brought his venture to an end with his capture and imprisonment.

Nearly 70 years were to elapse before another well-documented English expedition reached the South Sea, that of naval captain John Narborough in 1670. It was then almost a further 25 years before the journal of his voyage, through the Straits of Magellan to Valdivia, appeared in print, a reflection of an English interest in suspense rather than a judgement of the worth of the text. On the contrary, in a highly conscientious manner, Narborough fulfilled to the letter his instructions to carry out without provocation a mainly geographical and commercial survey of lands on the southern fringes of Spanish power in Peru, producing numerous descriptions of the animal, human and plant life of the coasts of Patagonia and of Chile as far as Valdivia, together with a detailed and accurate annotated map of the Straits of Magellan. The work of Narborough, and of his companion John Wood, was to become the standard English guide to the region for decades.[2]

Taking commercial aspirations first, Narborough concluded on the basis of his visit to Valdivia, 'I am of the opinion that the most advantageous

[2] British Library, Sloane MSS, 46A, fols 139–168; 46B, fols 144–188, descriptions of the Straits by Wood; Sloane MSS, 3833, John Wood's journal of the voyage; Additional MSS, 5414, art. 29, Narborough's map of the Straits, published in 1673; Archivo General de Indias (Seville), Mapas y Planos, Buenos Aires, 226, 'Tabla del procedimiento del viaje de una fragata y un patache ingleses al Estrecho de Magallanes, que es la primera que ha repasado dicho estrecho'.

trade in the world might be made in these parts' (110). 'It is my whole desire', he wrote, 'to lay the foundation of a trade there for the English nation for the future; for I see plainly this country is lost for want of the true knowledge of it'. The ease of his passage through the Straits both outward, and more significantly homeward, certainly helped to dispel fears of the perils then traditionally associated with the route, which would deter anyone contemplating investment in a commercial enterprise. Furthermore, at San Julián, now a port on the Argentine coast where he spent part of the winter of 1670, he appears to have found a site suitable to be used as an English base. 'It is a country capable of containing a great number of inhabitants and which promises great advantages to those who might wish to come and settle, for everything which grows in Europe would do well here, and the animals find abundant pasture' (42–43). Not only the land, but also the climate appeared to recommend it:

> The air is cold tonight but very healthy for strong men; I have not had my finger ache as yet; a man hath an excellent stomach here; I can eat foxes and kites as savourily as if it were mutton ... not one man complains of cold in his head, or of coughs' (49).

Such unqualified optimism, however, found no widespread support amongst his fellow countrymen until the birth of that disastrous speculative venture, the South Sea Scheme.

The few extracts above indicate that Narborough's words ideally suited the purpose of those who so fraudulently claimed that there were limitless possibilities for English trade in the South Sea. But as his work of reconnaissance and recording continued after entering those waters, there was yet further material to tempt those already hooked on the venture. Santa María clearly impressed him due to the availability of wood and water, but especially since it was a producer of fruits – apples, pears, plums, oranges, peaches, quinces, apricots, melons and olives. 'These Spaniards report it to be the finest country in the whole world, and that the people live with the greatest luxury of any on earth; they enjoy their health with so much delight, and have so much wealth and felicity, that they compare the land to Paradise' (96).

As for Valdivia, which proved to be his final destination, the town fulfilled his expectations in various ways:

> The people a-shore both men and women of the Spaniards are well-complexioned people, of a ruddy colour, and seem to be mighty healthy. Some of the men are very corpulent, and look as if they came from a very plentiful country, where there is a great store of provisions, and abundance of gold and silver (96).

On the basis of his own observations, together with the tales of his men who had disembarked, returning to recount how they were served from silver stewpots, had eaten from silver plates and washed in silver basins, and from reports of gold to be found at Osorno and Castro, Narborough felt confident enough to proclaim 'the most of gold in all the land of America is in Chile' (92). As further confirmation he adds, 'the Spaniards say that the Indians have much gold, and that their armour for their brest [sic] is fine beaten gold' (88). In fact, as with the reference to paradise above, almost as persistently as Columbus in the West Indies in 1492, Narborough had been recording regular, but hitherto frustrated, searches for signs of gold on the Patagonian coast and through the Straits of Magellan. Likewise, his hopes were continually kept alive by the slenderest of evidence, as on the occasion in the Straits when after Narborough showed him his ring, an Indian pointed in the direction of the hills, prompting Narborough to write, 'I do verily believe that in these mountains there is some metal, either gold or copper' (69). Narborough's words, with their juxtaposition of boundless wealth and luxuriant nature, seem still not to have strayed far from the mythical portrayal of distant, unknown lands in medieval and Renaissance accounts of travel.

On the other hand, Narborough further pandered to the commercial interests of his day and to those lobbyists in England who had backed his venture, by drawing attention to the scarcity of European goods in Peru, acquired legally via the Isthmus of Panama or as contraband from the River Plate. He outlined the patterns of trade along the entire coast, specifying the merchandise carried, and alluding to the transpacific trade to Manila. By implication, it was believed that there was a role for English commerce in those parts. Any strategic worries were answered by a dismissive attitude towards the Spaniards' ability to defend Valdivia from its forts, whose locations were considered ill-suited to the task. Narborough's tactical probing, therefore, although not immediately productive, does denote a swing towards commercial aspirations, but they would not, however, challenge French supremacy in the South Sea early in the following century, nor replace English privateering expeditions during the same period. The reason is the fact that he failed to take account of the reality that dreams of English commerce would founder unless guaranteed Spanish permission to do so, an unlikely proposition. Consequently, despite periods of popular and government enthusiasm, no substantial commercial benefits would emerge until the nineteenth century.

Lastly, in reviewing Narborough's optimistic conclusions for English prospects in the southern cone, it is instructive to consider also how he viewed an Indian response to further English intervention. The detailed orders clearly referred to this aspect of his voyage:

> You are also to mark the temper and inclination of the Indian inhabitants, and where you can gain correspondence with them, you are to make them sensible of the great power and wealth of the prince and nation to whom you belong, and that you are sent on purpose to set on foot a trade, and to make friendship with them' (10-11).

His close observation of them and communication with them on the coast of Patagonia and during the passage of the straits, quickly dispelled myths of giants or savages, with words that convey a favourable picture. Admittedly, as in North America, this was a necessary requirement if investment in some form of settlement was to be canvassed and won, but it was by no means uncommon for the English in Peru or North America to register traits that constitute elements of physical attractiveness in the makeup of those otherwise termed heathen savages. 'They are people of a middle stature, and well shaped; tawny olive-colour'd black hair, not very long'. Again later, 'these people are of a middle stature, both men and women, and well limbed, and roundish faces, and well shaped, and low foreheaded' (50 and 64). They are also active, nimble, and hardy because of the cold. Unlike much of his other reports, such bland and commonsensical descriptions would not prevail against the ingrained popular legend of lusty, naked, wild and monstrous savages, until a much later age when sober scientific enquiry prevailed.

Once in Chile, apart from employing the testimony of the native population in support of his unrestrained eagerness to believe in deposits of gold, and noting that they are treated like slaves, as do Richard Hawkins and the Dutch, Narborough in his turn re-affirms the notion of future mutual co-operation based on a common animosity towards the Spanish. At the end of an episode where Indians are said to weep pitifully as they prepare to leave his ship and return to what they call the Spanish 'devils', he comments, 'I verily believe that these poor innocent creatures speak truth, for they (the Spanish) are great devils in abusing these poor souls so unmercifully as they do' (102).

The endeavours of navigators from the Low Countries in seeking Peru were first made available in English with the publication, in 1619, of the popular journal recording the momentous exploratory labours of Willem Schouten and Jacob Lemaire, which led to the re-drawing of the coastlines south of the Straits of Magellan. For those embarking on round-the-world navigation by a westerly course, or merely seeking Peru, the unprecedented consequence of their venture was Schouten's tracing of their route to reveal both a new strait, to be named Lemaire, between Tierra del Fuego and Staten Island, and an open sea passage into the South Sea around what henceforth would be known as Cape Horn. In future the Straits of Magellan could be circumvented, albeit by an often treacherous alternative voyage which denied sailors access to fresh provisions. However, by following the new course and continuing further out to sea, Schouten also spread awareness of a fresh landfall in the South Sea from which to recuperate from the rigours of the long ocean passage, namely the Juan Fernández Isles, the future haunt of many types of intruders. Although the smallest (Más Afuera) was barren and mountainous, the largest (Más a Tierra) was hilly, wooded and fruitful, with good anchorages, fresh water, supplies of fish and populated by pigs and goats.

The publication a few years later of the translation of an account of the Jacques l'Hermite expedition to Peru in 1624, the first to put to the test the Cape Horn route, revealed more of Dutch overseas intentions and aspirations than it did about Peru, citing the seizure of the silver galleons at Arica as one of the main objectives. It further solemnly and piously stated that they came to deliver Indians, Blacks and Mulattos from Spanish slavery.

It was during the penultimate decade of the seventeenth century that the waters of the viceroyalty were infiltrated for the first time by a very different breed of intruder, namely considerable numbers of buccaneers from the West Indies. The rousing accounts of their tumultuous, reckless and intrepid exploits served not only to broaden knowledge about Peru and excite popular enthusiasm, but sparked off a vogue for literature of travel. Their eyewitness accounts range along the entire coastline from the Isthmus of Panama to the Straits of Magellan, above all narrating their visits to offshore island haunts and their assaults on minor ports which had in some cases hitherto escaped the attentions of previous interlopers.

The greatest popularity was without doubt achieved by the vivid and at times violent work of Alexander Exquemelin, which in its English edition of 1685 incorporated the journal of Basil Ringrose, a companion of the buccaneer Bartholomew Sharp in the South Sea from 1680 to 1681. Generally speaking, it is the individuals and their exploits which dominate this narrative, driven by their heartless and relentless greed for booty and ransom, each acquisition of which and its frequently bitterly disputed distribution is duly noted. It placed in the hands of armchair readers in England tales which were previously only exchanged between men of the sea in the taverns and inns of any port in the land – the thrill and the dangers of adventures on the high seas during which unruly and fractious bands of their compatriots, often resorting to the most brutal and cruel torture of their opponents, dared to challenge the might of Spain in the wealthiest and most renowned of her possessions. For readers more accustomed to the static presentation of geographical treatises or the third person narratives of historical events, the shores of Peru came to life through actions in which their narrators participated, rather than through description. Descriptive material, therefore, is limited to that which is of practical importance. Nevertheless, the ports and islands are remembered in the context of their relevance to the buccaneers' way of life in the South Sea, their survival far from a home base, their raids and the opposition they encountered – Arica where a landing was always difficult because of high seas and where as at Paita they lay in wait for treasure galleons; Guayaquil where ships were built and the exports of Quito stored; islands such as Juan Fernández for fresh herbs, crayfish and goats; Gorgona, Gallo and La Plata as secure havens, to careen and repair their motley craft, or in the latter's case also to fish and salt the meat of its goats and turtles; Ilo for its sugar, figs, olives, oranges, lemons and cattle; and Coquimbo similarly for its fruits, as well as for the wealth of its churches and rumours of gold dust in a nearby river.

Relating to the same phase of buccaneer activity is the edition of Sharp's exploits by Philip Ayres, which at the outset plainly sets down the motives of all those who shared his lifestyle. 'That which often spurs men on to the undertaking of the most difficult adventures, is the sacred hunger of gold; and t'was gold was the bait that tempted a pack of merry boys of us' (1–2). Only after the frustration of their 'expectations of fraighting home our coffers with Spanish gold, and pieces of eight' (4), at Santa María in Darién, did they head for Peru. In this text, latitudes and sailing distances between places are dutifully recorded, but descriptive information is once more sparse and practical, marking prominent coastal landmarks and the best locations for wood, water and provisions. Coquimbo again impresses the writer for its gardens of apricots, strawberries, apples, pears and cherries. Ilo likewise is 'an extraordinary fruitful valley with five olive yards, two pretty vineyards, [and] a great sugar work' (70).

A second wave of more numerous and lengthy buccaneer intrusions into the South Sea was under way by 1684. One of its participants, in fulfilment of a self-professed inclination to travel, was the Frenchman Raveneau de Lussan. His journal similarly narrates the barbarous and cold-blooded deeds of his fellow countrymen in their quest to enrich themselves, in what he plainly considers to be one of the richest countries in the world. In Peru, he assures us, everyday objects made in France of iron, steel or copper were instead made of silver. Although he repeatedly berates the bad luck which always seems to rob him of the riches so enticingly close at hand, he remains forever prone to believe in fantasies and displays a fertile imagination. For instance, he tells us that during the assault of April 1687, the women of Guayaquil were 'perfectly beautiful', but the clergy lived in a state of moral laxity and so hated the buccaneers that they had persuaded the female population that they did not even have the shape of humans, and ate women and young children.

Interesting in a different way, as the product of more reliable observation and genuine curiosity in all around them, were the journals of the buccaneers Lionel Wafer and William Dampier, both of whom spent some time with Sharp and then returned to Peru in 1684. Wafer has especially achieved renown for the account of his enforced stay of some four months amongst the Cuna people of Darien in 1681, following an accident during his return to the Caribbean after abandoning the Sharp expedition. Fortunately, the powers of observation and memory which he displayed on that occasion were valuably exercised in his recording of later experiences, so that although his journal still primarily narrates actions with lists of the booty and prizes taken, he does at times pay greater attention to the detailed representation of the settings in which they occur, and the peculiarities of Peru which left a lasting impression on him.

Visits to the various groups of islands feature regularly in this narrative

– Juan Fernández, the Lobos, La Plata, Puná, the Galápagos where giant land tortoises (or hicatees) and iguanas were used for food, and Gorgona where Wafer marvelled at how monkeys, which partly lived on a diet of oysters, opened them by placing them on a stone and hitting them with another (116). Mocha off the Chilean coast was as usual valued for its fresh water, maize, barley, wheat and fruits. Like his predecessors, Wafer was clearly fascinated by the island's llamas, 'an innocent and very serviceable Beast, fit for any Drudgery' (118–19). He describes them and their uses as sure-footed carriers at length, recalling how they searched their innards for bezoar stones, prized for their supposed medicinal powers, and made sport by riding them two at a time. However, when they returned both to Mocha and to Santa María towards the end of 1687, they discovered that the Spanish had deliberately emptied the islands of humans, animals and supplies of fresh food, to deny future interlopers help and sustenance (126). Similarly at Juan Fernández, there were clear indications that wild dogs had been landed to hunt down and kill goats.

If we turn to the mainland, it is 'barren and desolate, and so on each side all along both Chili and Peru', as for example at Copiapó, where Wafer searched for water to the point of exhaustion with no success, remarking on the vast numbers of sea shells to be found in the sand as much as eight miles inland. 'Nor did we see any sort of Fowl, nor Beast, or other living Creature' (120). Coquimbo is once more renowned for its nine churches, large, deep bay and the alluring tales of gold:

> The Sands of the River by the Sea, as well as the whole Bay, are all bespangled with Particles of Gold; insomuch that as we travelled along the Sandy Bays, our People were covered with a fine Gold-dust; but too fine for any thing else; for 'twould be an endless Work to pick it up (116).

From the point of view of a seaman, the merits and drawbacks of the bay of Arica, 'handsomely seated in the bending of that Coast' (121), its anchorages and the great swell of the sea 'continually rowling in upon the shore', noted too by Ringrose, are also listed. Further to the north, on account of features consistently mentioned by several buccaneer accounts, Ilo now merits the accolade of the 'finest Valley ... on all the Coast of Peru ... pleasanter for the dismal barren Mountains that lie all about, and serve as a Foil' (121–2).

Elsewhere, Wafer's inquisitiveness and keen observation lead him to record details missing from other reports. At Nazca he observes how the rich, strong wine, similar in taste to that of Madeira, was stored in the open air exposed to the sun, in jars containing eight gallons each bearing the identification symbols of their owner. After walking four miles inland from Bermejo (the port of Huarmey), he came across the bodies of men, women and children, thick on the ground so that 'a Man might, if he would, have walked half a Mile, and never trod a Step off a dead human Body' (122), which looked as if they had been only one week dead, 'as dry and light as a Spunge or piece of Cork' (123). These were, of course, the occupants of a Chimú cemetery, rather than as Wafer suggests the remains of Indians who had buried themselves alive to avoid submitting to the Spanish. His plan to take the body of a boy back to England for further study was frustrated by the superstitions of his companions 'having a foolish conceit' (122), fearing that the compass would be affected. At Santa he was confronted by the strange sight of three ships of between 60 and 100 tons deposited inland 'lodg'd there, and very ruinous' (123–4), a fact which he attributed to the effects of an earthquake and tidal wave. Indeed, before leaving the South Sea he was to experience at sea the shock waves of the tremor which struck Lima and Callao on 20 October 1687, his ship shuddering as if striking a rock, the sea foaming, the guns jumping in their carriages and several men being thrown from their hammocks. But certainly the most intriguing comment at this stage of his travels, was his sighting of land 500 leagues west of Copiapó, firstly 'a small, low, sandy island', and 12 leagues beyond it 'a range of high land' (125). This has led to much speculation that the latter could have been Easter Island, traditionally found by Jacob Roggeveen in 1722, when trying to locate what Wafer himself had first believed was the *Terra Australis Incognita*.

What we have seen so far of Wafer are examples of the material published in the *New Voyage* of 1699. However, eleven years earlier he had also addressed to the Duke of Leeds what is known as the 'Secret Report' (133–51), whose purpose was specifically to identify those locations which he considered useful for settlement or trade. It focuses on ports throughout the Viceroyalty of Peru, and responds to a re-generation of English interest in the region associated with the intrusion of the buccaneers. Thinking now in terms of longer range objectives, the strategic concerns of defence would be an important factor in reaching a conclusion on the suitability of such sites. Equally vital, though, was the clear establishment of the most viable sea route from England to Cape Horn. In this regard, at the River Plate 'a Factory wold [sic] be of great use to us'. Moreover, it would offer access to 'the Trade of Paraguay, Chilliae, and that part of Peru which is next the neck of that River', as well as to the 'high mountains which as I have been told containes in their Bowells great Quantitys of Gold and Silver' (134).

On the basis of what we have already extracted from Wafer's own journal, as well as from several other sources, it is no surprise that the coasts of Chile again receive the highest level of approval in the context of these new aims. 'I must say I find no place more convenient for a form'd settlement than Baldivia in Latt$^d$ 40 and Coquimbo in Latt$^d$ 30 or some other port betweene the two' (144). This evaluation rests on several factors: their proximity to Cape Horn, thereby it is hoped allowing a return voyage from England within a year, the expectation of a welcome from the indigenous population with their continuing support against the Spanish, and the similarity of the region to the valleys of Wales with a climate suited to the English constitution. In response to proposals for occupation and to strategic goals rather than periodic raids and plunder, Wafer optimistically adds to previous descriptions of Coquimbo that:

> the citty is soe situated by nature that itt might easely be made almost impregnable by art, nature as itt were pointing to several places adapted for building of forts ... Whosoever is master of this citty and hath but a good port betwixt itt and Baldivia may not onely be master of all the adjacent places but also the greatest part of Chillia (138).

Other places favoured or critically assessed for diverse reasons are the silver town of Arica, 'from whence that vast quantity of Bullion comes that Supplyes almost the World' (135), the disadvantages of the heavy swell at sea outweighed by its good soil, fine river and good harbour, and still defended only by a 'small Fort with verry few gunns on itt' (139–40); Callao which he had not visited and therefore could not comment upon the present condition of its defensive perimeter; Paita, a good port but lacking fresh water and therefore considered unsuitable for settlement; and Guayaquil 'for to gitt or Build Ships or Boats as being the onely Place on this Southward Coast for that use' (135), 'well fortified' (141), enjoying an important export trade in cacao, timber, cloth, guanaco wool and gold dust, but not fit for settlement because of its location upriver and its unhealthy mangrove swamps. Although also unhealthy, most optimistically and damaging of all, if Panama were taken and could be settled by the English 'wold undoubtedly Distroy the whole Trade of Peru and Chili and cut of [sic] the Communication they have with Portobell and Consequently ruine the whole Trade of Old Spaine' (142).

Amongst the places which completely failed to gain Wafer's approval was Valparaíso, 'a good port and no bad landing', with food and water, 'but here is no gold river nor is itt in my opinion fitt to settle in' (138). Huasco also failed to win his recommendation, even though 'here is a river of fresh water and a very good harbour ... it affords many good sheepe and some goats' (139). The importance of the wine trade at Pisco and Nazca was duly noted, but the former was protected by a fort and was an 'open road', whilst the latter was rejected for want of a good landing (140). Huaura 'has a good landing' yet it is not a port for settlement (140), Santa is 'a very Poor Towne' (141), the rocky island of La Plata lacked a reliable supply of water, and Buenaventura was turned down despite having the basic necessities of wood and water and even some gold dust washed from the river by the local population.

The scope of Wafer's experiences, ranging along the coasts from the northern to the southernmost limits of the Viceroyalty of Peru, together with his inquiring mentality and recording of detail both factual and quaint, enabled him to write both entertaining and informative accounts which appealed to those looking to South America for longer term goals such as trade or settlement. In the last years of the seventeenth century he was

listened to and his unbridled optimism unquestioned by those planning
the Scots' Darien Scheme on the Isthmus of Panama, of which more later,
whilst at the same time he doubtlessly shaped the views and enlivened the
zeal of those in England who were becoming attracted to the growing
fashion for stories of foreign lands.[3] Disappointingly absent, however, in
a text otherwise so rich in information, is the native population, except in
the expression of a desire for some future alliance with those living between
Coquimbo and Valdivia. 'We may Gain the Inhabitants the Chilians our
Friends, who are Inviterate Enimys and at Continuall Warrs with the
Spainards [sic]' (145). Clearly, any productive long-term English interest
in the region would depend on some form of accommodation with them.
They were favourably portrayed, therefore, as being 'Brave, Valiant, Ge-
norous and Warlike People and Very Populuse' (ibid.). Elsewhere, however,
from Valdivia to the Straits of Magellan, in a land lacking in mineral wealth
and less amenable to settlement, the judgement is rather less sympathetic.
'The Inhabitants are onely a Parsell of Poor Wild Indians and have neither
Commerce nor Trade, Liveing more like Salvages then Men' (144).

Nevertheless, although Wafer's journal of a buccaneering life off the
coasts of Peru is fuller in its themes than most, the most impressive
achievement of all is marked by the work of William Dampier, first
published in 1697 and immediately reprinted in 1698 and 1699. For whilst
it is still inspired by daring and sometimes exciting deeds and atrocities
in far-flung and, from the English perspective, exotic locations, the descriptions are accurate, more abundant in detail, and likely to satiate the
sharpest curiosity of any reader captivated by foreign travel. In fact, when
addressing matters pertaining to the environment, Dampier alerts the
scientists who followed him, like Charles Darwin, to the natural wonders
and singularities of South America. At the same time, through his careful
recording of climate, winds, the sea, the heavens or matters such as the
variation of the compass, his work constitutes at the same time a valuable
practical guide for those seamen who chose to sail the course he carefully
charted to the South Sea. Finally, by way of introducing Dampier's text,
its popularity is further evidence of the growing vogue for travel literature,
gaining him admittance to learned society such as that of Samuel Pepys.

The arrival at Juan Fernández may be chosen as typical of Dampier's
treatment of places he visits, reflecting a sailor's needs and acute observation:

> March the 22nd 1684, we came in sight of the Island, and the next Day got
> in and anchored in a bay at the South end of the Island, and 25 Fathom
> water, not two Cables length from the Shore (112) ... This Island is in lat.
> 34 d. 45 m. and about 120 Leagues from the Main. It is about 12 Leagues

[3] The historical romance by Bartholomew E. G. Warburton, *Darien; or the merchant prince*
(3 vols, London: 1852), demonstrates the continuing appeal of such exotic and tropical
settings for British readers.

round, full of high Hills, and small pleasant Valleys; which if manured, would probably produce any Thing proper for the Climate. The sides of the mountains are part Savannahs, part Woodland (114).

Characteristically, at this point he breaks off both to explain what savannahs are and for comparative purposes to describe others he has seen elsewhere in the New World or Old, a pattern he repeats whenever reporting on animal and plant life. He continues:

> The grass in these savannahs at John Fernando's is not a long flaggy grass ... but a sort of kindly Grass, thick and flourishing the biggest part of the year. The Woods afford divers sorts of Trees; some large and good Timber for Building, but none fit for Masts. The Cabbage Trees of this Isle are but small and low; yet afford a good Head, and the Cabbage very sweet (115).

He goes on to explain how goats were first introduced into the island, describes seals and sea lions and their habits, finally comparing varieties of fish such as the snapper and grouper.

Virtually unknown to his readers were the Galapagos Islands, 'laid down in the Longitude of 181, reaching to the Westward as far as 176, therefore their Longitude from England Westward is about 68 degrees. But I believe our Hydrographers do not place them far enough to the Westward' (127). An outline of the flora of dildoe and mammee trees, with bushes of burton wood 'which is very good firing' (127), is followed by a lengthy discussion of the local tortoises, and of tortoises in general, comparing the excellence of their flesh. The weather is considered to be 'temperate enough considering the Clime. Here is constantly a fresh Sea-breeze all Day, and cooling, refreshing Winds in the Night' (134). Obviously uppermost in his mind on this occasion, are the needs of those who like himself needed to find safety, seclusion and sustenance in order to remedy their own ailments and repair their ships.

With regard to the mainland, Dampier endeavours to record faithfully the outstanding traits of coastal towns. Paita is:

> A small Spanish Sea-Port in the lat. of 5 d. 15 m. It is built on the Sand, close by the Sea, in a Nook, Elbow, or small Bay, under a pretty high Hill. There are not above 75 or 80 Houses, and two Churches. The Houses are but low and ill built ... The Walls are built of Brick, made with Earth and Straw kneaded together ... They never burn them, but lay them a long time in the Sun to dry before they are used in building. In some places they have no Roofs, only Poles laid a-cross from the side Walls and covered with Matts (163).

He accounts for this design by pointing out the lack of timber and stone, as well as the fact that it never rains. As to Paita's defences:

> At one end of the Town there was a small Fort close by the Sea, but no great Guns in it. This Fort, only with Musquets, will command all the Bay, so as to hinder any Boats from landing. There is another Fort on Top of

the Hill, just over the Town, which commands both it and the lower Fort (164).

Nor does his seaman's eye neglect the importance of Paita as a port:

> One of the best on the Coast of Peru. It is sheltered from the South West by a point of Land, which makes a large Bay and smooth Water for ships to ride in. There is room enough for a good Fleet of ships, and good anchoring in any depth, from 6 Fathom Water to 20 Fathom (164).

But Dampier seems to have been particularly fascinated by the Indian seamen of nearby Colán, who supplied Paita with its provisions of fish, other food and water from its river. To do so they use what he calls bark-logs or rafts, 'fit only for these Seas, where the Wind is always in a manner the same, not varying above a point or two all the way from Lima, till such time as they come into the Bay of Panama' (166). His account of how these craft are built and sailed, for fishing or as cargo carriers, is particularly detailed. However, apart from this and a couple of other occasions, the native population of Peru disappointingly remain in Dampier's account no more than a vague shadow against the clearer profile of their environment.

Although he failed to travel far inland, like most English visitors, even from the coast Dampier was in awe of the mountains of Peru and Chile:

> The Land ... is of a most prodigious Heighth [sic]. It lies generally in Ridges parallel to the Shore, and 3 or 4 Ridges one with another, each surpassing other in heighth ... They always appear blue when seen at Sea: sometimes they are obscured with Clouds, but not so often as the high Lands in other parts of the World, for here are seldom or never Rains on these Hills, any more than in the Sea near it; neither are they subject to Fogs (121).

Before heading for Mexico and the East Indies, Dampier concluded his work of diligent recording along what he correctly terms 'the less frequented coasts' in the far north of the viceroyalty, beyond La Plata island. Using captured Spanish pilot books, he rounded capes San Francisco and Pasado, described Gallo and Gorgona islands, and visited river estuaries and villages such as Tumaco on the mainland. Correctly again, he identified the very different climate and landscape of these northern coasts

> The Land in the Country is very high and mountainous, and it appears to be very woody. Between Cape Passao and Cape St. Francisco, the Land by the Sea is full of small Points, making as many little sandy Bays between them; and is of an indifferent heighth covered with trees of divers sorts; so that by sailing by this Coast you see nothing but a vast Grove or Wood; which is so much the more pleasant, because the Trees are of several forms, both in respect to their Growth and Colour (184) ... All this Country is subject to very great rains, so that this part of Peru pays for the dry Weather which they have about Lima and all that coast (188).

There is a danger, however, that these few examples of Dampier's powers of observation and description, akin to scientific analyses, might obscure his own principal purpose in the South Sea. This can be rectified by recalling his disclosure of a scheme he had concocted to make himself rich. This involved transporting to Darien Black slaves taken from the Spanish off Guayaquil, and employing them in the gold workings at Santa María. He reported that 'besides what Gold and Sand they take up together, they often find great Lumps wedg'd between the Rocks as if it naturally grew there. I have seen a Lump as big as a Hen's egg' (215). After fortifying the mouth of the river, he claims 'we might have been Masters not only of those Mines ... but of all the Coast as high as Quito'. Obviously, these were, as Dampier himself rightly suggests, 'but Golden Dreams' of the sort that still enticed men to Peru (181).

The turn of the century was to witness the commencement of a period of intensive intrusion by French merchants into the commercial life of Peru, a consequence of the demise of the Habsburg dynasty in Spain and its replacement by a Bourbon monarch. The English, however, also continued to demonstrate their re-awakening of interest, now doubtlessly sharpened by their envy of French commercial enterprise, with the translation of two French works. One of these referred, in fact, to travels undertaken between 1657 and 1659 by Acarete du Biscay who claimed to have arrived from Cadiz by hiding his true nationality. What made it particularly valuable was that it offered a rare foreigner's view of the Viceroyalty of Peru from within, rather than merely from the coast, since it was an account of travels overland from the River Plate to Peru, the first such document in English.[4]

Its author, therefore, could confirm the growing involvement of foreigners in Spanish American trade, having found 22 Dutch and two English ships at anchor off Buenos Aires. Temptingly he lists the contraband cargoes of hides, wool and silver for which they had they traded. But far more than this, he personally followed the illegal route via Córdoba, Santiago del Estero, Salta and Jujuy to Potosí, even itemising freight charges

[4] Information about the overland route from the River Plate to Peru had been acquired and circulated by the English, if not yet published, by various means. For example, in the diary of his participation in Edward Fenton's voyage to the Atlantic coast of South America during 1582 and 1583, Richard Madox set down the information he had compiled from the crew of a boat captured off the coast of Brazil, amongst whom was the Englishman Richard Carter. The latter, locally known as Juan Pérez, had apparently left home 24 years previously and spent half that time at Asunción in Paraguay. He describes two routes with distances from town to town: the first from Buenos Aires via Santa Fe, Córdoba, Santiago del Estero, Potosí, La Plata, Cuzco and Huamanga to Lima, the second to Santiago de la Frontera and Coquimbo on the Chilean coast. Elizabeth S. Donno (ed.), *An Elizabethan in 1582. The Diary of Richard Madox* (Hakluyt Society, 2nd series, vol. 147, London: 1976), pp. 252-253. Ironically, by force rather than by desire, the first of these routes was followed in part to Lima by Francis Drake's cousin, John, who was captured by the Spanish in the River Plate after his ship foundered following his desertion of Fenton, ibid., pp. 40-42

and the additional payments to be handed over in order to secure exemption from being visited and searched before their return to Spain. Even so, his expectation was of profits estimated to be 250 per cent on the re-sale of goods he had acquired. Once in Potosí he found a few other foreigners (from Holland, Ireland, Genoa and his native France), women reportedly excessively addicted to the taking of coca, and 'the best and finest silver in all the Indies', 'in prodigious quantities', whose mining, refining and minting he described at the cost of Indian deaths through illness, the chewing of coca and the harshness of forced labour conditions (47). The picture was rounded off with an account of the timing of the operations of the silver fleet in the South Sea between Arica and Panama, and a sketch of trade between Peru and Chilean ports, including 'a great quantity of dust of gold' from Copiapó, Coquimbo and Valdivia (57).

Interestingly, the volume which contains the above account, namely *Voyages and Discoveries in South America*, also placed before English readers another rare glimpse of the interior of the continent, a record by Cristóbal de Acuña of his journey in 1639 from Quito to Pará in Brazil. Like the first English translation of 1661, this longer version of 1698 was derived from a French edition. Its author weaves an intriguing story which knits together the various elements that long ago had already come to constitute the dream of South American mineral wealth, somewhere at the hidden heart of the continent – the legend of the Amazons, the land of the Omaguas, mountains of silver and gold, a golden lake and El Dorado, 'whose inhabitants were cover'd with plates of gold' (10), all set in 'the richest, most fertile and best peopled country of Peru', through which flow rivers 'filled with a sand of pure Gold, and the waters that always wash them are continually discovering mines of gold and silver in the bowels of the earth' (49–50). In short according to Acuña, when added to its fertility, the abundance of trees, medicinal plants, tobacco, animals and fish, the region he visited was an Earthly Paradise.

The second of the French works translated at the end of the century, and the last of the travellers' accounts, was that of François Froger, journalist of the expedition of Jean-Baptiste de Gennes (1695–96). Its inspiration came from the exploits of French buccaneers in the South Sea, but it was intended also to serve as a reconnaissance of ports, peoples, animal and plant life, as well as of the prospects for commerce. However, as Froger states, 'we were not so happy as to see those fortunate coasts of Peru, from whence we are supply'd with what is generally esteem'd most precious' (80). Failing provisions caused them to turn back from the Straits of Magellan, and so the labours of close observation, drawing and recording extend no further than the Atlantic approaches to Peru and the ever-challenging perils of reaching its remote situation. What Peru continued to promise, what would attract Frenchmen and Englishmen in the following century, and how great was the disappointment at failing to fulfil the hopes, is summed up by Froger:

It may be easily imagin'd in so lamentable a Conjuncture, how great a Mortification this Disappointment was to Persons who hoped to make their Fortune by so noble an Enterprize. There was not one Mariner of the whole squadron who did not choose rather to perish with hunger, than to be diverted from the right Course (80).

# CHAPTER FOUR

# Collections of Voyages and Travels

There is only one place to commence a discussion of the translation, compilation and presentation of materials from history, geography, travellers' tales, letters and other documentary sources, and that is with Richard Hakluyt. His unsurpassed reputation as a collector, translator and editor was laid, and has been maintained throughout history, by three works of increasing scope and size. The first, *Divers Voyages* (1582), was conceived with the general intention of promoting overseas expansion in fulfilment of the ultimate object of colonisation. It was probably intended specifically to gain support for a proposed voyage by Humphrey Gilbert to North America. Granted these aims, one would be correct to assume that Peru does not figure directly in the text. In the present context, we simply need to recognise its significance for our understanding of the growth of English interest overseas at the time of its publication, especially the preoccupation with a North-West passage to Cathay and proposals for colonies on the Atlantic seaboard of North America. However, the highly desirable commodities expected to be found in North America, particularly the precious metals already so avidly sought by Martin Frobisher, would soon become a major motivation for interest in the South Sea. The work also contained Michael Lok's map of North America, the first to show Drake's visit to California after sailing along the coasts of Peru and New Spain.

By the time that the first, single volume edition of the *Principal Navigations* appeared in 1589, Hakluyt was able to include in this intended record of all English voyages and travels, the entry of his fellow countrymen into waters off the shores of Peru, namely John Oxenham into the Gulf of Panama in 1577, followed by Drake and Thomas Cavendish during their respective circumnavigations in 1577–80 and 1586–88. When each of the three sections of this original work became a separate volume in the much expanded, definitive edition a decade later, Hakluyt could extend coverage of the South Sea, and hence of Peru, to include narratives other than those written by Englishmen. Although, despite this enlargement and despite the pamphlet written by him on the colonisation of the Straits of Magellan which we shall come to later, it is probably fair to say that Hakluyt's main concern in respect of the South Sea was directed towards its significance as a maritime route leading to the East Indies and above all to Cathay. Nevertheless, in practice, his work served as the earliest compendium of information in English referring to Peru, thereby recording for his readers the images and anecdotes that others would perpetuate. True to the aims of literature promoting colonisation, Hakluyt's compilation confirmed the mineral wealth of Peru, identified sites such as Potosí and Arica associated with the mining and commerce of silver, fashioned the long-enduring images of Chile's gold and the fertility of its soil in references to Arauco, Valdivia and Santa María, provided accurate locations and notes on ports as far north as Buenaventura, and resolved a geographical controversy. Like the propagandists of settlement in North America, he was also conscious of the need to remove potential drawbacks for those who might be interested in the region. Hence, Spanish defences were not strong, one could return to England through the Straits of Magellan, the indigenous population were mortals of average stature and furthermore implacably opposed to the Spanish.

Since most of what was included in the first edition was retained in that of 1598–1600, we shall concentrate on the latter, listing relevant entries and marking those previously published in 1589 with an asterisk:[1]

1)  * 'The voyage of Sir Thomas Pert and Sebastian Cabot [in] the yere 1516 to Brasil ...': refers ruefully to 'that rich treasurie called Perularia' brought from the 'newfoundland of Peru', which but for the lack of courage 'might long since have beene in the tower of London' (2).

2)  * 'The voyage of John Oxnam (i.e. Oxenham) of Plimmoth ... over the streight of Dariene into the South Sea, Anno 1575': from the 'Discourse' of Lopes Vaz (see item 8 below). Enticed by stories of Peruvian silver disembarked at Panama for onward transport to Spain, Oxenham briefly held tangible evidence of mineral wealth by seizing 60,000 pesos of gold from Quito, although the claim to have added a further 100,000 pesos in silver ingots from the Peruvian treasure fleet seems to have been wishful thinking recorded only by Hakluyt (65).

3)  'A letter of Frier [sic] Alonso ... written in the citie de los Reyes the first of March 1590': describes Arica, 'where they imbarke all the barres of silver', with special reference to its recently constructed defences against English interlopers, namely 'a little fort made hard by the waters side, with certaine small pieces of ordinance', and an assessment of what is felt still to be needed for the port's security (136–37).

---

[1] The following items are to be found in volume III of the 1598–1600 edition of the *Principal Navigations*, and volumes VII (items 1–4) and VIII (items 5–12) of the Dent edition of 1927–28. For an introduction to the man and his work, see David B. Quinn (ed.), *The Hakluyt Handbook* (Hakluyt Society, 2nd series, vols 144–145, London, 1974).

4) 'A letter of Don John de Miramontes Suasola (Zuázola) ... from Arica ... the tenth of March 1590': records the presence of four galleons of 350 tons in the port following rumours of an impending English intrusion into the South Sea, and describes the port as 'the best harbour in all the South Sea: for all the silver which commeth from the mines of Potossi, is shipt in this harbour' (138).

5) * 'The famous voyage of Sir Francis Drake into the South Sea, and therehence about the whole Globe of the earth, begun in the yeere of our Lord, 1577': in which Hakluyt reprints with minor changes the brief account he had added at the last moment to the first edition of his work. It remains a relatively sparse record of the route sailed and booty taken along the coasts of Chile and Peru, with not unfavourable impressions of the Straits of Magellan comparable to those in Fletcher's notes. Although anchorages might be difficult and the cold forever extreme, the trees not only 'are greene continually, and many good and sweete herbes doe very plentifully grow', but also they 'found great store of foule which could not flie, of the bignesse of geese' (56). These again are the features which continued to secure a preference for the straits amongst English navigators as the best route to Peru. This text does, however, make an important correction to a common but erroneous configuration of the coast of Chile on maps of the time, the elimination of the westward bulge on the southern coast of Chile as portrayed, for example, on the famous world maps of Gerard Mercator (1569) and Abraham Ortelius (1570) (58).[2]

6) 'The voyage of Nunno da Silva': by a Portuguese pilot captured by Drake. Mainly a record of ports visited in Peru, and their location, with little descriptive material.

7) 'The voyage of M. John Winter into the South Sea' [1577]: an account by Edward Cliffe of the voyage of the *Elizabeth*, which returned to England after traversing the Straits. In contrast to Fletcher's account of Drake's passage, this emphasised the perils and isolation to be suffered by those sailing for Peru, proved false Spanish reports that the Straits were not re-passable from west to east, and reported to little avail that the Patagonians were 'of a meane stature' and not giants, 'much given to mirth and jollity' (94).

8) 'A discourse of the West Indies and South Sea': written by the

---

[2] The protuberance was eliminated by Ortelius from his famous *Americae sive Novi Orbis Nova Descriptio* and *Typus Orbis Terrarum* (1587). It still bulges westwards into the South Sea, however, in other well-known maps, e.g. Rumold Mercator, *Orbis Terrae Compendiosa Descriptio* (1587 and 1597), re-issued by Michael Mercator, *America sive India Nova* (1595); the world maps of Cornelis de Wytfliet (1597), Matthias Quad (1596), and Cornelis de Jode (1589); and Theodore de Bry, *Americae Pars Magis Cognita* (1592), although not in his *Americae sive Novus Orbis* (1596).

Portuguese Lopes Vaz, covering the period from 1572 to his capture by the Earl of Cumberland's expedition off the River Plate in 1587. This is undoubtedly one of Hakluyt's most comprehensive sources of information about the Viceroyalty of Peru. Vaz discusses the history of Spanish exploration and conquest from the South Sea to the River Plate, giving some attention to Indian resistance, especially in Chile, where he too perpetuates the tale of the death of Pedro de Valdivia forced to drink a cup of molten gold. He records expeditions to the Straits of Magellan, including that of Magellan himself, Drake, and Pedro Sarmiento de Gamboa who 'hath carried the name to be the best navigator in all Spaine' (191–92). It was he who was entrusted with the wearisome, woeful and ultimately tragic task of establishing Spanish settlements within the Straits of Magellan between 1579 and 1584, following Drake's passage. During the latter's proceedings off the coast of Peru, Vaz gives particular attention to the landings, the collection of booty and its final detailed tally. The fortification of Arica (100 houses) is again noted as a reaction to Drake's visit, but Vaz adds that 'they have built towers by the sea side, whereon, seeing any saile that they doe mistrust, they presently make smokes, and so from tower to tower they warne all the countrey' (202).

The discourse is notably useful for its compilation of rarer geographical data relating to areas of the interior of the viceroyalty, such as the New Kingdom of Granada and the River Plate. The former is 'very fruitfull, and bringeth forth much corne & other victuals, and hath many gold-mines, and great quantitie of emeralds, wherof they send so many into Spaine, that now they are become little worth'. Popayán is similarly 'rich of golde, and withall very fruitfull', whilst in the region as a whole the 'Indian people [are] so meeke and gentle of nature, that they are called flies' (160). In the River Plate rather than the recently re-founded Buenos Aires, it is the pre-eminence of the city of Asunción (2,000 houses) that is clearly established, 'one of the greatest in all the Indias', 'exceeding fruitfull, abounding with all kinds of victuals, & with sugar and cotton' (175), whilst from Santa Fe 'there lyeth an open highway leading into the land of Peru' (176). The first town on entering the South Sea is Castro, 'situate upon the worst place of all the coast, for there is small store of golde with scarcitie of victuals, and a sharpe colde ayre' (192). However, save for one further reservation, Chile's growing renown is confirmed for its 'rivers are the cause of divers valleys the fruitfullest in all the worlde, where bread, wine, and other victuals mightily abound: and the sayd rivers are very rich of gold'. The temptation to suggest that it is an earthly paradise is marred by one sad reality, 'it lacketh one onely commoditie, and that is peace' (192–93).

The coast of Peru proper is characterised as a land where 'did never drop of raine fall, since the flood of Noah' (197), yet despite that still agriculturally productive and conducive to the grazing of cattle. Furthermore, 'this countrey of Peru is full of people well apparelled and of civill behaviour. It hath many mines of gold and more of silver, as also great store of copper, and tinne-mines, with abundance of salt peter, and of brimstone to make gun-pouder' (199). For some of the coastal settlements as far as Panama, Vaz offers a descriptive phrase, and occasionally an estimate of their size. Valdivia (150 houses) 'hath twise bene burnt and spoyled by the Indians; so that now it is waxen poore' (196), a fate it shares with Concepción (200 houses), having been burnt four times. At Camaná (200 houses), 'they make store of wine, and have abundance of figges and reisins'. Lima (2,000 houses) 'is very rich', whereas at its port Callao (200 houses) 'a strong fort [was] built since Captaine Drake was upon the coast' (202). After Santa, Trujillo (500 houses) and Paita (200 houses), we reach Guayaquil 'the first place where it raineth, and here they gather Salsaperilla ... and build many shippes'. Puerto Viejo, once rich from its emeralds is now 'waxen poore' since they have been devalued by their very abundance. Lastly, at Buenaventura (20 men), despite its name, 'whosoever go thither must needs meet with evill fortune, the place it selfe is so waterish and unwholesome' (203).

9) 'The admirable and prosperous voyage of ... Master Thomas Cavendish': a narrative of the second English circumnavigation (1586–88) written by Francis Pretty, more detailed and more colourful than that by N. H. in the first edition, which it replaced. After witnessing the wretched remnants and survivors of Spanish attempts to fortify the Straits, Cavendish's landing at the island of Mocha, where like Drake and his men they were mistaken for Spaniards, was opposed by Indians from 'a great place called Arauco', 'wonderfull rich, and full of golde mynes, and yet could it not be subdued at any time by the Spaniards' (216). At Santa María they were impressed by the plentiful supplies of food such as wheat, potatoes, fruits, pigs, hens, maize, and barley, 'as faire, as cleane, and every way as good as any we have in England'. In common with many of diverse nations who were to follow them, they were pre-disposed to believe, and consequently readily convinced by Indians 'held in such slavery' whose language they did not understand but who 'made signes, as neere as our Generall could perceive, that if wee would goe over unto the mayne land unto Arauco, that there was much Golde' (217).

Further north the journal makes some acute and detailed observations of ports, bays and their inhabitants, for example: Quintero (33° 50′) where they travelled seven or eight miles inland, finding many cattle and horses and 'faire fresh rivers all along full of wilde foule', before being halted by 'monstrous high mountains' (219); and

Morro Moreno (23° ½') 'an excellent good harborough' whose
Indians 'are in marvellous awe of the Spaniards, and very simple
people, and live marvellously savagely', whose 'diet is raw fish, which
stinketh most vilely' (220). They investigated the contents of graves,
visited Indian dwellings, and marvelled at the boats they used, 'made
of two skinnes like unto bladders, ... blowen full at one ende with
quilles' (221). At Paita they claimed to have seen 200 houses, 'very
well builded, and marvellous cleane kept in every streete' (226).
However, in a lengthier and well-drawn passage of a place he enjoyed,
Pretty conveys a favourable impression of the Island of Puná, including the furnishings of the *cacique's* palace. Its chambers were constructed with galleries looking both to the sea on one side and the
land on the other, set around a great hall beneath and decorated
with hangings 'of cordovan leather all guilded [sic] over, and painted
very fair and rich' (226). Outside there was a garden of fig trees,
melons, cucumbers, radishes, rosemary and thyme, an orchard of
'orenges sweete and sower, limmons, pomegranates and lymes' (228),
and surrounding pastures where horses, bullocks, oxen and sheep
grazed. Of the owner of such luxury and agreeableness, he writes
that he 'doth make all the Indians upon the Iland to worke and
drudge for him: and hee himselfe is an Indian borne, but is married
to a marvellous faire woman which is Spaniard' (226).

10) 'Certaine rare and special notes most properly belonging to the voyage
of M. Thomas Candish': written by Thomas Fuller. These usefully
list the latitudes of ports on the coasts of Chile and Peru, record a
few soundings taken in the Straits and along the Chilean coast,
describe the lie of the land from different locations, note distances
and sailing times, and finally describe anchorages. Typical is the
following: 'From the bay of Cherrepe unto the bay of Paita it is 45
leagues, the course is 20 leags Westnorthwest unto two islands that
be called The ilands of Lobos, and from thence unto the bay of Paita
it is 25 leagues' (266).

11) * 'A letter of M. Thomas Candish to the right honourable the Lord
Hunsdon, Lord Chamberlaine': summarises Cavendish's first expedition and leaves one in little doubt as to Cavendish's expectations of
the outcome of a voyage to Peru. 'I navigated alongst the coast of
Chili, Peru, and Nueva Espanna, where I made great spoiles: I burnt
and sunke 19 sailes of ships small and great. All the villages and
townes that ever I landed at, I burnt and spoiled: and had I not bene
discovered upon the coast, I had taken great quantitie of treasure'
(279).

12) 'The last voyage of M. Thomas Candish intended for the South
sea ...' [1591–93]: written by John Jane who sailed with the former
Arctic explorer John Davis in the *Desire*. In contrast to Drake's

passage, this account becomes a catalogue of the worst dangers and bitterest privations which could frustrate the ambitions of those steering a course for Peru through the Straits of Magellan with such buoyant hopes. 'Wee indured extreeme stormes, with perpetual snow, where many of our men died with cursed famine, and miserable cold, not having wherewith to cover their bodies nor to fill their bellies, but living by muskles [sic], water and weeds of the sea' (291). On 14 August [1592] it also records the sighting of 'certaine Isles never before discovered by knowen relation' (298), generally considered to be the Falkland Isles, thereby anticipating the sighting by Richard Hawkins.[3]

Although Hakluyt did not add to the *Principal Navigations* before his death in November 1616, he most certainly continued to collect documents and narratives of travels. These, together with some of his published material, were incorporated into the works of a man who has been called his self-appointed successor, Samuel Purchas, compiler and editor of *Hakluytus Posthumus or Purchas his Pilgrimes*, published in 1625.[4] Of the material printed by his predecessor relating to Peru, Purchas reproduces items 5, and 8 to 12 above, generally abbreviated or with minor changes. These we do not need to consider further.

The English reader could glean fresh knowledge about Peru from Purchas's publication of documents relating to Dutch expeditions, which set course for the South Sea en route to the East Indies. They are as follows:[5]

a) 'The Voyage of Oliver Noort ... extracted out of the Latine Diarie' [1598–1601]: the fourth circumnavigation (187–206).

b) 'Of Sebald De Wert his Voyage to the South Sea' [1598–1600]: part of the Jacob Mahu and Simon de Cordes expedition (206–10).

c) 'The Voyage of George Spilbergen ... gathered out of the Latine journall' [1614–17]: the fifth circumnavigation (210–31).

---

[3] A companion of Cavendish on this voyage was Thomas Lodge, who in 1596 published his most successful romance, *A Margarite of America: For Ladies Delight and Ladies Honour*. On the basis of a story said to have been found in the Jesuit library at Santos in Brazil, he claimed to have written the book in the Straits of Magellan. Its dedication refers to 'many wondrous Isles, many strange fishes, many monstrous Patagones' to the south of the Straits.

[4] Previous to this, in 1613, Purchas had published his *Pilgrimage*, swiftly reprinted twice in the following year and in 1617. See Steele, *English Interpreters*, pp. 22–51, and Loren E. Pennington, *The Purchas Handbook* (Hakluyt Society, 2nd series, vols 185–186, London, 1997), for the man and his work.

[5] The Dutch journals can be found in the McLehose edition, Glasgow: 1905–07, vol. II, pp. 187–285, and the letters of Adams, pp. 326–46. An English version of the last Dutch venture to enter the South Sea in the seventeenth century, that of Hendrick Brouwer (1642–44), was only published much later as, *A Voyage to the Kingdom of Chili in America*, in *A Collection of Voyages and Travels*, ed. Awnsham and John Churchill (London: 1732), vol. 1.

d) 'The Sixth Circum-navigation, by William Cornelison Schouten of Horne' [1615–16]: the discovery of Cape Horn (232–84).

e) 'William Adams his Voyage by the Magellan Straights': by an English pilot of the Mahu/Cordes expedition (326–39).

f) 'A Letter of William Adams to his Wife from Japan': less detailed than the previous account (340–46).

In a number of ways the various accounts of Dutch experiences in reaching Peru are similar. As records of the first exploratory intrusions by seamen of that nation into the South Sea, there is a particular care to record the conditions met on land and at sea, both down to and through the Straits of Magellan. Hence, it might be possible, for those so tempted in Holland, to estimate the viability of a western route to the East Indies, assess any opportunities for trade en route in South America, and perhaps even find locations for commercial outposts. This is especially the case in the accounts of those who either wintered in the Straits or along the Patagonian coast. Typical of the former is Purchas's account of the suf- ferings of de Weert and his crew. 'Alway [sic] the storme founde them worke, and miserable was their toyle without any furtherance to their intended Voyage. Raine, Winde, Snow, Hayle, Hunger, losses of Anchors, spoyles of Ship and Tackling, Sicknesse, Death, Savages; want of store, and store of wants, conspired a fulnesse of miseries' (208). It is hardly surprising that they turned back, never to see Peru.

But the most striking and diverse descriptions are those offered by the first Dutch circumnavigator, in respect of places such as Puerto Deseado on the Patagonian coast, Cabo Vírgenes, and Puerto Hambre within the Straits of Magellan. For in addition to the ceaseless torments of the winter, van Noort accurately records sightings of abundant wild life such as penguins and ostriches which sustained them through their deprivation, and similarly the vegetation, such as 'two trees of sower Plumbes which cured the sicke [of scurvy] in fifteene dayes' (189). He demonstrates at the same location an acute interest in the local populations encountered, describing their appearance, dwellings, dress, weapons and social organi- sation, even attempting to note down names of tribes and words from their languages. Despite this, confounding the evidence of his eyes, he was unable to free himself from the conviction that elsewhere in the region lived a race of giants, mentioned in all these accounts of Dutch voyages with the exception of those written by William Adams. In a phrase remi- niscent of medieval European legends about brutish and mal-formed men of the woods, the de Weert narrative refers to 'wilde men, of ten or eleven foot ... with red bodies and long haire' (208–09). Spilbergen's men claimed to have seen a man of 'giantly stature' (212) on a hilltop, and Schouten 'found mens bones of tenne and eleven foot long' (241). The latter journal is also a vivid record of teeming marine life, telling how they found the 'horn' of a 'sea monster' sticking into their ship when they careened it, and how they sighted thousands of whales, 'so that we were forced to looke well about us, and to winde and turne to shunne the Whales, least we should sayle upon them' (243).

The first Dutch expeditions to pass into the South Sea established the Chilean islands of Mocha and Santa María as their preferred place of rendezvous and refreshment after passing the Straits. Here, like most foreign intruders into the South Sea, they were perforce keen to barter items like knives, hatchets and cloth for fresh provisions in the form of sheep, hens, maize, wine and fruits, to combat what Adams calls their 'wonderfull hunger' (342). Van Noort again is the most colourful but also prejudiced observer, referring to the natives 'drunken feasts' and 'Bacchanall mysteries' at which they drink chicha, 'somewhat sowerish, made of Mays, which the toothlesse old women chew'. Disapprovingly, he comments that men have many wives purchased from their parents and that 'their life is loose, scarcely subject to any law' (194), a clear indicator of their inferiority.

Nevertheless, doubtlessly in anticipation of some future opportunity to exploit the situation, the Dutch journalists like their English counterparts are prompt to note the state of war existing between Spaniards and indigenous people on the mainland. In fact before van Noort's arrival, over 50 members of the Cordes expedition had been killed at Punta de Lavapié south of Concepción, and others, as Adams reports, at Mocha by Indians who presumably at first assumed them to be Spaniards. From captured Spanish correspondence, van Noort himself was able to record the reason for such a hostile reception, namely the great revolt which coincided with this period of Dutch intrusion and culminated in the destruction of Valdivia in November 1599. In doing this he resurrects and extends the scope of the story of the death of the city's founder, describing how Spaniards were killed by Indians who 'thrust gold into their mouthes, and bid them satiate themselves with that for which they had raised such persecutions' (196).

Apart from these initial setbacks, Dutch recollections of the coasts of the Viceroyalty of Peru are as favourable as the English. Santiago is a 'towne fertile of Wine much like Claret in tast and colour. There are plenty of sheepe which they kill onely for their sewet, wherewith they lade whole shippes' (195). Indeed, in phrases comparable with those of Narborough as an invitation to settlement:

The region of Chili, from S. Iago to Baldivia, is the most fertile in the world, and of most wholesome ayre, insomuch that few are there sicke: yea, a sword put up into the scabbard all wet with the dewe, doth not therewith rust. Fruits, Mays, Hogges, Horses, Kine, Sheepe, Goats, are plentifull and wander in great herds, besides Gold-mines' (196).

For Spilbergen's fleet Quintero was a 'faire and secure harbour' (214) where they found ample wood, water and fish and saw many wild horses.

Arica, though attractive and verdant, detained them very little because the silver galleons they had hoped to find were not in port. Huarmey was judged to be 'a pleasant place with a large Haven. Neare unto it is a Lake of standing water' (217). Paita, which commonly drew the attention of intruders, in Purchas's version was now surprisingly considered to be 'strong and impregnable'. There were in it 'two Churches, one Monasterie and many goodly Buildings, an excellent haven to which all the ships of Panama resorted' (218).

In general, Spilbergen's journal is concerned with recording the events which befell the expedition, but Purchas did append to his extract a resumé of a description of Peru by a captured *limeño*, whose name he recorded as Pedro de Madriga, with notes from a second shorter description of Chile. The former outlines the system of government by viceroys and *audiencias* and its seat in Lima, lists hospitals and colleges and describes ecclesiastical foundations, their personnel and their revenue. Some attention is also directed towards the capital's population, both Spanish and Indian, with their trades and occupations. Callao is claimed to have a population of 800 inhabitants, Cuzco and Arequipa 6,000 and 2,000 Spaniards respectively. The Bishop of Chuquisaca has an income of 30,000 ducats and 'at Potosí live fifteen hundred shifting Card-players, and nimming companions which live by their wits'. But since, according to Purchas, 'it were tedious to relate the full story' (221), he cuts short his version of Madriga's account and for similar reasons even more drastically reduces the list of Chilean ports. 'Coquimbo hath store of brasse whereas Baldivia is rich in Gold', for example. Nevertheless, he does preserve two colourful episodes relating to the Indian rising of 1599. The first explains how the wives of 800 Spaniards were captured, 'which they offered to exchange, giving for each, a pair of Shooes, a Bridle, a Sword, and a paire of Stirrops'. Whereas the second further embroiders the tale of death by molten gold. 'They powred molten Gold into the Governours mouth, made a Cup of his skull, and made pipes of his shank-bones, in memory of their victory' (222).

The records of Dutch voyages to Peru display a certain coherence and a sense of gradual progress in the broadening of knowledge and experience, now passed on through translation to English readers. In general, they confirm the English reports of great mineral wealth and fertile soils in the south. Likewise, the Dutch are equally prone to believe in fantastic tales, but at the same time they can be reliable providers of facts about the natural environment, and especially about geographical realities. Although the western route to the East Indies they inherited from Drake would never eclipse that via the Cape of Good Hope, collectively over a period of forty years, various Dutch ventures, some of whose experiences were quickly available in English, demonstrated to the enemies of Spain the albeit perilous accessibility of Peru by alternative sea routes. Other accounts collected by Purchas are more the story of individual experiences. This is the case of the following:[6]

a) 'The Relation of Peter Carder of St. Verian in Cornwall' (136–46).

b) 'Master Thomas Candish his Discourse of his fatall and disastrous voyage towards the South Sea' (151–77).

c) 'The admirable adventures and strange fortunes of Master Antonie Knivet' (177–274).

d) 'A Briefe Note written by Master John Ellis' (199–203).

e) 'A briefe Relation of an Englishman which had beene thirteene yeeres Captive to the Spaniards in Peru' (205–06).

f) 'The Relation of Alexandro Ursino concerning the coast of Terra Firma, and the secrets of Peru, and Chili' (207–12).

When read together, whilst still rich in strange and diverting detail, as individual struggles for survival against dreadful adversity the above accounts constitute a sobering reminder and sombre warning of the true trials to be overcome by those lured to seek the legendary wealth of Peru, or foolish enough to discount the severity of the obstacles presented by such an undertaking. Whether myth or reality in English eyes, the quest for Peru was an exploit fraught with risk, and in Cavendish's case at least, one which drove him to the uttermost despair. Of the first three writers above, only Peter Carder actually succeeded in reaching the South Sea. His tale is significant as a matter-of-fact record of separation from his ship with seven companions on the southern coast of Chile during Drake's circumnavigation, the manner of his survival on a diet of oysters, mussels, crabs, roots and the salted meat of penguins, and the re-passing of the Straits of Magellan in a pinnace, further early proof that a return to England was possible by that route. The rest of the story is one of remarkable experiences 'as well among divers Savages as Christians' (136) in the River Plate and Brazil, the former allegedly including cannibals.

Cavendish, by contrast, in addition to the motives for his personal bitterness and sorrow, repeatedly records the perils of the southern Atlantic and how 'we were beaten out of the Strait with a most monstrous storme' (156):

> Such was the furie of the … windes [that] we had a new shift of sailes cleane blowne away, and our ship in danger to sinke in the Sea three times (153) …
> [I] found that besides the decay of my men, and expence of my victuall, the snow and frost decayed our sailes and tackle, and the contagiousnesse of the place to bee such … as there was no long staying, without the utter ruine of us all (154).

[6] Purchas, *Pilgrimes*, vol. XVI, pp. 136–289, contains the accounts of Carder, Cavendish and Knivet, whilst vol. XVII, pp. 199–212, has those of Ellis, the anonymous Englishman and Ursino.

Anthony Knivet, a gentleman adventurer who accompanied Cavendish on his last voyage, perhaps merits even greater renown than Carder for the copious, vivid and harrowing details of the hardships endured and overcome during his long captivity in Brazil. Yet it is a grim and dark tale forever intermingled with his private fears, famine, the customs of cannibals, rumours of fighting women, and lightened only by the dreams of neighbouring lands rich in gold and precious metals. 'When we saw the peeces of Gold and those Stones', he wrote, 'we made accompt that we were very neere Potasin' (220). At Port Desire the 'giants' were now 'of fifteene or sixteene spans of height' (265), with feet four times a normal length. Moreover, at Port Famine in the Straits, there lived a 'kinde of strange cannibals, short of body, not above five and six spans high, and very strong and thicke made: their mouthes are verie bigge, and reach almost to their eares' (266). But whereas Knivet provides amply uncommon entertainment for those with a taste for the extraordinary, his illustrations of the rigours of the climate and the extremes of cold in the Straits are unforgettable reminders of the hardships. The first is an incident of personal misfortune, for having gone ashore 'I was nummed, that I could not stirre my legs, and pulling off my stockings, my toes came with them, and all my feete were as blacke as soote' (186). The second involved a companion called Harris, interestingly described as a goldsmith, who 'lost his Nose: for going to blow it with his fingers, cast it into the fire' (187).

The note by John Ellis lists ports he visited as one of Richard Hawkins's captains. This is above all a seaman's record of the course sailed from the Straits of Magellan to Atacames, with anchorages and latitudes. Lima, however, is an exception, being 'neere as bigge as London within the walls: the houses are of Lome baked, for want of stone. There are neere twentie thousand negros in Lima' (201). Following his imprisonment, he was one of the few Englishmen of his time to travel inland, to Huamanga and Cuzco, describing the Inca roads and *tambos*. Of Cuzco he writes that it is 'about the bignesse of Bristow [i.e. Bristol], without a wall, having a Castle halfe a mile off on the side of an Hill, builded with stones of twentie tuns weight strangely joyned without morter' (201). He concludes with reference to Indian labour at Potosí and the wool and cotton trade of Quito. 'They drive sheepe to Lima twentie thousand in a Flocke, and be halfe a yeere in the Passage' (202). Sadly, his fellow Englishman who had also been a captive in Peru for some thirteen years, produced nothing more than a sketchy diary of his voyage to Mexico in 1602, and from there to Spain.

Writing in 1581, the Italian Ursino claimed to be drawing on 34 years of travels in the New World. His 'secrets' are the names of towns, with some rough estimates of their Spanish population, comments on the terrain, and above all assessments of the amounts of precious metals mined and the routes by which they are shipped to Spain. Continuing the comparisons, Cuzco now appears 'bigger then Rome: there is a Bishop and about 1,000

Spaniards', the same number as in Lima. Panama by contrast is estimated to have 400 Spaniards, Trujillo, 'a very wealthy town' and Arequipa 200 each, Paita, 'the harborough for all the Fleete for fresh provision', 100 men, Puerto Viejo 'another harborough where the Fleete taketh in fresh victuals ... not three Spaniards', and in the whole of Chile 'not above 1,300 Spaniards'.

Concerning the movements of the South Sea fleet, which the Spanish crown presumably would have preferred to keep as secret as possible, and which was one of the most irresistible attractions to foreign interlopers of whatever nationality or occupation, Ursino notes that 'in February the silver comes from Potossi and Porco to Lima: about the same time the Ships returne from Chili to Lima with Gold. In Aprill they set forth from Lima foure Ships, and in fifteene dayes they arrive at Panama'. Why the fleet continued to exercise such a fascination from the time of Drake to the age of the buccaneers and beyond is demonstrated by Ursino's estimate that the crown proportion of Chilean gold was 'one million', presumably pesos, that of private individuals one and a half million, and the total amount of gold and silver brought to Lima about twelve millions. In addition, a further five million pesos of crown gold was taken by river from New Granada to Cartagena, with an equal amount belonging to merchants.

As for the terrain, Ursino repeats the contrast of extremes of dryness and fertility, heat and cold. 'From the point Saint Helen to Copiapo it never raineth', but in Lima and Trujillo are cultivated oranges, pomegranates, citrons and melons. Whilst 'La Loma de Camana is a very fertile soile, yeelding abundance of grasse' (211).

If we turn to material translated by Purchas from Spanish, *His Pilgrimes* includes extracts of varying length from some of the major chroniclers of Indian and Spanish Peru:[7]

a) 'Notes of the West Indies, gathered out of Pedro Ordonnes de Cevallos' (212–17).

b) 'Observations of things most remarkable, collected out of the first part of the Commentaries Royall' (311–412).

c) 'Briefe notes of Francis Pizarro his conquest of Peru' (412–18).

d) 'The conquest of Peru and Cuzco ... by Francisco de Xeres' (419–28).

e) 'Relations of Occurrents in the Conquest of Peru ... by Pedro Sancho' (428–36).

[7] The notes from Ordóñez de Cevallos are in Purchas, *Pilgrimes*, vol. XVII, pp. 212–17, and the remainder pp. 311–436. A new edition of Ordóñez was published in Biblioteca de Viajeros Hispánicos, 8 (Madrid: Miraguano, 1993). Purchas also includes abridged versions of the works of authors already discussed above: Acosta, vol. XV, pp. 1–148; Richard Hawkins, vol. XVII, pp. 57–199; and Lopes Vaz, vol. XVII, pp. 247–92.

Unfortunately, Purchas chose severely to restrict his selections from the
*Viage del mundo* of Ordóñez de Cevallos, published in 1614, with the result
that they only give a hint of the disparate nature of the text, particularly
with regard to the northern inland regions of the viceroyalty. Amongst the
list of towns, Muso in the New Kingdom of Granada owes its fame to a
'store of the best Emeralds taken out of a rocke', in particular one priceless
gem sent to Clara Eugenia, daughter of King Philip. In Quito we learn
that two things are dear, wine and asses, with the result that 'it is a proverb
– what is dearest in Quito? An asse'. Of Lima he states that 'no houses
are covered with roofes, bee they ever so large, because they never have
raine. No Citie in India is richer then it'. Potosí is naturally singled out
as the origin of so much wealth, its hill overhung by a cloud, 'even in the
cleerest dayes, as it were marking and pointing out the riches thereof'.
But some hint of the perils and the human cost of mining emerge in the
statement that 'the entrance and Myne-works are so dangerous, that they
which goe in, use to take the Sacrament of the Altar, as if they went to
their death, because few returne' (212).

In a resumé of the racial groups in society, Ordóñez candidly reveals
that 'the Spaniards in these parts neither plow the ground, nor worke in
the Mynes ... Scarcesly shal you find any Spanish youth, which will betake
himselfe to the service of any man, except the Vice-roy'. Indians, on the
other hand 'are base minded, ... wittie, liers, and strong drinkers'. But he
admits, 'they are very expert in the Arts which they learne, although it be
writing or reading, which yet is not granted them to learne'. Finally,
mestizos 'wander up and downe poore and beggarly, nor give their minds
to learne any handicrafts. It were good they were forced to labour' (215).
The rest of Purchas's extracts from Ordóñez relate to church revenues and
their distribution, as well as those of the crown.

Already concerned by the vast volume of material which he was pro-
cessing, when it came to one of the truly indispensable early texts on Peru,
Garcilaso de la Vega's *Comentarios reales*, Purchas was obliged to sift out
what he considered new and appealing to English readers. However, despite
the abridgement, one must applaud the initiative which at least rendered
sections of the substantial text into English, making accessible information
on language, history until the first Túpac Amaru revolt, religious beliefs
and rites, culture and crafts. English readers saw before them the glittering
and sumptuous spectacle of the Temple of the Sun in Cuzco, its golden
image, its 'chamfred worke of gold, in forme of a crowne' (341), its garden
of gold and silver, and its associated chapels similarly adorned. As we have
already seen, they would have to wait a further 60 years for a more complete
version of the text.

When taken together, the extracts from the remaining three Spanish
chroniclers cover the historical period from the initial exploratory venture
of Pizarro and Almagro in 1524, until several months after the occupation
of Cuzco a decade later. In fact, this is the same period as that covered

by those earliest accounts of Spanish exploits in Peru, translated in 1534 into European languages other than English. Although Purchas now rescued these important narratives from the ignorance of all but readers of Spanish, they were not re-published in English for between 250 and 300 years. The first of his extracts, from Cristóbal de Mena, relates the confrontation of Pizarro and Atahualpa, the arrangement of the latter's 'ransom', its collection from sites such as the temples at Cuzco and Pachacámac, and its value. It incorporates the tale of how the shoes of Hernando Pizarro's horse were worn down by the stepped Inca roads, with the result that he 'commanded the Indians to shooe his Horses with Gold and Silver' (411).

Xerez, perhaps the best of the early chroniclers, is again much abbreviated to relate the voyages of discovery to Peru, but again mainly to concentrate on events at Cajamarca and somewhat more precisely on the 'ransom'. Using Sancho de la Hoz, Purchas is able to extend his coverage to Cuzco, the looting of its riches and the creation in 1534 of a Spanish municipality. The precious artefacts collected included 'a chaire or throne of most fine Gold', 'a Fountayne of Gold of excellent workmanship' (429), 'sheepe of fine Gold very great', and ten or twelve 'Statues of women in their just bignesse and proportion, artificially composed of fine Gold (432)'. But although here as elsewhere Purchas's selections seem above all intended to convey the splendour and magnitude of Peru's mineral wealth, he does take from Sancho some descriptions of the mountains, of Cuzco and especially of its 'faire Fortresse of earth and stone'. 'Many Spaniards which have beene in Lumbardie and other strange Kingdomes, say that they have never seen such a building ... being of stones so great, that no man would imagine them layd there by the hands of men, as great as pieces of stonie Mountaynes and Rockes (434).

The final collection, of rather more modest intention and proportions than those hitherto considered, is that of William Hacke. It consists of three parts:

 i) 'Cowley's voyage round the globe' [1683–86].
 ii) 'Sharp's journal of a voyage to the South Seas' [1680–82].
 iii) 'Wood's voyage through the Straits of Magellan' [1669–71].

From his acquaintance with buccaneers in Wapping by the River Thames, Hacke was able to compile documents related to their activities in the South Sea in the 1680s. The first of these, by a self-professed reluctant participant, does not add to the description of events and settings provided by Dampier and Wafer, although Hacke did include a chart of the circumnavigation and a map of the Galapagos based on Ambrose Cowley's survey and naming of the islands.[8] Like Cowley's, Sharp's journal

[8] Alec McEwen, 'The English Place-Names of the Galápagos', *The Geographical Journal*, vol. 154, 1988, pp. 234–42.

which is considerably abridged mainly deals with buccaneering episodes also previously recounted and published, this time by Basil Ringrose in Exquemelin's *Bucaniers of America* (1685). John Wood's log, of course, was compiled during the Narborough expedition to Valdivia. Its interest lies in its often detailed observations on the approaches to the Straits and their passage in both directions, constituting a valuable practical guide for seamen.

# CHAPTER FIVE

# Geographies and Atlases

## World geographies [1]

In this category we find the earliest description of the coasts of the New World by an English writer, Roger Barlow, presented in the form of a manuscript geography to Henry VIII. Naturally, as a consequence of its early composition in 1540 the references to Peru are few in number, but already indicative of the trend others would follow. The work is essentially a translation of Martín Fernández de Enciso's *Suma de geographia* (Seville: 1519), to which Barlow has made additions with particular reference to the region of the rivers Plate and Paraná. This is an area he was one of the first Englishmen to visit in 1526, as supercargo in the expedition of Sebastian Cabot diverted from its aim of reaching the East Indies by rumours of precious metals in the interior of South America. Therefore, supported by personal observation of native women wearing ornaments of gold and silver, knowledge of the progress of Spanish exploration southwards from Panama along South Sea coasts, and the reports of survivors from the expedition of Juan Díaz de Solís to the River Plate a decade previously, Barlow sketches out the description of a 'sierra or mount where they say is a king where is a great abundance of gold and silver', ruled by a monarch whose 'vessels and stoles that he sitteth on is of gold and sylver'. 'This lond' he continues, 'and the lond of Pirro, wᶜʰ is in the southside that the Spaniards have dyscovered of late, is all one lond, wheras thei had so grete riches of gold and sylver' (162). Barely was Pizarro's conquest complete, when these were the tantalising ingredients that would shape the lure of Peru for Englishmen drawn to its remote coasts during the coming centuries. The artful interweaving of legend and fact would be confirmed by tales of a fabulously wealthy 'white king',[2] the arrival of

---

[1] For analysis and listings of geographical literature, see Eva G. R. Taylor, *Tudor Geography, 1485–1583* (London: Methuen, 1930), and *Late Tudor and Stuart Geography, 1583–1650* (London: Methuen, 1934).

[2] Aleixo García had travelled from the coast of Brazil, probably in 1524, to the River Paraguay and then towards Upper Peru (Bolivia) in search of this monarch. Charles E. Nowell, 'Aleixo García and the White King', *Hispanic American Historical Review*, vol. 26, 1946, pp. 450–66.

Atahualpa's ransom in Spain, the pillaging of Cuzco's Temple of the Sun and the discovery in 1545 of a mountain of silver at Potosí.

The earliest offering of the next century was the first English translation of Giovanni Botero's *Le relationi universali* (Rome: 1591). At once a popular text, it was soon followed by several enlarged, revised editions. These were probably valued more for their material on Asia and the East Indies rather than America, at a time of growing English commercial interest in those parts. As for Peru, brief comments on the region's location, its size and Inca history are followed by the now commonplace references to 'incredible treasures of gold and silver' (39). Potosí, it is claimed, had yielded III million pesos in revenue to the crown in the space of 40 years, and only two thirds of its miners had paid their dues.

Gold, according to Robert Stafforde, in his geography of 1607, was so plentiful when the Spaniards arrived in the land of Peruana, 'that they shooed their horses with it', a tale as we have seen which was recounted by the chronicler Cristóbal de Mena. But this penchant for the fanciful rather than the 'real' embraces also the native inhabitants of that land, in phrases chosen to pander to the hankering of readers of the age for such material. In short, they are cruel, rude, barbarous, man eaters and idolaters, who 'if they take any man captive, they slice his body out into collops, and broile it upon the wales, making merry so long as that it indures them'.[3] It is no surprise, then, to learn that they were also giants, since the Spanish had found teeth 'three fingers in breadth, and foure in length'. In comparison with these remarkable imaginings, he finds little worthy of note in Chile except to recall, via Gómara and Zárate, the story of a river which flows by day but not at night (63–64).

Judging by the number of editions (twelve by 1664), the widest readership for geographies of the early seventeenth century seems to have been won by Bishop George Abbott, later Archbishop of Canterbury, whose original work of 1599, rather sparse in respect of Spanish America, appeared in an enlarged version from 1605. It is also somewhat primitive in its depiction of 'that huge and myghtie countrie' whose people are 'very barbarous and without God, men of very great stature', the latter comment traced by him to Cieza de León (T2). It is certainly predictable in its recording of fabulous mineral wealth, illustrating this by reference to Atahualpa's so-called ransom. Nevertheless, it does raise themes of contemporary relevance when alluding to the consequences of Spanish cruelty in employing Indians as miners 'as if they had been beastes' (from Las Casas), as well as by recording the wider impact of the influx of American precious metals into Europe. Recalling the inflation that had spread beyond the Iberian Peninsula to many states, Abbott surmises that this is 'the true reason wherfore

[3] Harry C. Porter, *The Inconstant Savage: England and the North American Indian, 1500–1600* (London: Duckworth, 1979), p. 14, cites a rather similar episode whose victim was a Spanish sailor, included in Eden's *Newe India* and taken from Vespucci.

all things in Christendome ... do serve to be sold at a higher rate, than they were in the daies of our forefathers'. He adds, 'it is the plenty of Gold and Silver which is brought from this America, that maketh mony to be in greater store' (Rv–R2v).

In 1657, Robert Fage showed a minimal interest in America, listing cities and rivers whilst limiting his interest in Peru to Atahualpa's 'ransom'. In the same year, the Reverend Samuel Clarke outlined a mainly dry and mountainous land whose rivers irrigated vineyards and cornfields. Some attention was also paid to individual cities such as Cajamarca whose 'streets are as strait as a line' (176), or Cuzco and its fortress, 'that may rather seem the work of devils than of men' (175). But the entire section on Peru, using Spanish sources via Purchas, is dominated by frequent references to gold and silver, on this occasion exemplified by a detailed and glowing account of the Temple of the Sun and its fabled garden in the former Inca capital. Chile too is 'fruitful and watered with many rivers', but the chief quality of the latter, in the manner of Richard Hawkins's version, is that 'every shower is a shower of gold: for with the violence of the water falling from the mountains, it brings from them gold along with it' (179–80). In keeping with the marked anti-Spanish tone of the Cromwellian age in which it was written, there is also a section on Spanish cruelty based on Las Casas.

A little over a decade later, and therefore coinciding with the period of English interest in the west coast of South America which culminated in the Narborough expedition to Chile, a more professional-looking, folio geography was published, with much improved illustrations. Its author, Richard Blome, acknowledged a debt to Nicholas Sanson, geographer to the French king, and displayed a knowledge of the Inca Garcilaso. The text lauded the prestige of Peru, 'so rich, and great, that All America Meridionalis ... sometimes takes the name Peruviana' (40). Set amidst a thinly sketched background of wooded and forested Andes, well-watered plains and sandy, dry coast, this volume offers a much wider coverage of coastal and inland cities and towns, many now beyond the frontiers of modern Peru, although in most cases the descriptions are limited to a single phrase.

For example, Cuenca now in Ecuador is reported to be 'seated in a country well stored with mines of gold, silver, copper, iron and veins of silver'. Loja is set 'in a sweet and pleasant valley between two rivers', and close to Manta 'is a rich vein of emeralds' (41–42). Guayaquil as ever is remembered for its sarsaparilla, Quijos for its cinnamon, Oropesa in Peru for its vermillion or quicksilver and Santa Cruz de la Sierra (Bolivia) for its fierce people (the *chiriguanos*), its wheat, maize, wine, deer and ostriches. After giving similar attention to coastal towns, Lima and Cuzco are granted a little more space, the former noted for its 'pleasant valley, sweet fields, delightful gardens', well built houses and broad streets, and the latter judged to be 'of the greatest account in all this country, as well for its beauty, and greatness, as for its populousness'. But, inexplicably, according to Blome 'the inhabitants of Huánuco, and of Chachapoyas, are the most civilised of Peru' (42–43). Although Potosí remains 'the richest [mine] in the world', the unprecedented overall impression conveyed in this instance is one of decline, a rare reflection of the reality of diminishing output, for 'they have now exhausted all that was the best, and easiest to take away', with the result that despite the labours of 20,000 miners one *quintal* of ore barely yields but 2 ounces of pure silver (44).

Nevertheless, in Blome's descriptive list of towns the fame of Chile remains untarnished, a reputation in part due to its coastal valleys, 'healthful, serene, temperate', with fertile soil and 'capacious' harbours such as Concepción and Valdivia. But it is the region's mineral wealth, especially its gold, that for over a century, and certainly since the time of Drake, had provided English writers with the main motive for their adulation. Blome in turn perpetuates the fame of Valdivia and Osorno in this respect, adding that there is 'throughout all Chili, so great a quantity of sand-gold ... that a certain author hath been bold to say, that Chili was but a plate of gold' (45).

The mix of fact and fiction, however, still remains, for although the 'giants' of Chile are now somewhat reduced to merely 'well proportioned, strong, active, warlike and cruel' individuals over six feet tall (47), renowned for their resistance against the Spanish, an interest in the oddities of Peru lingers in the references to plants with remarkable qualities. One of these has the power to prophecy either death or recovery for the sick, whilst another produces flowers on different parts of the plant in summer and winter (44).

In the penultimate decade of the century, the translation of the work of another geographer at the French court, Pierre Duval, shows some curiosity in the southern Atlantic approaches to the South Sea and the *Terra Australis Incognita* (the 'Southern Indies' or 'Third World' he suggests) (7), significantly at a time of growing commercial interest by his countrymen in Peru. The courses sailed by Magellan, Lemaire and Hendrick Brouwer are usefully compared. The legend of Patagonian giants is laid to rest on the evidence of recent English reports. Even so, the persistent and ever adaptable legends of Old and New World origin live on in the form of Lake Parima, where descendants of the former emperor Huayna Cápac are reputed to live, in the Amazons who remain 'great women who make war with an admirable dexterity and valour', and at Manoa which 'is called El Dorado, by reason of the quantity of gold, which is said to be there so great, ... that the inhabitants make their arms of it, [and] cover their bodies with it, after having rubbed them with oyl or balm' (44). The dazzling golden and silver splendours of the Indian past (Atahualpa's 'ransom', Cuzco and its Temple of the Sun, 'wainscoted with silver') (13) are duly recalled, as are those of the Spanish colony (Potosí which has 'all the conveniences and delights of life' (48), the mines of Chile still believed to be producing 'the purest gold in the world' (49), and the trans-isthmian trade route with Spain (40–44). All of these lead to a conclusion that might well have gained wide approval amongst many of the English commentators we have been citing, namely that 'Peru is without contradiction, the richest countrey [sic] in the world' (45). However, anticipating developments that would occur nearly a century later, Duval looks ahead from the legends and sources of wealth associated with the past. Despite official Spanish prohibitions, he recognises the future in the potential for commercial growth at Buenos Aires, on the basis of expansion in the area's already existing trade with Brazil and Europe.

Three years later in 1688, Robert Morden covered the same topics at times word for word, dithering perhaps more than most over his readiness to accept the most widespread legends. He struggles against the idea of a whole army of warrior women or Amazons, but still recalls that some Indians are 'remarkable for the bigness of their ears' (522), and certainly upholds and repeats the view that 'Peru is certainly the richest country in the world', where 'the very Earth is oftentimes nothing but gold and silver' (527). His main novelty was to incorporate detailed material on the tides, vegetation, animals and ports of the South Atlantic and Straits of Magellan, undoubtedly derived from Narborough's voyage. In doing so he repeats the latter's favourable expectations of the prospects for 'a very advantageous trade in those parts, by reason of the abundance of gold and silver' (517). To a lesser extent, he draws also on the first buccaneer intrusions into the South Sea, for example reporting their sea battle with the Peruvian squadron off Perico Isle in the Gulf of Panama in (1685), and how La Serena was taken and burnt by them despite their taste for its 'stawberries as big as walnuts' (520–21).[4] Finally Edmund Bohun, using an alphabetical arrangement of place names, writes rare sceptical notes under the heading 'Peru', deducing that 'what the Spaniards report of the fertility, wealth, and government of this kingdom is scarce credible'.

## Geographies of the New World

The activities of Richard Eden as propagandist of empire and forerunner of Hakluyt are widely known and discussed, but generally only indirectly can they be related to Peru. His *Newe India* (1553) was, in reality, a translation of those parts of Sebastian Münster's *Cosmographia* (1544) dealing with the East and West Indies, the former more favourably than the latter. It drew on the voyages of Columbus and Vespucci to publicise themes his compatriots would later ascribe to the New World generally, namely vast mineral wealth, fertile lands, abundant rivers, an exuberant flora and fauna, and human rarities such as cannibals and Amazons. Two

---

[4] On the battle in the Gulf of Panama, see Peter T. Bradley, 'Los bucaneros en el Istmo y Bahía de Panamá', *Revista Cultural Lotería*, 378 (1990), 5–32.

years later, his edition of the first three decades of Peter Martyr's *Decades* (plus excerpts from Gonzalo Fernández de Oviedo and from Gómara), placed before English readers their first history of Spain's exploits in America, especially the West Indies, pre-dating the translation of the latter's complete work. In a sense it also turned English eyes more longingly westwards in search of fresh opportunities, perhaps even to the South Sea and Peru, for it contained an abbreviated account of Magellan's expedition of circumnavigation and the expeditions of others to the River Plate. Following Eden's death in 1576, it was left to Richard Willes to edit the *History of Travayle*. He used Eden's papers to address themes established by his predecessor, but added his own notes on Peru and the River Plate. These were the first put into print by an English author, some eight years after the translation of Thevet and over a decade before the first publication of Hakluyt's compilation of writings. Thus, Peru 'is taken to be the rychest land in golde, silver, pearles, precious stones, and spices, that ever was founde yet to this day. For gold is there in suche plentie that they make pyspots thereof, and other vessels applied to fylthy uses'. Similarly, in the style of Columbus, the fruitfulness of the land on the one hand, is conveyed by the phrase 'it seemeth in a maner an earthly paradise', whilst on the other a fascination with the region's perceived oddities is expressed in the statement that 'theyr sheepe are of suche heyght, that they use them insteede of horses'. Willes, finally, is particularly generous to the people of Peru, judged to be 'witty, gentle, cunning in arts, [and] faithful of promise' (226–226v).

By the middle of the next century, Puritan England under Oliver Cromwell had turned to the New World, in part for the exploitation of its resources and as a challenge to Spain. International rivalry and propaganda underlies the now common allusions to the human cost of Spain's imperial enterprise. Even so, after affirming the value of geography in his preface, by stating that 'nothing [is] so pertinent to a man's felicity, next to the enjoying of happy places, as to know where they are', George Gardyner wrote a text which immediately states his own predominant interest in the New World, by reference to the 'treasures that are yearly drawn from the bowels of the Spanish Regions' (38). Likewise, Chile as ever is a region 'wholsome above all other in the Indies', and the descriptive list of its towns confirms the common view of abundant mineral wealth, cattle and grain, 'excellent pleasant wine' and an 'excellent temperature, as neither too hot nor too cold' (171). As regards Peru, Potosí still 'is much to be admired' for the great quantities of silver. But its caves are 'so intricate and far in the earth, that those that go in take the popish sacraments, the danger of death is so great' (174–75), a comment reminiscent of Purchas's notes taken from Ordóñez de Cevallos. Further description of Peru emphasises this wealth, but also more rarely draws attention to the region's production of wine, sugar and oil. Settlements, mainly ports, are listed as far north as Quito, with brief but practical characteristics of each. Arequipa is a 'rich and flourishing place, and in a wholesome climate' (179), though plagued by earthquakes. Lima, with 4,000 houses, is in a 'rich and pleasant valley' (177). Trujillo is a 'bay not very good for ships' (178), whereas Paita is considered to be 'a good and great harbour' (183). A touch of the fantastic as ever remains, however, in Gardyner's account of 'three wonderfull springs of water, ... a water that turneth so soon as it is stopt to stone. If a man or beast drink of it, it turneth to a stone in his body, and killeth him' (180).

The documents collected and published by N.N. (perhaps Thomas Peake[5]) in 1655, in the very year when Cromwell's 'Western Design' was taking unplanned-for shape in the West Indies, again concentrated on exploitable riches, whilst at the same time linking Spanish wealth from mines such as Potosí to Spanish cruelty towards native societies. This popular theme of the mid-seventeenth century is again alluded to by Gorges, in his recollection of the 'cruel massacres and slaughters of above twenty millions of innocent heathens' alleged by Las Casas (52), whose own work had just been re-published in English as *The Tears of the Indians*. However, although the allusion to Spanish barbarity towards the indigenous population served a political purpose, the latter still had not shed the traits of savagery in English minds. Indeed, the glaring frontispiece of Gorges's *America Painted to the Life* (1659) depicts an illustration of an Indian holding in his left hand the leg of a human being (minus the foot), entitled 'America'. Predominantly, however, in so far as it refers to South America, the text lists English and Dutch voyages to the South Sea (the latter from Johannes de Laet), with a particular interest in the islands frequented off the Chilean coast.

John Ogilby's *America* (1671), claims a wide range of sources but in the main draws on them via Purchas. It coincides with the Narborough expedition to Valdivia, and in Book 1 contains abbreviated narratives of earlier expeditions to the South Sea, from Drake to the Dutchman Hendrick Brouwer, recording important or unusual events and landfalls. These are supported by excellent engravings of America and its regions, although they are entirely fanciful in their depiction of Peruvian towns. Book 3 relates to 'Peruana or Southern America' with some reference to the Incas, the Spanish conquest, the giants of Santa Elena, episodes of foreign intervention in the South Sea, and a touch of misgiving concerning the productiveness of yet deeper veins at Potosí, all soberly done and without notable originality.

## Maps and atlases

Whilst our main intention has been to concentrate on descriptive texts relating to the New World and Peru in particular, it is perhaps appropriate

---

[5] Steele, *English Interpreters*, p. 65.

to end this section devoted to geographical concepts with a brief mention of maps and atlases. Obviously, these offer general information about the global location of Peru, whilst to a varying extent they mark the sites of human settlement and notable geographical features such as bays, headlands, mountains and rivers. Furthermore, they chart the evolution of knowledge about the routes to Peru and the correct delineation of the entire western coastline of the viceroyalty. What is abundantly clear, moreover, is the fact that the various legends and titles added to these maps, together with their decorative features such as sketches of animals and people, constitute a further important source of information regarding general perceptions of Peru. Moreover, in some instances they are very early records of these ideas and, in the case of their pictorial data, they transcend the limitations on accessibility imposed by the written word, especially when it is in a foreign language.

Without doubt, following the initial ascendancy of Spanish, Portuguese and Italian mapmakers in the second half of the sixteenth century, it was the output of mapmakers from the Low Countries which became most accessible to English writers and readers, in some cases in their own language. They include not only the labours of the renowned world mapmakers and first compilers of atlases, such as Ortelius, Mercator, Jodocus Hondius and Willem J. Blaeu, but also the maps and descriptive accounts of those who were the first to give special prominence to the New World – Laet, Jan van H. Linschoten, and Cornelis van Wytfliet who in 1597 produced the first printed atlas whose text deals exclusively with the geography, natural history and discovery of America, illustrated with regional maps.[6]

---

[6] For comments on maps known in England in the late sixteenth century, see Raleigh A. Skelton, 'Hakluyt's Maps' in *The Hakluyt Handbook*, ed. David B. Quinn (Hakluyt Society, 2nd series, vols 144–45, London: 1974), pp. 48–73. In addition to those mentioned in the text, this reproduces and discusses two maps used by Hakluyt: the map of the Americas by F[ilips] G[alle] (1587), and in an appendix by Helen Wallis, the world map of Edward Wright (1599) which was added to Hakluyt's *Principal Navigations*, being an accurate representation of the state of English knowledge about the world, and incorporating the discoveries made by Drake and Cavendish in the South Sea. As an excellent catalogue, for analysis and for illustrations of maps, see Rodney W. Shirley, *The Mapping of the World: Early Printed World Maps, 1472–1700* (London: New Holland, 1993). Still a valuable and detailed survey of the cartography of Peru from diverse European origins, with some examples of the legends figuring on such maps, is Raúl Porras Barrenechea, *Fuentes históricas peruanas* (Lima: Instituto Raúl Porras Barrenechea, 1968), pp. 375–459.

# CHAPTER SIX

# Documents, Monographs and Theatre

The earliest advocates of English overseas expansion in the age of Elizabeth I were to produce, during the 1570s, various types of propositions recommending voyages to the west, to the South Sea and beyond to the East Indies. One of the most widely known and influential was Humphrey Gilbert's *Discourse of a Discoverie for a New Passage to Cataia*, composed in 1566 and published a decade later. Although it contained a world map portraying the Straits of Magellan and Peru, its main objective was to prove the existence of a North-West Passage leading by a short voyage to the East Indies, and to advocate the supposed commercial advantages of this route, a dream tenaciously pursued by generations of English navigators since the voyages of John Cabot. But before Gilbert's *Discourse* had come into print, in 1570 the Spanish ambassador in London reported that a Portuguese seaman, Bartolomeu Bayão, had presented to the Privy Council a project 'to occupy and colonise one or two ports in the Kingdom of Magallanes, in order to have in their hands the commerce of the Southern Sea ... as well as getting as near as they wish to Peru'.[1]

In 1574 this was taken a stage further, again in formulation if not yet in practice, by the proposal presented to Elizabeth by Richard Grenville, for the 'discovery, traffic and enjoying' of lands south of the equator not at that time in the possession of any Christian sovereign.[2] It identified the regions and the potential rewards that would remain a lure to Englishmen for centuries, albeit more fitfully sought than others in North America and, as we have seen, often imagined in terms of an extraordinary reality. Grenville envisaged exploratory work which it was anticipated might culminate in trade and coastal settlements between the River Plate and southern Chile, perhaps the province of Arauco, an area also favourably alluded to later in texts compiled by Hakluyt. The scheme furthermore held out 'the likelihood of bringing in great treasure of gold, silver and pearl into this realm from those countries', that is Peru. Two years later in 1576, following the queen's rejection of his plan on the grounds of fears

---

[1] Eva G. R. Taylor (ed.), *The Original Writings and Correspondence of the Two Richard Hakluyts* (Hakluyt Society, 2nd series, vols 76–77, London: 1935), vol. 76, p. 87.

[2] Alfred L. Rowse, *Sir Richard Grenville of the 'Revenge'* (London: Cape, 1937), p. 90.

that it might damage Anglo-Spanish relations, and in response to Gilbert's alternative project, in a 'Discourse' presented to Lord Burghley, Grenville counselled the need for an English expedition through the Straits of Magellan along the entire western seaboard of America.[3] This implied a novel vision of English control both of the north-western and south-western entrances to the Pacific Ocean, and perhaps of some of the lands and seas in between. Francis Drake sailed to Peru and California a year later.

At the end of the same decade, the pamphlet prepared by Richard Hakluyt is surely the most optimistic and enthusiastic expression at that time of English expectations in and beyond the Straits of Magellan, 'the gate of entry into the tresure [sic] of both the East and the West Indies' (140). The source of his information was the crew of the *Elizabeth* under the command of John Winter, who had sailed for the South Sea with Drake in 1577 but returned to England two years later after becoming separated in a storm. The propagandistic purpose of Hakluyt's words mean that either he did not heed, or perhaps did not hear, any opinions from his informants which might have suggested the true hardships and hazards of the passage of the Straits, let alone their settlement. They are the antithesis of the record of Cavendish's experience during his last voyage, published in Hakluyt's own *Principal Navigations*, and of others compiled by Purchas. Hence, Hakluyt assures his readers that there lay a land rich in seals, fowl, mussels 'of mervelous bignesse and most delicate, in suche plentie as were able to victuell an armie for ever' (145), limpits 'as broade as halfe orenges' (141), hard and sound wood to build houses and ships, fresh water, and if it were lacking 'we have a devise of the sea water to make greate plentie'. It was a land fit to grow corn or graze cattle and goats. Since its bays were considered ample to shelter 'the greatest Navie in the worlde', and since 'all the tract of America on Mar del Sur is voyde of fortification and of ordinaunce' (140), he can confidently proclaim that 'there is no doubt but that we shal make subjecte to England all the golden mines of Peru and all the coste and tract of that firme of America upon the Sea of Sur' (142).

---

[3] Ibid., pp. 89–105, based on documents in State Papers. The complete set of documentation was first published by R. Pearse Chope, 'New Light on Sir Richard Grenville', *Transactions of the Devonshire Association*, vol. 49, 1917, pp. 210–82. For the development in England of this early information about Peru, see Kenneth R. Andrews, 'Beyond the Equinoctial: England and South America in the Sixteenth Century', *Journal of Imperial and Commonwealth History*, vol. 10, 1981, pp. 4–24, and 'On the Way to Peru; Elizabethan Ambitions in America South of Capricorn', *Terrae Incognitae*, vol. 14, 1982, pp. 61–75. These projects of the 1570s were not, however, the first examples of an English interest in Peru, extending beyond merely an awareness of its existence and the attraction of its treasures. Sebastian Cabot reported that in 1550 he had been consulted by the Duke of Northumberland and the French ambassador in London concerning a joint proposal to capture Peru in a surprise attack, by sending 4,000 men up the Amazon in pinnaces. *Calendar of Letters, Despatches and State Papers, relating to Negotiations between England and Spain* (13 vols, London: 1862–1954), vol. 11, ed. Royall Tyler, pp. 361–62, 15 November 1553.

The truly unreal and far-fetched quality of the scheme, however, which also affirmed English attitudes to those of other races, if not in this instance the natives of America, resides in Hakluyt's suggestions for the practical implementation of his project. The initial work of occupation and fortification, he asserts, could be entrusted to the pirate Thomas Clarke on the promise of a pardon, although 'to culler [i.e. colour] the matter he may go as of himselfe, and not with the countenance of thenglish state'. But the settlers, apart from some condemned Englishmen and women, might be cimarrones transported from Panama by Drake, 'to live subject to the gentle government of the English'. For although born in a hot climate, unlike the Spaniard who 'for his breeding in a hote region and for his delicacie in dyett and lodging' (142) would not be able to endure the cold, the cimarron 'has been brede as a slave, in all toyle farre from delicacie, he shalbe able to endure the climate, and think himself a happy man when as by good provision he shal find himselfe plentifully fed, warmly clothed, and well lodged and by our nation made free from the tyrannous Spanyard' (143).

In 1584 Hakluyt wrote his *Discourse of Western Planting*. As a document intended to furnish the Queen with information designed to persuade her to support colonisation in North America, it remained unpublished until 1877. Although in theory Hakluyt could have drawn on Drake's circumnavigation in making very brief references to Peru, in reality he merely alludes to the voyage in support of his belief that Spanish coastal settlements are weak, linked by 'simple shippinge' and 'afflicted by the Inhabitauntes' (251). The southern limits of Spanish control are in error, on the evidence of the world map of Ortelius (1570), stated to extend no further south than the Tropic of Capricorn, an opinion that would continue to foster the belief in some form of English presence in an unpopulated southern cone. Indeed, in notes of 1598 ascribed to him, Hakluyt is still keen to stress the lack of European coastal settlements from São Vicente in southern Brazil to the Straits of Magellan, within the Straits themselves, and thence as far north as the island of Santa María off the Chilean coast (422). He is more specific, however, with regard to what might attract the English both to the latter island, namely its 'greate store of golde', as well as to Nombre de Dios, cited as the town to which is brought 'all the golde, perle, stones, and Jewells that cometh from Chile, Peru and Panama oute of the South Sea' (253).

The fabulous mineral wealth of Peru is mentioned to a varying degree in all the early accounts in English referring to Peru. In two, however, it is the main focus of attention. As curate at Potosí, Alvaro Alonso Barba was ideally located to scrutinise and chronicle diverse aspects of mining operations, in the first book of his *Art of metalls* (1670). Additionally, he gives wide coverage to mining in many other areas and for metals other than silver, as well as to the hitherto neglected search for precious stones. Barba compiled reports of amethysts near to Potosí, of 'a pure transparent

Chrystalline stone' near Aguascalientes, Callapa and Julioma – 'exposing them to the sunbeams, they looked all like so many several suns' (57), of stones as transparent as diamonds at Arica and Camata, of authentic diamonds at Lipes and at Atacama, which also 'produces stones of such various colours, and beautiful gloss, and lustre' (60), like turquoises, worn in necklaces and bracelets.

Naturally, much of Barba's work is given over to the sources of precious metals in Peru: gold 'the most perfect of all inanimate bodies, and the most esteemed' (107), at Carabaya, Oruro and Chuquisaca, and silver from Porco, Andamarca, Lipes and 'the wonderfull mountains of Potosí, of whose treasure all Nations of the world have liberally participated' (116). He recalls, 'the very streets of the town when I was curate there, were full of small grains of rich oar [sic], which I swept up, and made profit of' (121). Metals which much later would become the future target of international exploitation, copper from Atacama, lead and tin are briefly included. Finally, one should not forget that in the second book of the *Art of Metalls*, Barba produced an invaluable text on the processes of mining, smelting and refining of metals in Peru, especially the mercury amalgamation process for silver-bearing ores.

By comparison, William Waller, whose real purpose was by example to encourage the development of mines and associated settlements in Wales, resorts to a few colourful images and impressive statistics relating to Potosí at the peak of its production. By his own admission they are largely derived from Acosta and N. N.

If it has sometimes been impossible to separate fact from fantasy in the supposedly veracious texts of history and geography which we have been studying, the works of William Davenant and John Dryden weave an unashamedly fictional plot against a setting rich in elements which epitomise the English response to the Spanish in the New World at the time. Into his masque *The Cruelty of the Spaniards in Peru*, presented daily at the Cockpit in Drury Lane in 1658, with 'instrumentall and vocall musick and by art of perspective', Davenant vigorously incorporated images of the reality of Peru as conceived by his compatriots of the Cromwellian era. Three aims he states by way of introduction underlie the work: firstly 'to represent the happy condition of the people of Peru antiently, when their inclinations were govern'd by nature', secondly to represent 'the cruelty of the Spaniards over the Indians', and finally to 'infer the voyages of the English thither and the amity of the natives towards them, under whose ensignes ... they hope to be made victorious, and to be freed from the yoke of the Spaniard'.[4]

Quite clearly, the representation of historical events in Peru, and above all the portrayal of the native population and their relations with the

---

[4] The sources for the first two aims are clearly to be found in the works of Las Casas and the Inca Garcilaso.

English, carry a political message at a time of war with Spain. Spain is the defeated, unjust and cruel oppressor, whilst England emerges as the victorious and well-intentioned liberator. One can legitimately speculate that the opinions which were expressed in the presence of Davenant's theatrical audience by word and image, were shared en masse by the generally unrecorded popular sphere of English public opinion, in whatever environment it flourished. The setting against which this is done is described as one of 'parcht and bare tops of distant hills ... sands shining (with gold?) on the shores of rivers, and the natives in feather'd habits and bonnets, carrying, in Indian baskets, ingots of gold and wedges of silver'. The flora and fauna is a luxuriant one of pines, palms, coconuts, monkeys, apes, parrots and sugar canes.

The Priest of the Sun enters to lament the loss of a time of innocence, even before the age of the Inca empire, which is echoed in the words of the first song:

> Whilst yet our world was new,
> When not discover'd by the old;
> E're beggar'd slaves we grew,
> For having silver hills, and strands of gold.

Whereupon he next recalls the prophecy that bearded peoples, 'cruell men, idolaters of gold, / should pass vast seas to seek their harbours here' (second speech), a vision fulfilled by the Spanish in a conquest aided by the Inca civil war. Consequently, to the accompaniment of 'doleful' music, we are presented with a scene inside a prison filled with the 'racks and other engines of torment, with which the Spaniards are tormenting the natives and English marriners which may be suppos'd to be lately landed there to discover the coast', and where on a spit a Spaniard is seen 'basting an Indian Prince, which is rosted at an artificiall fire' (fifth entry).

Against the background of Indians still carrying their baskets of silver and gold, but now limping along in silver fetters and being brutally beaten by the Spanish, it is the priest who expresses both fear and an incomprehension grounded on a rational response to Spanish behaviour:

> What dark and distant region bred
> For war that bearded race,
> Whose ev'ry uncouth face
> We more than Death's cold visage dread? (fourth speech).

And he continues, 'What race is this, who for our punishment / Pretend that they in haste from Heav'n were sent, / As just destroyers of Idolatry?' (fifth speech).

The setting to the sixth and final entry of the Priest of the Sun is a joint army of Englishmen and Indians, the former 'imaginary English forces' in the vanguard, explained as 'a vision discern'd by the priest of the sun, before the matter was extant'. This dream of an alliance, shared already

by Hawkins, the Dutch and later by Narborough and Wafer in Chile, held
out the prospect of a future in which:

> Those whom the insulting Spaniards scorn,
> And slaves esteem,
> The English soon shall free;
> Whilst we the Spaniards see
> Digging for them.

As the 'Spanish eagle darkly hov'ring' overhead yields to the English lion
of liberty which 'does still victorious grow', the chorus concludes that:

> After all our dysasters
> The proud Spaniards our Masters
> When we extoll our liberty by feasts,
> At table shall serve,
> Or else they shall starve;
> Whilst th'English shall sit and rule as our guests.

This is no doubt a stirring dramatisation of English national antagonism
towards Spain in the Cromwellian era, founded on evidence derived from
the works we have been considering, but also embracing the fanciful
aspirations of co-operation with the indigenous population. The historical
context of the work was recent English intervention in the Caribbean, the
capture of Spanish Jamaica, war and the embargoing of English ships in
Spanish ports. Although not specifically thinking in terms of Peru, amongst
the several arguments put forward by the former Dominican Thomas Gage,
now converted to the Church of England, which had induced Cromwell
to embark on the enterprise we know as the 'Western Design', there
featured the suggestion that indigenous peoples would welcome the English
to free them from Spanish exploitation, and particularly that of the Catholic
church.[5] Moreover, embedded in their cyclical construct of historical eras,
there lay the prophecy of strangers arriving from afar to rule their land.
In Mexico, of course, one inevitably remembers the identification of Cortés

---

[5] Gage's recommendations are in a memorandum to Cromwell based on his best-seller,
*The English American: A New Survey of the West Indies* (London: 1648, rep. 1655). For example,
'the Spaniards might very well fear that if their country (he refers here to Guatemala) should
be invaded, the multitude of their Indian people would prove to them a multitude of enemies,
either running away to another side; or if forced to help, they would be to them but as the
help of so many flies', J. Eric S. Thompson (ed.), *Thomas Gage's Travels in the New World*
(Norman: Oklahoma UP, 1958), p. 213. The year 1656 also saw the re-printing with the title,
*The Spaniards Cruelty and Treachery to the English in the Time of Peace and War*, of Thomas
Scott, *An Experimentall Discouerie of Spanish Practises* (n. p.: 1623), derived from Las Casas.
See Steele, *English Interpreters*, pp. 33–34 and 67. For the general question of Amerindians
on the English stage, see Virginia M. Vaughan, ' "Salvages of Men and Ind": English Theatrical
Representations of American Indians, 1590–1690', in *New World of Wonders. European Images
of the Americas (1492–1700)*, ed. Rachel Doggett (Seattle: Washington UP, 1992), pp. 114–124.

with Quetzalcóatl. There is also some evidence that precisely at the time when Davenant was writing, sections of the native population of Campeche in Central America gave new life to the belief, by turning to the English buccaneers who came to cut logwood in the hope of forming joint enterprises to free them from Spanish domination.[6] Similarly, in Chapter 9 of this present volume, David Cahill discusses kindred beliefs and hopes amidst the Indians of Peru in the late eighteenth century, with specific reference to English aid in seeking their liberation from oppression.

Finally, in the preface to *The Indian Emperor*, Dryden clearly states that 'in it I have neither wholly follow'd the truth of the History, nor altogether left it'. In fact, themes of love and honour clearly take precedence over historical accuracy in this heroic play, as indeed they do in *The Indian Queen*. Nevertheless, the American setting of each work is inspired here and there by motifs which we have seen to be characteristic of the representation of Peru in a number of works in English. This is as much the case of the scene set in the 'Temple of the Sun all of Gold' in the latter play, as it is in the former when Almeria urges 'Go and beget them Slaves to dig their Mines, / And groan for Gold which now in Temples shines'. In the latter work too, Vasquez's allusions to the abundance of mineral wealth are a close re-working of those used by geographers and travellers in the context of Chile:

> Methinks we walk in dreams on fairy Land,
> Where golden Ore lies mixt with common sand;
> Each downfal of a flood the Mountains pour,
> From their rich bowels rolls a silver shower.

Lastly in each play, in common with Davenant and of course Las Casas, Dryden sympathetically compares a naturally idyllic and fruitful Indian way of life in the past, lost through the Spaniards' pursuit of mineral riches, with a present of suffering and torture at their hands.

---

[6] Jorge Victoria Ojeda, 'La piratería y su relación con los indígenas de la península de Yucatán', *Mesoamérica*, vol. 14, no. 26, 1993, 209–216.

# CHAPTER SEVEN

# Conclusion

By and large, the works we have been discussing were circulating in the English language by 1700. Obviously, neither these diverse types of material, nor the English fascination with South America and especially with Peru, ceased abruptly at that moment. In fact, it has been our purpose not simply to shed light on the elements of Peruvian reality which provoked such attention, but even more importantly to convey an idea of the depth to which concepts of the region, in an enduring amalgam of the 'imaginary' and the 'real', became profoundly ingrained in the minds of authors, compilers and editors. From them they were transposed into the dreams, proposals and enterprises both of men of action and investors in overseas enterprise. By the end of the seventeenth century, perceptions of Peru had been widely consolidated into an image whose essential features would not suffer a radical transformation for at least a further 150 years. Without doubt, even before the early nineteenth century, the prospect of Peru's political independence from Spain had generated somewhat modified concerns, such as an awakening in Britain of imperialist interest in South America, in part out of fear of rival French involvement. The post-independence period would also bring in its wake new patterns of economic relationships. But essentially, the lure of Peru continued through the eighteenth century to remain potent and largely unchanged from that expressed in the works we have examined – remote, with elements of the strange and even fabulous, and above all a land offering extravagant prospects for exploitation in pursuit of personal or national gain and enrichment. Since the first descriptions gathered from translations of Spanish chroniclers, and from the earliest English eyewitness accounts in the age of Drake until the nineteenth century, what really occurs is a gradual but steady formulation of beliefs and fancies, followed by a constant regeneration of the basic attitudes in a variety of different guises.

Even before the seventeenth century drew to its close, some of the most inhospitable terrain on the northernmost fringes of the Viceroyalty of Peru was to witness the unfolding tragedy of one of the most foolhardy schemes in the name of Scottish pride and envy of the English, the Darien enterprise

(1698–1700).[1] Its objective became the founding of the colony of New Edinburgh on the northern coast of the Isthmus of Panama, near the buccaneer haunt of Golden Isle. So powerful were the attractions of creating a trans-isthmian trading enterprise to link the oceans, that the Scotsman William Paterson, founder of the Bank of England, and others who backed the venture, were blinded to the realities: disease, an unhealthy climate, potential starvation and Spanish opposition that reduced the settlers to a wretched end, the total antithesis of their hopes, dreams and aspirations. For information, guidance and assurance they had turned to the descriptions of Dampier and Wafer, the latter having been invited personally to Scotland to explain his views and offer the benefits of his experience, which no doubt he did with characteristic optimism. Although the site of so many Scottish deaths was on the Caribbean coast rather than the South Sea, there is no shred of doubt that it was the prospect of what lay across the Isthmus of Panama on the coasts of Peru which persuaded so many to countenance such a perilous venture.

Within a decade and this time in London, during the negotiations to end the War of the Spanish Succession, Englishmen were beginning forcefully to pursue tempting opportunities to avail themselves through commerce of the legendary wealth of Peru. The British government declared its interest in establishing a permanent presence in South America by creating four fortified ports, two on the Atlantic coast and two in the South Sea, for the purpose of gaining access to and ultimately controlling the trade into that sea.[2] The ports would be located in those southern zones first identified to be of interest by Richard Grenville in 1574, and subsequently explored intermittently from the time of Drake and by Narborough through to the buccaneer expeditions at the end of the seventeenth century. The link with the latter can be observed in the purchase by the South Sea Company of a copy of the captured Spanish charts brought to England by Bartholomew Sharp and copied by William Hacke.[3] The Company's charter received royal assent in June 1711, awarding it a monopoly of British trade from the mouth of the River Orinoco, around Cape Horn and along the west coast of America. In practice, although Britain's demand for some form of permanent base was rejected during

[1] There is a popular account of the venture by John Prebble, *The Darien Disaster* (London: Secker and Warburg, 1968), and a shorter study in David Howarth, *The Golden Isthmus* (London: Collins, 1967), pp. 102–44.

[2] Glyndwr Williams, 'The Inexhaustible Fountain of Gold. English Projects and Ventures in the South Seas, 1670–1750', in *Perspectives of Empire*, ed. John E. Flint and Glyndwr Williams (London: Longman, 1973), pp. 27–52, discusses this and other projects at pp. 35–45.

[3] *Description of a Buccaneer's Atlas by W. Hacke* (London: 1914), p. 12, one of *A Collection of Monographs and Miniatures offered for Sale by B. Quaritch* (London: 1904–1914). The interest in Chile and the route to the South Sea also resulted in the translation for the first time in a shortened version of Ovalle's account of the Kingdom of Chile in 1706, and the re-publication of Narborough's journal in 1711.

the peace negotiations at Utrecht, in 1713 it was agreed to hand to the South Sea Company the *asiento* to supply slaves, with the right to dispatch to the Indies one trading vessel per year.[4] Of course, what began in such a whirlwind of optimistic speculation as the South Sea Scheme ended disastrously in 1720 with the bursting of the South Sea Bubble. Above all, the unreal and inflated dreams of investors rested on the illusion that English manufactured goods could be sold with vast profit in ports from the River Plate to the coasts of Chile, obviously filling the markets which Narborough had assured them were there.

Consequently, with these precedents, strengthened by the stimulus of commercial rivalry with the French who were now trading profitably and in large numbers on the coasts of Chile and Peru, a variety of analysts applied themselves to the inducements for a continuing English interest in the region. In search of details that would furnish the background for *Robinson Crusoe* (1719), Daniel Defoe would have recourse to buccaneer accounts such as that of Dampier, and more particularly the journal of Woodes Rogers's privateering voyage to the South Sea, in which the story of Alexander Selkirk's solitary sojourn on the island of Juan Fernández was developed as an incentive to capture sales. However, through his *Review of the State of the British Nation* (especially from late June to the end of August 1711), *The Essay on the South-Sea Trade* (1712) and other writings, Defoe would also become actively involved in the South Sea debate.[5] After ridiculing the apparent ease and total disregard for the Spanish response, with which the government and South Sea investors spoke of destroying Spanish exclusivity and capturing their commerce, he re-stated a proposal he had first put forward a decade earlier. With the connivance of the native population in regions not effectively controlled by Spain, this envisaged a settlement on the fertile and minerally rich soils of Chile, with a further supporting base located between the River Plate and the Straits of Magellan, in short not an encroachment against Spanish settlements, although certainly an unwelcome close presence. This scheme would also appear to imply the end of the age of privateering incursions that preyed on coastal towns and their commerce by sea (which in practice would still continue into the third decade of century), in favour of maintaining an English foothold in locations where the Spanish themselves might even choose to trade. But ultimately, in his elaboration of a fictional account of a *New Voyage round the World* (1725), Defoe re-worked his ideas on Chile, since he was already looking further afield to the west in

---

[4] John Carswell, *The South Sea Bubble* (London: Cresset Press, 1960); John G. Sperling, *The South Sea Company* (Boston: Kress, 1962).

[5] For the South Sea debate and the involvement of Defoe, see Glyndwr Williams, *The Great South Sea. English Voyages and Encounters, 1570–1750* (New Haven and London: Yale UP, 1997), pp. 161–70.

advance of actual trans-pacific expeditions of discovery in the second half of the century.

Others were less critical and more traditional in their recollection of the attractions of the southern fringes of the Viceroyalty of Peru. In 1712, Robert Allen who had been at the settlement of his Scottish compatriots in Darien, would list the prizes to be gained as 'gold and silver in vast quantities, costly pearls, emeraulds, amethists, and several other sorts of precious stones, copper and other metals'.[6] In the previous year Thomas Bowrey, a widely experienced merchant who had met Dampier in the East Indies, had recommended like Narborough the need for a settlement in the Atlantic, perhaps at Port St. Julian or Port Desire, as a pre-requisite for the seizure of Valdivia in order to establish a site for a commercial base. In part this latter choice rested on its southerly location and cold climate which presented an opening for the sale of English woollens, together with manufactured goods. But he selected it principally because 'Baldivia produces ye most gold of any place in ye S° Seas'. As enduring as this long-outdated and long-mistaken belief, was that shared by the Dutch in the creation of an alliance with the local population, who 'may profitably joyn with us against them [the Spanish]'.[7] Ironically, when in 1720 the South Sea Company collapsed, it had not managed to dispatch even a single ship to trade off Peru. Nevertheless, not even a fiasco of those proportions, which threatened to bring down the entire system of finance and credit in London, could deter others from sustaining their enthusiasm and pursuing fresh goals in the region by means of maritime ventures. A brief recollection of the actual contacts made during the eighteenth century, and their motivations, must suffice to explain how this continuing English appetite for Peru was maintained until the period of independence.

For a little over twenty years, first by the return of Dampier (1703–07), then by the expeditions of Woodes Rogers (1708–11) with Dampier as pilot, and John Clipperton and George Shelvocke (1719–22), English aspirations continued to be founded both on the opportunistic short-term goals pursued by the buccaneers of the previous century, as well as longer range commercial prospects in imitation of the French. Although now generally clothed in a mantle of legality through the concession of letters of marque to attack French and Spanish shipping, they craved profit for themselves and their investors, dreaming of shipments of gold being transported from Valdivia to Callao, hunting the now rarer silver galleons bound for Panama, plundering lone prizes at sea, recklessly raiding ports such as

---

[6] Robert Allen, *An Essay on the Nature and Methods of Carrying on a Trade to the South Sea* (London: 1712), from British Library, Additional MSS, 28140, fol. 29. Allen had been a prisoner in Quito from 1702–07.

[7] British Library, Additional MSS, 28140, fols 31–31v, 'Proposal for taking Valdivia in ye South Seas', and 'Proposal for settlement in ye way to ye South Seas', 10 and 11 September 1711.

Paita and Guayaquil, and in the case of one of Dampier's former associates, returning home to tell fanciful tales of treasure left buried in Peru.[8] The published accounts of their adventures and their descriptions of the coasts of the viceroyalty, now gaining a wider and more enthusiastic readership for what were more readily available examples of eyewitness testimony, turned English eyes in increasing numbers to the South Sea.[9] They saw opportunities both old and new.

Without doubt, the financial returns of Rogers's venture, the first English expedition to return with substantial profits from the South Sea since the Elizabethan age, were opportune for those planning future investment gambles in those waters. Moreover, by 1726 if not earlier, since Rogers had advocated a Chilean settlement, following the publication of journals written by those who participated in the Clipperton-Shelvocke voyage, there had been governmental discussion of some form of settlement, apparently based on proposals for the conquest of Chile.[10] Although as yet no one realised the potential, Shelvocke in his journal did refer to two activities which in the nineteenth century would play a role in the economy of the new Republic of Peru. These were his observation of large numbers of whales off the coast of Patagonia, commented on over a century previously by the Dutchman Schouten, and the capture near Arica in February 1720 of the *Rosario* laden with a cargo of guano, which he correctly describes as an aid to the fertility of the soil. From the 1840s the Peruvian guano trade would, of course, attract a substantial level of British shipping. But also simultaneously, though more briefly, in less troubled times than those we have been discussing, the much assailed port of Paita would become a base of operations and support for North American whaling fleets.[11]

---

[8] This was Thomas Stradling who had been imprisoned in Lima. Several years later he was transported for further confinement to Normandy in northern to France, from where he escaped by telling false stories of treasure he had buried in Peru.

[9] The main journals are: William Funnell, *A Voyage round the World* (London: 1707, rep. Amsterdam: N. Israel, 1969), for Dampier's voyage; Woodes Rogers, *A Cruising Voyage round the World* (London: 1712), and Edward Cooke, *A Voyage to the South Sea and round the World* (2 vols, London, 1712, rep. Amsterdam: N. Israel, 1969); George Shelvocke, *A Voyage round the World* (London: 1726) and William Betagh, *A Voyage round the World* (London: 1728). On these and later voyages, see Williams, *The Great South Sea*, pp. 133–160, 197–205, 214–250, and Bradley, *Navegantes británicos*, pp. 277–313. For a critical analysis of the genre of voyage-literature which began with Dampier and those who followed him to the South Sea, see Philip Edwards, *The Story of the Voyage: Sea Narratives in Eighteenth-Century England* (Cambridge: Cambridge UP, 1994).

[10] Williams, *The Great South Sea*, pp. 202–203.

[11] As Williams, *The Great South Sea*, p. 203, has pointed out, Shelvocke was not the first to refer in English to guano, since there is a mention in the translation of Amedée F. Frézier's account of his voyage of 1712–1714, *A Voyage to the South-Sea, and along the Coasts of Chili and Peru* (London: 1717), p. 147. For Paita's new role see William L. Lofstrom, *Paita Outpost of Empire: The Impact of the New England Whaling Fleet on the Socioeconomic Development of Northern Peru, 1832–1865* (Mystic Seaport Museum, Conn.: 1996).

For the time being the pattern of plundering activity did not change with the entry of the first naval squadron into the South Sea under the command of George Anson (1740–44). Beset by angry storms around Cape Horn, his fleet dispersed, his men ill and dying from disease and want of food, Anson was left no other recourse than to employ His Majesty's ships in the profession of privateering off the coasts of Peru. One must admit that he performed the role as if born to it, returning with the greatest haul in plunder from the South Sea since the time of Drake. Subsequently in 1745, some silver coins minted in the English capital bore the inscription 'Lima', a further testimony to the lingering lure of Peru, since the silver from which they were made had been seized from a Manila galleon in the Philippines and was undoubtedly of Mexican origin. Nevertheless, in all of this, Anson at least went some way towards the fulfilment of what were surely the common hopes of many of his officers and men. One of them, Philip Saumarez, had written optimistically even before they had reached Cape Horn: 'We now began to look upon the conquest of the Peruvian mines and principal towns in the Pacific as an amusement which would naturally occur'.[12] Likewise, the aspirations were still those of the age of Drake in Walter's journal of the Anson voyage, as they dreamed of Peru, 'those opulent coasts, where all our hopes and wishes centred'. 'Our most sanguine dreams were upon the point of being realised; and hence we indulged our imaginations in those romantic schemes, which the fancied possession of the Chilian gold and Peruvian silver might be conceived to inspire'.[13]

However, it is not solely with these aspirations, by the nature of his actions, through the outcome of the enterprise, nor by the reminder of the dreadful and deplorable human cost at which the riches of Peru were sometimes won, that Anson brings to mind the contents of journals of voyages to the South Sea written in the previous century. During the planning of the enterprise, amongst the various objectives voiced by those consulted were the opinions that Buenos Aires or Montevideo might be taken, Chile conquered with the help of native allies, Chiloé or Juan Fernández settled, fortified and garrisoned, and Valdivia 'taken and made an arsenal or magazine for the English men-of-war and merchant ships'.[14] Several of these propositions, together with the suggestion of plundering Lima and seizing defenceless ports such as Guayaquil and Trujillo, confided in him in England and later cast aside by the force of circumstance, were also a clear legacy of an earlier age. The instruction to explore

[12] Glyndwr Williams (ed.) *Documents Relating to Anson's Voyage round the World, 1740–44* (Publications of the Navy Records Society, no. 109, London: 1967), p. 165.

[13] Richard Walter, *Anson's Voyage round the World*, ed. Geoffrey S. Laird Clowes (London: Martin Hopkinson, 1928), p. 71, the definitive account of the voyage now generally believed to have been mainly written by the professional pamphleteer Benjamin Robins under Anson's supervision.

[14] Williams, *Documents*, p. 22.

suitable locations in which to establish a base to support future voyages, is an acceptance of the perils and hardships to be overcome, which his compatriots had earlier endured. That it should be located in the southern cone, again repeats the proposals already voiced before the end of the sixteenth century and supported a century later by Narborough. Similarly, the fact that he was urged to seek alliances or some form of understanding with the native population is yet further evidence of another long-standing feature of English aims. Although on this occasion, it was hoped that following the provision of arms and ammunition to the Indians of Chile, 'they would then, in all probability, open their mines, and gladly embrace a traffick of such mutual convenience to both nations'.[15]

There was, however, a novelty about Anson's orders, not present in the objectives and actions of those who had recently preceded him to Peru. This lay in the instruction that he should assess whether it might be possible to take possession of Panama, Callao and Lima, informing the *criollo* population of the advantages of trade with Britain, whilst urging them at the same time 'to throw off their obedience to the King of Spain, and set up for themselves'.[16] Thereby was appended to the former English fads concerning South America, the new delusion that after plundering their towns, sinking their shipping and wrecking their trade, a mere rallying cry would suffice to turn disgruntled American-born whites against their Spanish superiors. This was set out in a draft manifesto, which appeared to suggest that the British government believed that when given the chance freely to choose, the merchant community would welcome British trade as 'a free and happy people', if provided with guarantees such as freedom of worship and military protection.[17] It would still be many decades before the realisation of these dreams of commercial alliances in Peru was fulfilled. Yet, if Anson failed to stir *criollos* into insurrection, there still remained the long-cherished hope not only of being able to count on indigenous support, but of promoting rebellion amongst Black slaves by offering them freedom.

In total disregard of the appalling human losses to disease suffered by Anson's squadron, in the press reports which with such patriotic glee reported the passage of 32 carts transporting his booty of silver and gold to London before the gaze of bedazzled multitudes, he was dubbed 'our second Drake'. The journal of the voyage was at once a best-seller and repeatedly reprinted. Presumably, the lesson of just how remote Peru remained in that age of sail was not one which onlookers and readers

---

15 Walter, *Anson's Voyage*, p. 88.

16 Williams, *Documents*, p. 34.

17 Ibid., p. 41 from the manifesto, pp. 39–41. It states further 'that if you are disposed and willing to renounce the King of Spain as your lord and sovereign, and to set up a new form of government, we have orders to assist and protect you therein', in order to 'enjoy the same liberty and freedom as we do'.

were keen to heed. However, at last on Anson's advice, subsequent English voyages did demonstrate the Admiralty's concern with alleviating the trials and adversity posed by distance and the alien environment, by formally instituting enquiries into a mid-course base on the way to Peru. John Byron (1764–66) and John McBride (1766–70) were to become preoccupied with investigating whether the Falkland Islands might constitute this long-desired and much needed station to ease the passage into the South Sea, as well as for servicing the growing enthusiasm for a new age of trans-Pacific exploration. It was stated in England that the islands were 'the key to the whole Pacific Ocean', since from a base there Britain could 'command the ports and trade of Chile, Peru, Panama, Acapulco, and in one word all the Spanish territory upon that sea'.[18] As far as Byron was concerned they also fulfilled naval requirements, since 'all the navy of England might ride here together very safely'.[19] First French then Spanish rivalry put paid to these English attempts to settle the islands. Hence, Philip Carteret (1766–67) proposed as an alternative to assess the viability of the rocky and arid islands of San Félix and San Ambrosio adjacent to the Chilean coast, as suitable locations for refreshment, but failed even to locate them.[20]

However, with the participation of vessels belonging to the British Navy, this was also an age in which more rigorous and methodical processes of scientific enquiry and geographical exploration were to be consciously applied, to the testing and dismantling of myths given credibility since some of the earliest voyages to the South Sea and Peru. Seemingly all English writers of journals, half in wonder and half in fear, address the question of the existence of giants on the coasts of Patagonia, in the Straits of Magellan and occasionally along the Peruvian coast. Even though such quaint beliefs which mirrored Columbus's expectation of encountering monsters in 1492, appeared to have been laid to rest long ago, as early as Drake's incursion and again by the observations of Narborough, they were resuscitated by John Byron who wrote that the Patagonians came 'the nearest to giants I believe of any people in the world'. He added that one of the tallest of his men 'appeared comparatively speaking a mere shrimp to them'. In short, 'nothing in nature could appear more frightful than these people did both men and women'.[21] It was, therefore, left to Samuel Wallis a few years later to land at Cape Vírgenes in order to carry out

[18] Robert E. Gallagher (ed.), *Byron's Journal of his Circumnavigation, 1764–66* (Hakluyt Society, 2nd series, vol. 122, Cambridge: 1964), p. 161, from a letter of Lord Egmont to the Duke of Grafton, 20 July 1765, pp. 160–163.

[19] Ibid., p. 58.

[20] Helen Wallis (ed.), *Carteret's Voyage round the World, 1766–69* (Hakluyt Society, 2nd series, vols 124 and 125, Cambridge: 1965) p. 144.

[21] Gallagher, *Byron's Journal*, pp. 46 and 48, with an illustration of the 'giants'. On the topic in general, see Helen Wallis, 'The Patagonian Giants', ibid., pp. 185–196.

measurements to prove that the height of the tallest inhabitants ranged from six to seven feet.[22]

In a similar vein, despite hopes having been raised by the credulous Byron who observed flocks of birds heading south at dusk, within a few years Captain James Cook, during his second famous voyage (1772–75), by heading beyond the Antarctic Circle would once and for all discount any possibility of the existence of a vast, fertile and habitable southern continent, *Terra Australis Incognita*. Some historians for long have debated whether the search for this continent should be included amongst Drake's original objectives at the outset of his voyage to Peru. Most certainly it was portrayed on world maps drawn by the most prestigious cartographers in the Low Countries, and continued to be so, in some instances further south than hitherto, even though Drake's own course had revealed an archipelago rather than a large land mass.

In some senses, therefore, the application of scientific enquiry to the testing of long-standing beliefs and legends would appear to imply the waning of the strange, the extraordinary and the unknown, as also the curtailment of imagination. In fact, the scientific expeditions of the late eighteenth and nineteenth centuries to South America and the South Sea would promptly uncover a vast new world of wonders in the natural environment that would shake fundamental beliefs. Likewise, as Latin American nationhoods began painfully and spasmodically to coalesce, and although these years would bring the demise of the long but intermittent period of English privateering expeditions to Peru and South America in general, other forms of contact would emerge as new manifestations of the long-held English aspirations we have analysed in the seventeenth century.

This is not the place to become immersed in the debate about to what extent the statements of British ministers constitute a coherent foreign policy towards the political and social changes in Latin America, for example with regard to the advisability of direct intervention into affairs there, or simply the adoption of a more passive role whilst being ever alert to French objectives. A new age was dawning, and perhaps private individuals rather than the government were the first to recognise the consolidation of new opportunities for Britain in Latin America. It has been suggested recently that the turning point was the ultimate failure of Commodore Sir Home Popham's expedition to Buenos Aires in June 1806, which despite the initial surprising but short-lived capture of the city, marked the end of the periodic privateering voyages to South America initiated by Drake.[23] The venture was undertaken without the sanction of

[22] Hugh Carrington (ed.), *The Discovery of Tahiti. A Journal of the Second Voyage of H.M.S. 'Dolphin' round the World, 1766–1768* (Hakluyt Society, 2nd series, vol. 98, London: 1948), p. 24, a journal by her master George Robertson,

[23] John D. Grainger, 'The Navy in the River Plate, 1806–08', *The Mariner's Mirror*, vol. 81, no. 3, 1995, pp. 287–99, at p. 288, and *The Royal Navy in the River Plate, 1806–07* (Publications of the Navy Records Society, vol. 135, Aldershot: Scolar Press, 1996). On the Popham venture

the government, but it was undoubtedly a link with that past, with the ambitions expressed by Hakluyt and those echoed by Narborough. Remarkably, when it was enthusiastially accepted and still believed in London that Buenos Aires had been incorporated into the British Empire, additional British forces were dispatched not only to reinforce those in Buenos Aires but with the objective of launching diversionary campaigns on the coasts of Peru with the hope of proceeding to the conquest of Chile.[24] The orders issued to the commander of the land forces read: 'the object of your expedition is the capture of the sea ports and fortresses and the reduction of the province of Chili'.[25] Thereby, but for Popham's enforced withdrawal from the River Plate, the much debated scenario of British control of trade around the southern cone with bases on the Atlantic and Pacific coasts, most recently mooted in the aftermath of what by *force majeure* had become Anson's privateering incursion along the coasts of Chile and Peru, would have moved significantly closer to realisation. It had of course been Anson who carried the official authority which Popham lacked, but whose sentiments they both naively shared, to promote a rising of the *criollo* population of Peru by the temptation of free commerce with Britain. Although the opportunity was denied him through the loss of ships and men, Anson like Popham seriously underestimated and misjudged the degree and effectiveness of local resistance to such a proposal, at least at the precise moment of their respective enterprises. In the nineteenth century British influence would be exercised through commercial treaties and the enterprise and initiative of private commercial enterprises.

The failure of Popham's 'freebooting' adventure represents a landmark in Britain's relations with South America, and with Peru. 'It certainly cured the British of the delusion that South America was a fruitful imperialist field'.[26] However, as we have been suggesting throughout this study of representations in English of the former Viceroyalty of Peru, the perceived attractions and appeal were so deeply rooted that they were able to prevail not only against the ever-present obstacles of distance and danger at sea which barred the way to their realisation, but also despite recent foolish speculation leading to financial collapse, and finally military defeat. In the aftermath of the Wars of Independence, the myths would be recycled, and what has been described as 'the British mania for Latin America' would now be expressed in the form of the sale of British textiles in Peru, the import of guano, copper and nitrates from Peru and Chile, the provision of credit, insurance and marketing services, and investment in new mining

and its immediate consequences, see Henry S. Ferns, *Britain and Argentina in the Nineteenth Century* (Oxford: Oxford UP, 1960), pp. 17–66.

[24] This was to be the naval squadron of Rear-Admiral George Murray, carrying 3,000 soldiers under the command of Brigadier-General Robert Craufurd, Grainger, *Royal Navy*, pp. 112–113, 130, 134, 136–137, 143–144, 159–160.

[25] Ibid., p. 137.

[26] Grainger, 'The Navy in the River Plate', p. 298.

enterprises, 'a new El Dorado'.[27] Those who promoted these activities, who continued to look upon Peru as a field for exploitation, were the heirs of a perception of the region in England that had taken shape in the late sixteenth century, as a challenge to a Spanish monopoly. In reality, however, these new aspirations proved as difficult to realise as those of the past. Moreover, as the nineteenth century progressed, the appeal of Peru, the new and territorially diminished republic, past source of legendary mineral wealth, would be challenged as the focus of British attention by Brazil and the countries of the River Plate. The British merchants who had flocked to Buenos Aires with some 70 ships to sell goods worth more than a million pounds, in practice proved to be a more durable and influential invading force, commercially speaking, than the military forces in whose wake they had been so quick to follow. Perhaps only then, if by no means at once, can we say that the attraction of Peru began to fade in English eyes, at least in the sense of being a provider of opportunities for profit and wealth. Perhaps only then did the attractive and enduring image of the Viceroyalty of Peru start to become tarnished by the new reality of the republic.

---

[27] These are the views of Rory Miller, *Britain and Latin America in the Nineteenth and Twentieth Centuries* (London: Longman, 1993), p. 2.

PART II

# The Inca and Inca Symbolism in Popular Festive Culture: The Religious Processions of Seventeenth-Century Cuzco

David Cahill

# CHAPTER EIGHT

# Exploring Incan Identity

The Spanish conquest implied the capture of the Andean *imaginario* by the new overlords, an open-ended and variegated process still in train today. This capture is not merely an appropriation, however, but rather a continuing dialectic which is sometimes uneven, sometimes reciprocal. Multiple processes of acculturation have generated various degrees of hybridity, sometimes resulting in a true synthesis.[1] This process reaches beyond mutual borrowings, appropriations and impositions; it is often creative, so much so that the resultant hybridities sometimes border on the fantastic, such that were they fiction, they would easily fit under the rubric of 'magical realism'. And these outcomes either represent or at least involve the creation of new *imaginarios* – perhaps as good a definition of syncretism as any – which in turn evolve in new directions. In such encounters, Europeans gazed calmly from without, mulling over the stream of reports of the fabulous that impinged upon their consciousness, while the Andean Other scrambled furiously to construct an identity that would be acceptable to their new masters, and which might preserve some vestige of the erstwhile fealty accorded the former Incan elite by their native Andean subjects. It was a tall order to sell the notion of a post-colonial Incan aristocratic caste to conquerers and conquered alike, both of whom, it may be surmised, held this anachronistic nobility in some contempt, for different reasons but in roughly equal measure.

Memories are cheap, but all that the surviving Incas had to sell was their past. They were imagining a community, but it was a past community.[2]

---

[1] Such terms are capable of bearing several meanings: Peter Burke, *Varieties of Cultural History* (Cambridge and Oxford: Polity Press, 1997), p. 208, in the course of discussing what he calls the 'encounter model' of cultural history, notes the great variety of terms, many of which are synonomous: 'processes of cultural borrowing, appropriation, exchange, reception, transfer, negotiation, resistance, syncretism, acculturation, enculturation, inculturation, interculturation, transculturation, hybridisation (*mestizaje*), creolisation, and the interaction and interpenetration of cultures'. Nor do these seventeen terms exhaust the possibilities, e.g., the term 'cultural involution' is sometimes used by anthropologists to describe certain syncretic phenomena. Whatever one makes of such a variety, it is clear that there has been an over-production of neologisms.

[2] The notion of 'imagined community' is now a familiar historical theme, since Benedict

The success with which they drew on this memory and cobbled it to borrowings from the newly hegemonic culture would determine their place, their survival, within the new Spanish order. Their future was a 'future past'.[3] Save for a scattering of nobles who had materially assisted the conquest, either before or after the fall of the city of Cuzco, their claim to noble status was based principally on lineage and kinship.[4] Claims based on Incaic lineage were on the whole paltry and insufficient in Spanish eyes, for all that kinship and inheritance were themselves pillars of Spanish society and thus colonialism. Indeed, these qualities were at the heart of occidental notions of the aristocratic. Yet this commonplace serves to point up a further obstacle to the Incas' winning a place in the Spanish sun, namely that the conquerors already had their own ranked aristocracy, non-titled as well as titled. The colonial Inca nobility aimed, then, for a consubstantiality of aristocracies. If at first the crown was magnanimously amenable to this notion, in the long run colonial administrators often displayed little sympathy with the Incas' nobility, which had in the early sixteenth-century been recognised by the crown, especially by the Emperor Charles V, who had issued a plethora of decrees of *hidalguía* to prominent Inca noble families. Later viceroys and provincial administrators often looked askance at such titles, scorning the *cédulas de hidalguía* as dubious and their proud possessors as absurd, notwithstanding that they often found themselves legally constrained to honour such legal instruments.

Such ethnocentric disdain was in part a reflection of cultural misunderstanding, one alas sometimes reproduced by historians and other Andeanists.[5] The genuineness of the colonial Incas' claim to nobility did

Anderson, *Imagined Communities* (rev. edn, New York and London: Verso, 1991). For its application to Peruvian history, see Cecilia Méndez, 'República sin indios: La comunidad imaginada', in *Tradición y modernidad en los Andes*, comp. Henrique Urbano (Cuzco: Centro de Estudios Regionales Andinos 'Bartolomé de Las Casas', 1997); Mark Thurner, *From Two Republics to One Divided: Contradictions of Postcolonial Nationmaking in Andean Peru* (Durham and London: Duke UP, 1997), esp. chap. 2 ('Unimagined Communities'). The concept neatly collapses E. P. Thompson's distinction between 'being' and 'becoming' in the study of nationalisms.

[3] Reinhart Koselleck, *Vergangene Zukunft: Zur Semantik geschichtlicher Zeiten* (Frankfurt-am-Main: Suhrkamp, 1979); English translation as *Futures Past: On the Semantics of Historical Time* (trans. Keith Tribe, Cambridge, Mass. and London: MIT Press, 1985).

[4] It should be noted that there were several classes of nobles in the pre-1532 Incan elite, while after the conquest several non-nobles were granted *hidalguía* as recompense or reward for having assisted the Spaniards at various points during the conquest. The complexity of the pre-1532 nobility is discussed in R. T. Zuidema, 'The Inca Kinship System: A New Theoretical View', in *Andean Kinship and Marriage*, ed. Ralph Bolton and Enrique Mayer (Washington, D.C.: American Anthropological Association, 1977), pp. 240–292, esp. 276–279.

[5] In this respect, see the comments of Marshall Sahlins on scholars' disrespect towards the post-conquest history of colonial peoples, by which acculturation is considered to have tainted autochthonous cultures, thereby rendering these non-pristine and 'impure' cultures correspondingly less valuable for 'scientific' study. There has long been a widespread view

not only depend upon a family's receipt of either a formal grant of noble title or official affirmation of *hidalgo* status. Nevertheless, the lack of such corroborative documentation would, in the long term, have ineluctably consigned a family to historical oblivion. History, in Pareto's famous aphorism, is the graveyard of aristocracies; in colonial societies, the truism that social mobility can work in both directions tends to be writ large. Time and again in the course of three centuries, Inca noble families, and the nobility itself as a composite of lineages, were obliged to prove their noble status to crown administrators. The reason for this kind of structural uncertainty was not due solely to the customary exception from the poll-tax and personal service automatically attaching to noble status, but probably had as much to do with the thwarted social aspirations, envy and racial contempt of non-noble, Spanish colonial administrators. There was also the administrative messiness of it all: it was socially and administratively awkward, not to say absurd, to have two distinct aristocracies in the one society. All these considerations were manifest in the hostility toward the Inca nobles displayed by the Intendant of Cuzco, Benito de la Mata Linares, in the repressive aftermath of the Túpac Amaru rebellion.[6]

Spanish administrators and Inca nobles had conceptions of history and status validation that did not always cohere, for all that they displayed a remarkable degree of commensurability. The benchmark for official acceptance of noble status was the *probanza de nobleza*, a hurdle that peninsular nobles were obliged to negotiate within Spain itself, witness the magnificent genealogies that are such a notable feature of Spanish historical documentation.[7] Inca nobles were therefore obliged to cast their claim for noble status in the form of the *probanza*, i.e., in genealogical form, but family documention usually contained serious errors and lacunae that, in formal judicial proceedings, would have been adjudged insufficient. More than

that colonial Inca culture was degenerate and debased, and therefore that the colonial Inca nobles themselves were not quite 'kosher'. See Sahlins, 'Goodbye to *Tristes Tropes*: Ethnography in the Context of Modern World History', *Journal of Modern History*, vol. 65, no. 1, 1993, pp. 1–25.

6 This was especially the case in the aftermath of the Túpac Amaru rebellion; see. e.g., Archivo General de Indias, Leg. 35, Mata Linares to Gálvez (No. 11), 6 August, 1785; Mata Linares to Gálvez (No. 28), 19 March, 1786. For further discussion, David Cahill, 'After the Fall: Constructing Inca Identity in Late Colonial Cuzco', in *Constructing Collective Identities and Shaping Public Spheres: Latin American Paths*, ed. Luis Roniger and Mario Sznajder (Brighton and Portland: Sussex Academic Press, 1998), pp. 65–99.

7 On the Spanish nobility, see Antonio Domínguez Ortiz, *La sociedad española en el siglo XVII* (Granada: C.S.I.C., University of Granada, 1992 [1963]), vol. I, pp. 161–322, esp. p. 172ff on the *probanzas* ('el conjunto de diligencias necesarias para demostrar la hidalguía, tenían que adquirir una importancia desmesurada a partir de comienzos del siglo XVI, cuando la delimitación jurídica de los estados comenzó a tomar una importancia preeminente, al par que crecía el afán de *honra*, es decir, de distinción social'). The highpoint of the *probanzas* thus coincided nicely with the conquest and early colonisation of Peru; just in time, in fact, for the Inca nobles to make good use of them.

one noble claimant suffered that fate. For the Cuzqueño nobles, there was the further stumbling block that the customary *probanza* was a linear historical reconstruction, the very basis for recognition of nobility. The Inca nobility grounded their claims in a mixture of history, memory and myth, though they also argued that they were recognised as nobles by their peers, Native Andean as well as Hispanic elites. Effectively, they had to fit their own conception of nobility into its European homologue, formulate it so that it made sense in terms readily understandable to Spaniards. It was, in part, a matter of receptivity. To mix metaphors, the colonial context determined that they would have to put their own 'spin' on the received notion of Spanish nobility and return it to the Spanish authorities in a readily acceptable form, not to say formula. This, in turn, rendered the colonial definition of nobility perhaps a little more flexible than its peninsular equivalent; socially constituted in its colonial context, it gained in the telling. There was thus some latitude for error in the colonial *probanzas*, a circumstance doubtless congenial to creole holders of *títulos de Castilla* or *hidalguía*, some of whom had some genealogical problems of their own, ranging from missing documentation to illegitimate lines, present as well as past, which might vitiate the legal status of their titles.[8]

Even so, there were problems of compilation specific to the Inca nobility, above all that of rendering the *mélange* of history, memory and myth – usually conflated – acceptable to the Hispanic administrative and judicial hierarchies, from Cuzco to Lima to Madrid.[9] This was less a fiction or

[8] On the Creole nobility and other elites of Cuzco, see Michèle Colin, *Le Cuzco á la fin du XVIIe et au debut de XVIIIe siècle* (Paris: Institut des Hautes Etudes d'Amérique Latine, 1966); Bernard Lavallé, *Le Marquis et le marchand: les luttes de pouvoir au Cuzco (1700–1730)* (Paris: CNRS, 1987), also in translation as *El mercader y el marqués: Las luchas de poder en el Cusco (1700–1730)* (Lima: Banco Central de Reserva del Perú, 1988); Scarlett O'Phelan Godoy, 'Aduanas, mercado interno y elite comercial en el Cusco antes y después de la gran rebelión de 1780', *Apuntes*, vol. 19, 1986, pp. 53–72; David Cahill, 'Repartos ilícitos y familias principales en el Sur Andino: 1780–1824', *Revista de Indias*, vol. XLVIII, núms 182–183, 1988, pp. 449–473; Neus Escandell-Tur, *Producción y comercio de tejidos coloniales: Los obrajes y chorrillos del Cusco 1570–1820* (Cuzco: Centro de Estudios Regionales Andinos 'Bartolomé de Las Casas', 1997).

[9] There is a burgeoning literature on the theme of memory, the most obvious manifestation of which is the journal *History & Memory*. The key work is the French project under Pierre Nora (ed.), *Les lieux de mémoire* (7 vols, Paris: Gallimard, 1984–92). This is now being translated into a three-volume English edition: see Pierre Nora (ed.), *Realms of Memory: Rethinking the French Past* (trans. Arthur Goldhammer, New York: Columbia UP, 1996) vol. 1, esp. the introduction by Nora at pp. 1–20. See also David Lowenthal, *The Past is a Foreign Country* (Cambridge: Cambridge UP, 1985), pp. 193–210, who provides a useful introduction to the theme. Especially important is Jacques le Goff, *History and Memory* (trans. Steven Rendall and Elizabeth Claman, New York: Columbia UP, 1992), and Burke, *Varieties*, pp. 43–59, esp. pp. 58–59 on myth; Burke, *History and Social Theory*, pp. 101–103 on myth. Myth here is used in the sense of a particular construction of the past (e.g., a 'founding father' story) that provides a platform and 'charter' (Malinowski) for the present, or just a story with a social function.

fraud, as some royal officials had it, but rather a kind of ideological history, keenly felt and believed. It was an ancestral memory, something more than the sum of all the Incaic lineages, and it was juxtaposed with another, more conventional and derived European 'history'. Indeed, any Incan justification of nobility had to be imbricated in such a 'history', were a *probanza* to have any chance of success. As memory, it was partial, involving as it did an act of forgetting of some magnitude, an elision of erstwhile 'pagan' ways from the Incas' reconstructed ideological memory. Here, as in other known cases of 'ethnic memory', there is evident 'the same orientation of collective memory toward the time of origins and mythical heroes'.[10] The Inca nobles were grouped into twelve 'houses', each corresponding to a former Inca 'emperor'; depending on their kinship affiliations, many nobles might belong to more than one such lineage. These lineages, it seems clear, were a colonial reworking – a reconstitution – of the pre-conquest *panacas*, the stem-groups that had cared for the *momias* of former Inca rulers, had administered the wealth accrued during their respective reigns, and had constituted a fundamental social, political and ritual pillar of Tahuantinsuyu. Yet to speak of former kings is to speak of the independent reality of a 'king-list'. Here we touch upon a controverted theme in the historiography of the Inca. Some authors accept the twelve (in the colonial schema) Inca rulers as historical individuals, others view more than half of them as mythic (perhaps composite) personages, and scholars also differ as to whether they represent twelve successive monarchs or six successive diarchies (necessarily with some overlap).[11] The mythical element implicit in this grounding of the colonial self-image of the Inca nobles in ancestral tradition is, in the wider scheme of things, hardly novel. It was more generic than singular: Jacques Le Goff notes that in medieval Western Europe, 'when noble families, nations or urban communities become interested in giving themselves a history, they often begin with mythical ancestors who inaugurate the genealogies, with their legendary founding heroes'.[12] In colonial Spanish America, genealogy was no less inventive. Yet there is good reason to think that such mythic elements corresponded to pre-conquest, official 'historic' tradition. At some

---

[10] Le Goff, p. 56; see also p. 129: 'Just as the past is not history but the object of history, so memory is not history, but both one of its objects and an elementary level of its development'. This distinction – perhaps fairly tenuous in any case – is sometimes lost to view by Nora, 'Introduction', but is cogently delineated in Lowenthal, op. cit.

[11] This is perhaps to simplify a complex problem; the question of a diarchy involves consideration of the moieties of *hanan* and *hurin*, and of whether the ruling Inca had a 'brother' in the corresponding moiety who might replace the Inca absent on campaign ('hermano' cf. the colonial 'segunda persona'). A good starting-point and introduction to the several issues and to the literature on the subject is María Rostworowski de Diez Canseco, *Estructuras andinas del poder: Ideología religiosa y política* (Lima: Instituto de Estudios Andinos, 1983), pp. 130–180.

[12] Le Goff, op. cit., p. 134.

historical point, such myth is constructed: 'myth recuperates and restruc-
tures the outmoded leftovers of "earlier social systems"'.[13] To the extent
that it was fictive, it was nevertheless sincerely meant. It was the essential
foundation of the individual and group identities of the colonial nobles;
their *ayllus*, *panacas*, rites and social arrangements made little sense without
this identity net of founding heroes and 'kings'. Their status and prestige
depended upon it utterly.

The colonial *probanzas* that reflected this historical king-list thus con-
cealed considerable interpretive difficulties, evident already to some
contemporary observers. There is more than a suspicion that this schema
was due as much to the Inca nobles' awareness of Spanish historical texts
as it was to their own received tradition. That tradition was first and
foremost oral, and therefore difficult to recover; precisely how that memory
was kept alive – aside from its rememoration in colonial *probanzas* – is
unknown. Famously, the Incas had had the mnemonic device, the *quipu*,
as an administrative tool. The extent to which this might have been used
(by the *amautas*) to retain a historical *cum* mythic memory in pre-conquest
times is unclear, much less in the colonial era; indeed, this very question
is the subject of heated dispute among students of Tahuantinsuyu.[14] It is,
however, now abundantly clear that the nobles were capable of drawing
upon Hispanic and even universal history in order to buttress their claim
for a special place in the colonial sun.[15] This was not confined to their
introduction into their *probanzas* of the *topoi* and narratives of the classic
Hispanic accounts of the conquest, above all that of Garcilaso. They
accepted, for example, the notion of the 'behetrías', which was congenial
to (at least) the post-Toledan chroniclers, but in any case apparently a
trope of pre-conquest Incan ideology. To the standard accounts of the
conquest, they occasionally added their own group and familial traditions,
some of which materially expand our historical knowledge of the immediate
conquest and subsequent campaigns. More novel and enterprising, however, was a late eighteenth-century incorporation of the views of classical
authors such as Juvenal and Pliny. They drew, too, upon a comparative

[13] Ibid., citing Lévi-Strauss; cf. Burke, *Varieties*, p. 58, citing Malinowski's view that 'myth
functions as the "charter" of institutions'.

[14] Reference here is to the discovery of a supposedly new colonial Jesuit treatise concerning
a 'literary quipu' which, if authentic, would appear to support the thesis that the (pre-1532)
Incas had a system of writing: see Viviano Domenici and Davide Domenici, 'Talking Knots
of the Inca', *Archaeology*, Nov/Dec. 1996, pp. 50–56. The 'discoverer' is Laura Laurencich
Minelli, who presented the evidence for authenticity of this new source to the 49th International Congress of Americanists in Quito in July, 1997, as 'Una contribución a la etnohistoria
del Perú. El documento "Historia et Rudimenta Linguae Piruanorum"'. Both the validity
of the document and Laurencich herself have been attacked by Juan Carlos Estenssoro F.,
'¿Historia de un fraude o fraude histórico?', *Revista de Indias*, vol. LVII, núm. 210, 1997,
pp. 566–578.

[15] Cahill, 'After the Fall', pp. 65–99.

history of the aristocracies of past civilisations and their respective emblems of nobility, which buttressed their own 'founding-fathers' myth-history.[16] Some of these past aristocracies were as much mythical as historic, but this circumstance was similarly consonant with the Inca nobles' construction of history from mythic roots. In this, European and Incan lineages and genealogies dovetail neatly, and were expressed juridically in that classic Spanish institutional template, the *probanza de nobleza*. In retrospect, however, such a splash of Occidental wisdom in the Incas' group justification should occasion little surprise, because of their education in the Colegio de San Francisco de Borja, founded for the sons of 'Indios nobles y Caciques'; a Spanish foundation, Jesuit until 1767, it was in certain measure a continuation of the pre-conquest Inca institution, the *Yachay Huasi*. The College of San Borja was an important vector of Westernisation for the Inca nobles, and whether by design or accident provided the nobles with the array of cultural weapons necessary to defend their status and very existence against the manifold challenges to their welfare posed by the imperatives of colonial rule.

The signal mixture of memory, history and myth exhibited in the Inca nobles' *probanzas* was not uncharacteristic of the generic category known as 'ethnic memory'.[17] It was singular in the nature of its hybridisation, whether one conceives of this as acculturation, syncretism, appropriation or merely reception of Hispanic culture. These categories of scholarship, to the extent that they do not just describe the same phenomenon, were all no doubt present to a varying degree. Moreover, it should not be forgotten that these processes often involved a two-way transfer or appropriation,

[16] Ibid., pp. 80–83. Note the similar genealogical construction in medieval France mentioned by Le Goff, op. cit., p. 134, 'Thus in the medieval West, when noble families, nations, or urban communities become interested in giving themselves a history, they often begin with mythical ancestors who inaugurate the genealogies, with their legendary founding heroes. Thus the Franks claimed to descend from the Trojans, the Lusignan family claimed to descend from the fairy [!] Mélusine, and the monks of Saint-Denis attributed the foundation of their abbey to Denis the Areopagite, the Athenian converted by St. Paul'. Exactly, in fact, like the colonial Incas.

[17] Le Goff, op. cit., pp. 51–58, refers to 'ethnic memory' without writing ('primitive'), and then goes on to analyse the 'rise of memory'. Given that (see above note) there were close similarities between the construction of identities in medieval France and colonial Peru, the distinction between 'ethnic' and other memory appears rather false. Burke, *Varieties*, p. 47, criticises Nora's tendentious distinction between the 'spontaneous memory of traditional societies and the self-conscious "representation" of modern societies'. Certainly, in the case of the colonial Incas, the distinction is entirely false (even if we allow that such a thing as 'spontaneous memory' might actually exist). Such comparative ethnology or 'world history' has a tradition that stretches back at least to the sixteenth century: see, e.g., Anthony Pagden, *The Fall of Natural Man: The American Indian and the Origins of Comparative Ethnology* (rev. edn, Cambridge: Cambridge UP, 1988). Its influence continues through Voltaire, the Encyclopaedists, Herder and the Romantics: see the remarks of Isaiah Berlin, *Vico and Herder: Two Studies in the History of Ideas* (London: Hogarth Press, 1976), pp. 148–151.

nicely summed up in Crosby's phrase, the 'Columbian exchange' – nicely illustrated, too, by the manner in which the Inca nobles 'received' the Spanish formulaic institution of the *probanza* and subtly altered it by inserting criteria of social memory and myth, and then winning offical acceptance of their nobility on the basis of this documentary meta-morphosis. How far the colonial Incas were conscious of the extent to which they transformed the received criteria is, of course, an unknown, but it was probably a combination of passive reception and appropriation, consciously transformative actions, and just cultural misunderstanding of legal criteria – colonial masters and subjects often found one another mutually incomprehensible. However, a brief look at the nature of the colonial Incas' representative body, the 'Twenty-Four Electors of the Alférez Real', suggests that to a considerable extent, the Incas were con-scious of constructing a hybrid institution; this should occasion little surprise, given that scholars have long been aware, for example, of the creativity of indigenous communities in using Christian appearances, prac-tices and rites, in order to mask continued adherence to pre-Columbian beliefs and worship.

For all that it was more than the sum of its parts, the Incan electoral college can readily be parsed into its cultural elements and their respective provenances.[18] First of all, its autochthonous components are most obvious. The Twenty-four Electors were divided into twelve 'houses' (*casas*), each representing a former Inca ruler. There were thus two to each 'house', a circumstance that probably reflects the traditional Andean oppositional categories and the 'upper' and 'lower' Incan moieties of *hanan* and *hurin*, which had been so important in pre-conquest political, social and ritual arrangements. These twelve 'houses' almost certainly were a continuation of the aforementioned Incan lineage or clan groups, the *panacas*. The *panacas* had fulfilled a crucial ritual role during the Incario, so that there was a clear correspondence between their pre-1532 ritual function and their colonial (post-1555) function of electing the *alférez real de los incas* who, dressed in Incan raiment and adorned with Incaic symbolism, bore the royal standard on the Day of Santiago (July 25) during the Corpus Christi celebrations in the city of Cuzco. Here, then, was perfect ritual symmetry. There was an equal correspondence with Spanish institutions. First, the twenty-four electors appear to have reflected the institution of the *veinti-cuatros*, a Spanish civil and ecclesiastical body that derives from a synonym for the composition of a peninsular *cabildo*. In Cuzco, as elsewhere in the wider Hispanic world, 'los hermanos veinticuatros' – a kind of directorate – were those who administered some hospitals, *cofradías* and *hermandades*. Moroever, the Twenty-four Electors did not only choose the *alférez real*, the traditional bearer of the royal standard who, in the Hispanic world was usually a town councillor (*regidor*, *cabildante*, sometimes also *alcalde*), but

18 Cahill, 'After the Fall', pp. 65–99.

they elected also a distinct *alcalde mayor de indios* and *alguacil mayor de indios*, again, traditional Hispanic local-government officers.

In the course of addressing possible approaches to the interpretation of cultural encounters or 'contests', Peter Burke has underscored the need to understand the internal logic of syncretism, what he calls the 'emic' approach.[19] He argues that 'what the historian needs to investigate is the logic underlying these appropriations or combinations, the local reasons for these choices'. The above example of the colonial Inca electoral college is remarkable in that the 'fit' between Hispanic and Incaic was serendipitously perfect, on both civil and ecclesiatical criteria. In the aftermath of the conquest and civil wars, the surviving Inca nobility discovered Spanish institutional templates that were ready-made conduits for the preservation of at least some vestige of their pre-conquest, social and ritual roles. This Incan appropriation of Spanish institutions was a counterpoint to the Spaniards' own, well-known adaptation of Incaic institutions such as tribute, the labour corvée (*mita*), the communications system (*tambos* and *chasquis*), the network of chiefdoms (*kurakazgos*, *cacicazgos*), and so forth. However unequal the colonial power equation, borrowings and appropriations move in both directions. Contexts changed, the repertoire of borrowings was vast, and misunderstandings were rife. The end result of such cultural transferences was usually something more than the sum of tradition plus received novelties, its logic and function often thereby correspondingly amended.

Yet the institutional design of the Incan electoral body was not just a happy coincidence of traditional and received elements. Its now syncretic, primary function and inner logic were also commensurately reflective of Incan and Spanish cultural accommodation. Its ostensibly sole function was to elect the Incas' *alférez real* to accompany his Hispanic homologue during the Corpus Christi procession and on other civic and ecclesiastical occasions. This office thus reflected Spanish ceremonial and civic praxis, especially in its invocation of *cofradía* officer-holders and processional participation, again paralleled by the pre-conquest *panacas'* ritual responsibilities. The dualism of two matched *alféreces*, moreover, corresponded neatly to Native Andean conceptions of ritual space, with its intrinsic oppositions and complementarities; its numinosity would have been all the more potent if we accept the (albeit contested) view of some authors that Inca rule was a diarchy, each Inca of which represented separate moieties and ritual functions. Such ceremonial presence went beyond the strictly religious; Balandier's view of ritual seems especially apposite in this context: 'Ritual ... accentuates certain aspects of power. It evokes its beginnings, its roots in a history that has become mythic, and it makes this history sacred'.[20] In the religious processions of Cuzco, Incaic conceptions of

---

[19] Burke, *Varieties*, p. 209.
[20] Le Goff, op. cit., p. 55, citing Georges Balandier.

history and memory came together. These processions were something more than a *lieu de mémoire*, in the sense in which Pierre Nora used the term. It was the point at which history and memory intersected, where group memory was lived and celebrated and revalidated, before it became just history. The case study which follows, that of syncretic Incaic ceremonial at its colonial zenith, attempts to 'unpack' the extraordinary complexity of its religious symbolism and multiple meanings. The bald, contemporary descriptions of processions on which it is based invite reflection and provoke the historical imagination. They are of course texts, but their range of possible interpretations is severely circumscribed, because of their juxtaposition with other available evidence – other *texts* – of colonial as well as pre-conquest Incaic praxis, social structure and customs. In the final analysis, it is this documentary context which allows the historian considerable advance along the *via negativa* of the historically possible.

CHAPTER NINE

# The Inca and the Politics of Nostalgia

The Cuzco region was the principal theatre of protest, rebellion and sundry subversive activities in the Viceroyalty of Peru during the last half-century of colonial rule (c. 1770–1824).[1] Royal authorities considered it to be the military and political key not only to Peru itself, but also to Spanish South America in general. This view took into account the obvious symbolism of the city of Cuzco for indigenous groups who yearned (according to Creole and peninsula pundits of the age) for a return to the supposed Golden Age of the Incario (Tahuantinsuyu), but it had also to do with the city's symbolic importance for the region's Creole elites. They sought a degree of independence from *limeño* interference in their administrative, judicial, and especially commercial and fiscal affairs, as well as either a better political profile within the imperial structure or their own total

[1] There is now an enormous bibliography on colonial Andean rebellion, for an evaluation of which, see Steve J. Stern, 'The Age of Andean Insurrection, 1742–1782: A Reappraisal' in Stern (ed.), *Resistance, Rebellion, and Consciousness in the Andean Peasant World: 18th to 20th Centuries* (Madison: Wisconsin UP, 1987). The two principal works on the 'conjuncture' of rebellion are: Boleslao Lewin, *La rebelión de Túpac Amaru y los orígenes de la independencia de Hispanoamérica* (2nd edn, Buenos Aires: Librería Hachette, 1957); Scarlett O'Phelan Godoy, *Rebellions and Revolts in Eighteenth-Century Peru and Upper Peru* (Cologne and Vienna: Böhlau Verlag, 1984). Several recent works are valuable: Luis Miguel Glave, *Vida, símbolos y batallas: Creación y recreación de la comunidad indígena. Cusco, siglos XVI-XX* (Lima: Fondo de Cultura Económica, 1992); Scarlett O'Phelan Godoy, *La gran rebelión en los Andes: De Túpac Amaru a Túpac Catari* (Cuzco: Centro de Estudios Regionales Andinos 'Bartolomé de las Casas', 1995); Núria Sala i Vila, *Y se armó el tole tole: Tributo indígena y movimientos sociales en el Virreinato del Perú, 1784–1814* (Ayacucho: Instituto de Estudios Regionales 'José María Arguedas', 1996). See also the contributions in Charles Walker (ed.), *Entre la retórica y la insurgencia. Las ideas y los movimientos sociales en los Andes, siglo XVIII* (Cuzco: Centro de Estudios Regionales Andinos 'Bartolomé de las Casas', 1996). For overviews (apart from the titles by Glave and Sala i Vila cited above) of the period following the suppression of the *levantamiento general*, see especially John R. Fisher, 'Royalism, Regionalism, and Rebellion in Colonial Peru, 1808–1815', *Hispanic American Historical Review*, vol. 59, no. 2, 1979, pp. 232–257; Scarlett O'Phelan Godoy, 'El mito de la "independencia concedida": los programas políticos del siglo XVIII y del temprano XIX en el Perú y Alto Perú (1730–1814)', in Inge Buisson et al., *Problemas de la formación del estado y de la nación en Hispanoamérica* (Cologne and Vienna: Böhlau Verlag, 1984), pp. 55–92; Luis Durand Flórez, *Criollos en conflicto: Cuzco después de Túpac Amaru* (Lima: Lima UP, 1985).

emancipation from Spanish hegemony. There were still other, more prosaic considerations: Cuzco was then located at the centre of those provinces in which the indigenous population was most numerous, and it would have been difficult to send military reinforcements while at the same time providing the logistical resources necessary for successful prosecution of any campaign to crush an uprising or even a localised insurrection. Here, for example, is the advice proferred the crown in 1783 (conserving the original orthography) by the Intendant of Cuzco, Benito de la Mata Linares, who spoke of:

> lo importantisimo que es atender a esta cuidad del Cuzco, y con sólo decir ... que perdida ella se levantó todo el Reyno; y conservada, aunque se aniqilara Lima, y Buenos Aires no debia dar cuidado, se comprendera su importancia: el Yndio tiene tal entusiasmo con ella, que interín no la posea no cree conseguir cosa particular por aquella memoria que conserva de haber sido Capital de los Yncas: su disposición contribuye mucho para estar colocada entre las provincias mas numerosos de Yndios, y tener distante los recursos.[2]

In a later representation, Mata Linares referred to the 'consideracion que merece esta poblacion, pues segun asegure, como no se pierda se conserba el Reyno, pero si la ocupan los enemigos se extinguió la Dominacion'.[3] In this formulation, military and political domination are equated with control of hearts and minds, and in Mata's view the crown was losing the latter, thereby imperilling the former. Here, then, we have a royal functionary of the eighteenth century referring implicitly to that concept of *utopía andina* that historians have formulated only in recent years.[4] Such a *utopía* has to do with the yearning – at times messianic – for the return of the Inca to mark the inauguration of a new Golden Age, as well as to

---

[2] Archivo General de Indias, Audiencia del Cuzco Leg. 29, Mata Linares to Gálvez, letter of 30 June, 1783. There is more than a suspicion of plagiarism by Mata here, of the early eighteenth-century Peruvian savant Pedro de Peralta Barnuevo y Rocha (1664–1743), who argued: 'Quit Lima from Peru and no empire will remain ... With Lima defended, all is defended; with it lost, all is lost'. If one substitutes Mata's Cuzco for Peralta's Lima, the rhetorical resemblance is uncanny. For Peralta's views, see David A. Brading, *The First America: The Spanish Monarchy, Creole Patriots, and the Liberal State 1492–1867* (Cambridge: Cambridge UP, 1991), p. 397, citing Peralta, *Lima expugnable* (ed. Luis Antonio Eguiguren Escudero, 2nd edn, Lima: 1966), pp. xxv, xxxii.

[3] Archivo General de Indias, Audiencia del Cuzco Leg. 35, Mata Linares to Gálvez, 6 August, 1785.

[4] Alberto Flores Galindo, *Buscando un inca: Identidad y utopía en los Andes* (Lima: Instituto de Apoyo Agrario, 1987); Manuel Burga, *Nacimiento de una utopía. Muerte y resurrección de los incas* (Lima: Instituto de Apoyo Agrario, 1988). The concept was first delineated by Burga and Flores Galindo, 'La utopía andina', *Allpanchis*, vol. XVII, 1982, pp. 85–101. For related approaches, Juan M. Ossio (ed.), *Ideología mesiánica del mundo andino* (Lima: Gráfica Morson, 1973); Franklin Pease G. Y., 'Mesianismo andino e identidad étnica: continuidades y problemas', *Cultura* (Quito), vol. 5, no. 13, 1982, pp. 57–71; Wilfredo Kapsoli, *Ayllus del sol: anarquismo y utopía andina* (Lima: TAREA, 1984).

a whole gamut of indigenous projects for restoration of an autochthonous government. There is some reason to think that such projects and aspirations do exist, and become especially evident or activated at times of crisis – whether social, economic or political – but there are other interpretations which emphasise that such a regressive *utopia* comprises a permanent and immanent mental structure that is continually on view in traditional Andean iconology, whether in art, craft or ritual forms.

From around 1770, separatist movements in the Cuzco region had as context a new economic conjuncture which, for all that it was in part the result of structural weaknesses in the regional economy, had its roots fundamentally in a series of royal reforms (1776–1784) that destroyed the administrative and commercial bases upon which the region had founded its traditional prosperity. In economic terms, the region lost its 'comparative advantage' in the internal market of the southern Andes. There was a close, even symbiotic, link between that prosperity and Cuzco's location along the Lima-Potosí commercial axis. Thus it was that the century to *c.* 1770 had been an era of significant economic growth in the leading sectors of the colonial monetary economy. This *siglo de oro* had generated – best to say, consolidated – a coherent oligarchy *cum* aristocracy that dominated agrarian and pastoral production (beyond that produced by indigenous communities) and especially textile production and its commercialisation.[5] Moreover, it was they who controlled the local cabildo through their monopoly of hereditary offices, and they shared a *conciencia de sí* that represented an implicit social and political challenge to the aristocracy and commercial oligarchy of Lima and, potentially and ultimately, to the Spanish crown itself.

Between 1780 and 1815 the region was the scene of two attempted revolutions against Spanish overlordship, as well as of three failed conspiracies and desultory murmurings that shared the same separatist goal. All these attempts failed, and when independence finally came to the region, it was imposed from without, for between 1821 and 1824 Cuzco had been the seat of the rapidly disintegrating viceregal government. The uprising of 1780–83 was fundamentally an indigenous movement, while that of 1814–15 was essentially a Creole movement, notwithstanding that each witnessed important alliances which crossed barriers of race, ethnicity, class and estate. Such alliances, however, collapsed during the course of each

---

[5] Maximiliano Moscoso, 'Apuntes para la historia de la industria textil en el Cuzco colonial', *Revista Universitaria* (Cuzco), vols. LI–LII, nos. 122/125, 1962–63, pp. 67–94; Magnus Mörner, *Perfil de la sociedad rural del Cuzco a fines de la colonia* (Lima: Universidad del Pacífico, 1978), chap. 3; Scarlett O'Phelan Godoy, 'Aduanas, mercado interno y elite comercial en el Cusco antes y después de la gran rebelión de 1780', *Apuntes*, vol. 19, 1986, pp. 53–72; David Cahill, 'Repartos ilícitos y familias principales en el sur andino, 1780–1824', *Revista de Indias* vol. XLVIII, nos. 182–183, 1988, pp. 449–473; Neus Escandell-Tur, *Producción y comercio de tejidos coloniales. Los obrajes y chorrillos del Cusco 1570–1820* (Cuzco: Centro de Estudios Regionales Andinos 'Bartolomé de las Casas', 1996).

movement. Nevertheless, it was remarkable that any type of coalition between Creoles, mestizos and indigenes had been formed at all, given that the last half-century of colonial rule in the region had been marked by an intensification of the several modes of exploitation of the peasant (and especially indigenous) sector of the economy, and that the principal exploiters were those very same Creoles.

The common denominator of this welter of uprisings and conspiracies was the search for an Inca as leader of a movement that could provide a political alternative to continued Spanish domination, a search favoured as much by Creoles as by indigenes. This idea gathered considerable momentum in the southern sierra during the last fifty years of colonial rule, and appears to have been adopted – it was not an entirely novel idea prior to 1770 – by some members among the upper tiers of indigenous society. Now, the attractiveness of this concept of a new Incario for the surviving Incan and other indigenous nobility will be obvious, but its enchantment for the Creole elites of the region requires a more detailed explanation. Historians have traditionally ascribed the Creole acceptance of this concept either to romantic nostalgia for a supposed 'Golden Age' or to cynical opportunism, but any evaluation of the concept has always been impeded by the lack of any clear formulation of its content in the eighteenth century itself. While there is a corpus of evidence which indicates that Incaic symbolism was widespread in the separatist movements and conspiracies of the era, any explanation of its appeal for both indigenes and Creoles must necessarily rely on an inductive approach.

In no other place did colonial social stratification have more nuances than in the Cuzco region. There, above all in the erstwhile Inca capital, the complex and familiar social categories of Spanish American colonialism were interwoven with the now anachronistic lineage groups of the upper tiers of the quondam Inca society, a social sector that, for its part, also displayed considerable social differentiation. The pretensions and claims of these colonial Inca nobles within the eighteenth-century colonial order depended principally on their individual lineage or descent from one or more of the former Inca 'emperors' ('Sapay Inca'), and individually and collectively they jealously guarded their exclusive right to wear the *mascapaicha*, which had been the symbol of the Inca rulers, and which right, in its colonial context, demarcated the 'kosher' Incan nobles from their arriviste counterparts. Their representative body, the Twenty-four Electors of the Alférez Real, argued in 1785 that 'la mascapaicha es en realidad una antiquisima orden de Caballeros Yngas en demonstracion de su Regia Gentilicia extirpe'.[6]

In 1786 this indigenous nobility comprised 212 males (or *c*. 8 per cent of the urban *indiada*), while still others had fallen through the tribute net,

[6] Archivo General de Indias, Audiencia de Lima Leg. 35, Petition of Don Cayetano Tupa Guamanrimachi, Comisario de los Incas, n.d. but *c*. 1778.

that is to say, they had lost the most practically important noble privilege of the colonial era.[7] Nonetheless, most of this latter group were still recognised socially by their peers as nobles, and this was manifest in their participation, resplendant in Incaic raiment, in the principal festivals of colonial Cuzco. Yet authority within colonial indigenous society often lay elsewhere. Beyond this nobility, there existed a group of over 600 caciques or *kurakas* who governed the communities of the region, the power of each cacique depending, in the first instance, on the number of tributaries and communal lands under his or her control (female incumbency of the cacicazgos was not uncommon). There were caciques who governed ten families, others who were responsable for hundreds: a tier of nested units that stemmed for the most part from the erstwhile Incan decimal organisation.[8] Moreover, there was a further network of *cabildos de indios*, each one with its respective alcaldes and regidores, who probably comprised between one thousand and two thousand *cargueros* in the pueblos of the southern sierra.[9]

Now, the search for an Inca to lead a rebellion and/or to serve as titular head of a restored Incario was an idea that ran like a red thread through the separatist politics of the era. It was an idea that was obviously imbued with some messianic or millenarian content, for all that there is scant evidence in the extant documentation for such a quasi-religious dimension. In the wake of the 1780 rebellion, the Bishop of Cuzco criticised the availability of a popular and prophetic literature that foretold the restoration of Tahuantinsuyu. For example, a 1723 edition of the *Comentarios reales de los Incas* by Garcilaso de la Vega included a prologue by Gabriel de Cárdenas which recorded a prophecy of just such a restoration of the

[7] Archivo Departamental del Cuzco, Intendencia: Real Audiencia, Leg. 175, 'Expediente relativo a los tributos del Cuzco, matrícula hecha en el año de 1786 ...'. This document contains rough drafts of a *matrícula* that has not come to light. There are several ambiguities within the document, such that the figures quoted above must be taken as minimum figures for the total of indigenous 'nobles' within the city and Cercado of Cuzco. Specifically, there are separate lists of those exempt from tribute obligations, and those (not all nobles) who for various reasons were to be deducted from the *matrícula*. It is not clear, however, whether these names had already been removed from the *borrador* of the *matrícula* beforehand. Were that the case, then the corresponding number of male heads of noble households would rise to 457 (13 per cent of the urban *indiada*). Resolution of this ambiguity awaits discovery of the final version of the 1786 *matrícula*.

[8] See especially Karen Spalding, *Huarochirí: An Andean Society under Inca and Spanish Rule* (Stanford: Stanford UP, 1984), who skilfully elaborates these 'nested tiers'.

[9] David Cahill, 'Curas and Social Conflict in the *doctrinas* of Cuzco, 1780–1814', *Journal of Latin American Studies*, vol. 16, no. 2, 1984, pp. 241–276, esp. p. 258.

[10] The views of the Bishop, Juan Manuel Moscoso y Peralta, on these 'fantásticos vaticinios' (singling out Cárdenas) are to be found at: Archivo General de Indias, Audiencia del Cuzco, Leg. 29, Moscoso to Josef Antonio de Areche, 13 April, 1781. The importance of the Cárdenas edition of the *Comentarios reales* as a factor in the separatist sentiments of the era is underscored in Lewin, op. cit., pp. 282–285, 381–384; John Howland Rowe, 'El movimiento nacional inca

Incario, in this case with the protection of England.[10] The era appeared to favour such hopes, for in 1777 there was another rumour of a supposed prophecy by Santa Rosa de Lima (also by San Francisco de Solano, according to one source) that fixed upon the year of the 'three sevens' (1777) as the moment of the restoration.[11] This alleged prophecy of Santa Rosa appears to have been widespread in the taverns of Cuzco towards the end of the 1770s, and even José Gabriel Túpac Amaru, leader of the 1780–81 *levantamiento general*, believed it. He is also recorded as believing that England would come to his aid. This accords well with the 1723 Cárdenas prophecy, and in fact we know that Túpac Amaru possessed a copy of that particular edition of Garcilaso; it was also an inspiration for the leaders of the abortive Aguilar-Ubalde conspiracy of 1805. It should be emphasised that this concept of an imminent New Age or *pachacuti* appears to be a constant in Andean thought: it first comes to light with the nativist Taqui Onqoy movement of the 1560s, and is delineated at length in the *Nueva córonica* of Guamán Poma de Ayala of 1615. It reappears not only in the Aguilar-Ubalde conspiracy but also on the eve of the failed revolutionary attempt of 1814–15. Most notably, during the 1780 rebellion there were indigenous rebels who believed that Túpac Amaru was an ancient Inca whom God had resurrected to usher in a New Age.[12]

In the past two decades or so, numerous contemporary versions of the myth of Inkarrí have been registered in the several regions of Peru.[13] Inkarrí is at once Inca and King, at times messiah, at times a traditional hero

del siglo XVIII', *Revista Universitaria* (Cuzco), no. 107, 1954, pp. 17–47, follows Lewin on this point. For details of this edition, see Philip Ainsworth Means, *Biblioteca Andina* (Detroit: Blain Ethridge, 1973, reprint of 1928 Yale UP edn), p. 380.

[11] For the documentation on this 1777 episode, see *Colección documental del bicentenario de la revolución emancipadora de Túpac Amaru*, vol. II, pp. 241–244. For more details, see David Cahill, 'Crown, Clergy and Revolution in Bourbon Peru: The Diocese of Cuzco 1780–1814' (doctoral dissertation, University of Liverpool, 1984), pp. 208–209; Jan Szeminski, 'Why kill the Spaniard? New Perspectives on Andean Insurrectionary Ideology in the 18th Century', in Stern, op. cit., pp. 179–180. For the 1667 conspiracy, see Franklin Pease G. Y., 'Mesianismo andino', and for its juxtaposition with the subversive conjuncture of the late colonial period, David Cahill, 'Una visión andina: El levantamiento de Ocongate de 1815', *Histórica* (Lima), vol. XII, no. 2, 1988, p. 155.

[12] Archivo General de Indias, Audiencia de Lima, Leg. 1052, 'Testimonio [E] del proceso gral. informativo obrado sobre la rebelion del Reyno por el Alcalde de Corte comisionado en Arequipa. Años 1780, 1781', fol. 40v: 'Que en todos los pueblos de Alca Tomepampa y demas circumbesinos oio decir a los yndios con grande regosijo que gracias a Dios que havia resusitado su Ynga que hasta quando havian de estar vajo de la carga'. Alca and Tomepampa are located in the province of Chumbivilcas.

[13] Flores Galindo, op. cit., pp. 21–25. See also the essays in Ossio, op. cit., most of which deal explicitly with Inkarrí; also Pease, 'Mesianismo andino', passim; Henrique Urbano, 'Inkarri antes y después de los antropólogos', *Márgenes: encuentro y debate*, vol. I, no. I, 1987, pp. 144–154. Scholars frequently cite the several myths of 'Inkarri' as though they were always and everywhere present, but in fact there are few references to Inkarrí in the extant historical sources.

come to signal or to prepare the ground for a New Age. The myth is, then, a cyclical concept that prospers even today. If there is some indication that in 1780 Túpac Amaru was seen as Inkarrí, the belief in the dawning of a New Age did not necessarily connote the idea of an Inca *redivivus*. In a wider, more general form it may refer simply to the expulsion of any outsider or foreigner or even dominant class – in short, a generously defined 'Other'. Thus it was that during the 1780 uprising, a false and self-appointed 'Inca' appeared on the scene to proclaim that 'gracias a Dios havia llegado el tiempo de que recordasen de lo ciego que havian vivido todos estos años en servicio de todos los Cholos, y que ahora les llegava su tiempo de ser ellos servidos'.[14] In the uprising of 1815 an indigenous prisoner affirmed that the aim of the revolt was 'el de acabar con todo español, y mestizo, y existir solamente los yndios'.[15] Clearly, Andean rebellions cannot be explained without reference to the aspirations of *comunero* or *hatunruna*. On the other hand, the involvement of (elite and non-elite) urban Creoles, *españoles de pueblo*, mestizos and other castes in both major uprisings serves to underscore the hazards of interpreting Andean rebellion as an essentially indigenous phenomenon.

While it appears that such millenarian ideas are innate to Andean thought, they were far from being a necessary component of the Spanish or Creole 'mentality' of the eighteenth century. To the extent that 'Incan' ideology was a Creole concept, it was 'derived';[16] it appears for the first time in the Oruro conspiracy of 1737, when a group of indigenous nobles and prominent Creoles invited the most prestigious Incan noble of Cuzco to lead a reformist movement (although with apparent separatist tendencies).[17] In March 1780, following a number of rumours and apocalyptic prophecies in the preceding decade, there was a similar conspiracy in Cuzco that sought to impede the implementation of several Bourbon fiscal and administrative reforms; this plot gathered momentum when a Creole

---

[14] AGI Lima, Leg. 1052, 'Testimonio [B] ... del proceso gral. informativo ... por el Alcalde de Corte ...', fol. 57r.

[15] David Cahill, 'El levantamiento de Ocongate' pp. 133–159, esp. p. 144; David Cahill and Scarlett O'Phelan Godoy, 'Forging their Own History: Indian Insurgency in the Southern Peruvian Sierra, 1815', *Bulletin of Latin American Research*, vol. 11, no. 2, 1992, pp. 125–167, esp. p. 155.

[16] The allusion here is to George Rudé, *Ideology and Popular Protest* (London: Routledge, 1980), pp. 27–38, for the distinction between 'inherent' and 'derived' ideology. To simplify his distinction somewhat, the former may be said to consist of that learned by 'direct experience, oral tradition or folk-memory', whereas the latter is acquired from without, from books, sermons, or 'more structured' systems of political and religious ideas.

[17] Boleslao Lewin, La rebelión de Túpac Amaru, pp. 117–120; O'Phelan Godoy, *Rebellions and Revolts*, pp. 86–92; Oscar Cornblit, *Power and Violence in the Colonial City: Oruro from the Mining Renaissance to the Rebellion of Túpac Amaru (1740–1782)*, (Cambridge: Cambridge UP, 1995), pp. 63–64.

[18] The Farfán de los Godos-Tambohuacso conspiracy is variously treated in Lewin, op. cit., pp. 162–174; Manuel Jesús Aparicio Vega, 'El proceso seguido a los sediciosos de 1780',

leader was designated as 'Inca'.[18] The idea had, then, the potential to infuse any protest movement with a revolutionary, separatist character. It carried with it, moreover, the possibility of uniting – at least in the short term – the indigenous and Creole sectors, in other respects divided structurally by racial, cultural and class differences. The potential of this 'Incaic' concept to unite disparate groups politically was seen again in 1805 and 1815, when Creole groups employed it in order to attract indigenes to the separatist standard. Nevertheless, it is clear that the use of Incaic symbolism by the Creoles in 1805 and 1814 went beyond mere political cynicism, and it should be noted that such symbolism was more evident in 1814 than in the rebellion of 1780, which had been led by a lineal descendant of the Incas. Why was this so? How can we explain the attraction for Creoles of the idea of a restoration of the Inca?

First of all, it was the Age of the Enlightenment, and private and institutional libraries in the Cuzco region held examples of proscribed works of the *philosophes*, the novels of Marmontel and Mme. de Graffigney on the Incas among them; that is to say, the theme of the Incas was in fashion in Europe as well as in Peru, so that literate Cuzqueños were imbibing idealised, European romantic constructions of the Incario at the very time when they were becoming progressively alienated from an interventionist Bourbon régime. In the second place, it would appear that the regional oligarchy – including many who bore a *título de Castilla* – had developed a strong *conciencia de sí*, the better to confront the pretensions of their *limeño* counterparts, and it would seem that the memory of an Incaic heritage lent a special flavour to the Creole conscience of the *cuzqueño* elites.[19] Third, the region had produced a distinctive 'school' or style of painting that portrayed not only the conventional religious themes of the era but also indigenous nobles dressed in Incan raiment, adorned with Incan insignias; the products of this 'escuela cuzqueña' were commercialised throughout the entire viceroyalty (including Upper Peru or Bolivia) and most of its artists were native Andeans, some of them nobles.[20] Fourth, a strong regional identity gathered momentum from around 1804

*Revista del Archivo Histórico del Cuzco*, no. 12, 1967, pp. 204–235; Víctor Angles Vargas, *El cacique Tambohuacso: Historia de un proyectado levantamiento contra la dominación española* (Lima: 1975); Armando Sotomayor Farfán, 'El conato de Farfán de los Godos y Bernardo Tambohuacso Pumayalli' in *Jornadas peruano-bolivianas de estudio científico del altiplano boliviano y del sur*, ed. Carlos Urquizo Sossa (La Paz: 1976); Cahill, *Crown, Clergy, and Revolution*, pp. 216–224; O'Phelan, *Rebellions and Revolts*, pp. 194–203.

[19] The principal family of the Cuzqueño aristocracy *cum* oligarchy was the Ugarte y Celiorigo clan, who traced their colonial roots to Juan de Pancorvo, one of Pizarro's band of conquistadors. Pancorvo produced an illegitimate daughter, her mother being a *palla*, i.e., a noble. Of more moment was the marriage of Pancorvo's descendant, Diego de Celiorigo y Zúñiga, with the ñusta (princess) Doña Juana Asurpay, grand-daughter of Huayna Capac and sister of Huascar Inca. For the Ugarte clan's links with the network of other Cuzqueño elite families, see David Cahill, 'Repartos ilícitos y familias principales', pp. 453–458.

[20] José de Mesa and Teresa Gisbert, *Historia de la pintura cuzqueña* (2 vols, Lima: 1982).

with a proposal by Francisco Carrascón, a prebend of the cathedral, to make Cuzco the seat of a new viceroyalty, a proposal that still had not been rejected by the crown when revolution erupted there in 1814, a movement in which Carrascón played a prominent role as ideologue and cadre.[21] Finally, there was a long history of positive relations between Creole and indigenous elites, relations reinforced by links of *parentesco* and *compadrazgo*, which stood in marked contrast to the bitter history of Creole exploitation of native Andeans generally.

Now, such explanations of the allure of 'the Inca' for Creoles help us to understand the formation of political alliances between Creole and indigenous elites, but these alone are insufficient to clarify the phenomenon. It is certain that Creoles needed the support of the indigenous (apart from other 'peasant') masses – who comprised 73 per cent of the regional population – but at the same time it must be taken into account that the period after 1780 was characterised by an increase in the various modes of exploitation of indigenous groups by those selfsame Creole elites.[22] Perhaps we can locate the decisive factor in this Creole identification with the Incas in the nature of the kinship ties among the principal Creole families. The pre-eminent family was the Ugartes, which had links of *parentesco* with all other elite families. The political significance of such a kinship network resided in the fact that the Ugartes were held to be descendants of the Incas, a belief that was also shared by the indigenous groups of the region. It can therefore be seen that the desire of some Cuzqueño Creoles for the restoration of a *modernised* version of the Incario responded to a particular constellation of circumstances, among which the fact that the leading elite family of the Creole oligarchy was regarded as having Incaic roots was perhaps the key motive underlying this Creole 'incanismo'. With the Ugarte family having Incan descent apparent in its genealogical 'tree', its kinship links with all the other principal Creole families meant that *all* of these families would have Incas in their family 'trees' – at the very least, affines. One in, all in. It is worth mentioning in this context that the eighteenth century was especially marked by an inordinate attention to genealogy, and such concerns became especially prominent in regard to racial categories and affiliations.

---

[21] This was the *Plan del Perú* by Francisco Carrascón y la Sota, for which see John Fisher, 'Royalism, Regionalism and Rebellion', pp. 232–257; David Cahill, *Crown, Clergy and Revolution*, pp. 322–338, 372–383.

[22] David Cahill, 'Independencia, sociedad y fiscalidad: El Sur Andino (1780–1880)', *Revista Complutense de Historia de América*, no. 19, 1993, pp. 249–268. This is a revised version of that which appeared in *América: encuentro y asimilación* (Santa Fe de Granada, 2a Jornada de Historiadores Americanistas, 1989), comp. Joaquín Muñoz Mendoza (Granada: Diputación Provincial de Granada, 1990), pp. 141–156.

### The bishop's broadside

The great uprising of 1780 focused the minds of crown authorities won-
derfully, led as it was by an indigenous noble who claimed to be the rightful
successor to the last Inca and as such entitled not only to the advocacy
of indigenous welfare and associated reform, but also – as became clear
during the course of the rebellion – to sovereign rule, to a restoration
of a modernised version of Tahuantinsuyu. In the official recriminations
that followed the suppression of the insurgency, the question of how to
obliterate the nostalgic yearning for a return to a supposed Incan Golden
Age remained high on the agenda of royalist reprisals and counter-
insurrectionary strategy. The jeremiad of Intendant Mata Linares concerning the overriding emblematic importance of the city of Cuzco for Native
Andeans echoed similar evaluations by other leading crown functionaries
in the wake of the rebellion, notably the well-known representation of 1
May, 1781 made by the Visitor-General Joseph Antonio de Areche which
called for the iconoclastic suppression of all artistic, folkloric and cultural
vestiges, as well as privileges and ceremonial practices, that evoked the
memory of the erstwhile Inca emperors and thereby, ran the argument,
inculcated a veneration for the long-gone Incas rightfully due the Most
Catholic Monarch by his subjects. Such nostalgia was thus seen as not
only providing a fertile seed-bed for subversive and even separatist activities
but as also carrying with it the opportunity cost that fealty – frequently
compared to filial love – was imperilled by a kind of ancestor worship.
The analogy is apt, however exaggerated it may appear at first sight, for
it had been a fundamental function of the Incan *panacas* (lineage groups)
to worship and care for the *momias* of their respective Incan progenitors.[23] As the spirits of Inca rulers were regarded as animistically present,
perhaps omnipresent, Spanish authorities in the early post-conquest decades were particularly assiduous in hunting down every last *momia*. In
late colonial Cuzco, there is evidence that a version of the *panacas*, formally
extinct, was still in operation. It would do less than justice to the cluster
of royalist iconoclasts who oversaw the pacification of the Cuzco region
after 1780 not to appreciate that their policy, at first glance a paranoid
reaction, owed something to a realistic assessment of the quasi-religious
dimension of Andean politics, and of the extent to which the 'great uprising'
of 1780–83 was grounded in traditional Andean culture, with all its chiliastic

---

23 The *panaca* was in many respects the key Inca institution, and references to them abound
in the literature. Their centrality is best seen in the classic study of R. Tom Zuidema, *The
Ceque System of Cuzco: The Social Organisation of the Capital of the Inca* (Leiden: E. J. Brill,
1964). Good, condensed treatments of the institution are: María Rostworowski de Diez
Canseco, *Estructuras andinas del poder: Ideología religiosa y política* (Lima: Instituto de Estudios
Peruanos, 1983), pp. 138–150; María Concepción Bravo Guerreira, *El tiempo de los incas*
(Madrid: Editorial Alhambra, 1986), pp. 92–105; Fernando Iwasaki Cauti, 'Las panacas del
Cuzco y la pintura incaica', *Revista de Indias*, vol. XLVI, no. 177, 1986, pp. 58–74.

overtones. In a society permeated with animistic beliefs, an ancestor's spirit leaves the body only to continue in the world.

Areche's submission geared towards erasing the memory of the 'Gentile kings' resulted in a royal order of 27 April, 1782 which approved, though in much diluted form, the root and branch eradication of Incaic culture suggested by the Visitor-General. While Areche's report has often been cited by historians, it has not often been recognised that his proposals were but a pale epitome of the swingeing critique of the late colonial Incan elite and of indigenous society generally which the Bishop of Cuzco, Juan Manuel Moscoso y Peralta, had submitted to Areche just two weeks prior to the latter's own call for suppression of Incaic culture.[24] Moscoso's report drew on his own Creole background and considerable knowledge of the rites and customs of the southern Andes, a familiarity reinforced by his extensive pastoral visitation in 1780 of most of the 136 parishes within his remit. His submission indicates clearly the pervasiveness of Incaic symbolism and its deep roots in ceremonial and quotidian life, though the prelate's interpretations of their significance may stand only as hypotheses. There have always been ethnocentric views of Andean culture and, then as now, they have rarely failed to mislead.

The initiative for the Bishop's report came, however, from the Visitador-General. Moscoso had dictated it in response to an instruction from Areche ordering the removal of all portraits and likenesses of former Inca rulers from ecclesiastical institutions. He singled out in particular the *Colegio de Indios Nobles de San Francisco de Borja* – also called the *Colegio del Sol* – which had since 1628 provided the scions of the indigenous nobility and leading caciques (*kurakas*) with an education commensurate with their future administrative and political responsibilities – should they eventually succeed to hereditary *cacicazgos* – and which harked back to an analogous Incaic institution (*Yachay Huasi*).[25] Moscoso had removed such portraits from San Borja and from the church of Curahuasi (*partido* of Abancay), even presenting Areche with a portrait of Felipe Túpac Amaru. This Inca had led a war of resistance against the Spanish until his capture in 1572 by Martín García de Loyola, nephew of the founder of the Jesuit order, and whose lineal descendant José Gabriel Túpac Amaru had led the uprising of 1780–81. The portrait of Felipe Túpac Amaru had hung in the refectory of San Borja, there presumably to inspire generations of young nobles with his deeds, an extraordinary oversight on the part of college authorities. For Moscoso and Areche, at any rate, the portrait was pregnant

[24] See note 10.

[25] Bravo, op. cit., pp. 96–97; George Kubler, "The Quechua in the Colonial World', *Handbook of South American Indians* (New York: Cooper Square, 1963, repr. of 1944 Smithsonian Institution publication), vol. 2, pp. 408–409. On the Colegio de San Borja generally, see Monique Alaperrine Bouyer, 'Esbozo de una historia del Colegio San Francisco de Borja de Cuzco', in *Actas del XI Congreso Internacional de AHILA* (Liverpool, 17–22 September, 1996), vol. IV, ed. John R. Fisher, University of Liverpool, 1998, pp. 44–53.

with political connotations. Of perhaps wider import, the Bishop also ordered the removal of likenesses 'engraved in the wall of the lower angle' of the college. San Borja was centrally located, on a rise just above the main plaza of the city, and Moscoso's description suggests that such likenesses may have been on the exterior of the building. If so, they might have served as inspiration not only to the College's alumni, but to the entire indigenous sector, city residents as well as the numerous transients. In Moscoso's judgement, Native Andeans were 'a species of rational beings' on whom what they saw made more impression than what they heard. This was the dialectical keystone upon which he built his analysis of the diffusion of colonial Inca culture and his disquisition on the political ramifications of such perceived atavism.

The Bishop grounded his critique of the ubiquity of Incaic culture, with its concomitant veneration of the Incaic past, in a wide-ranging purview of the realms of indigenous material culture, dress, music, literature, and religious and ceremonial life. He averred that the Incan nobility and caciques of the southern sierra had no other images in their houses but those of former Inca emperors or their own ancestors dressed in Incan regalia. As George Kubler and John Rowe pointed out long ago,[26] the religious art of the Cuzqueño School of the seventeenth century gave way in the eighteenth to a marked concentration on Incaic representations of the indigenous nobility. There are, however, no grounds for supposing, *pace* Rowe, that this demonstrates a reversion to Incaic dress by nobles following their widespread adoption of European dress in the aftermath of the conquest; rather, Incaic dress had always been *de rigueur* on cere-monial occasions. What was new in the eighteenth century was that the nobility chose to have themselves portrayed in such regalia by a traditional school of painting that had always been dominated by indigenous and mestizo artists. The works of this school provided, in fact, an additional export industry for the region, enabling indigenous artists to diffuse their thematic preoccupations throughout the Andes. Where once thematic content had been mainly restricted to the religious sphere, it now took on a more secular tone and ominous political message. Other-worldly pre-occupations gave way to a concern with the past in relation to the present.

A further target of the Bishop's criticism was the Incaic heraldry boasted by the indigenous nobility. These coats of arms – still to be observed in the escutcheons of the houses of the town of Maras – appear to have been those awarded many noble families by successive Spanish monarchs

---

[26] Kubler, op. cit., p. 350; Rowe, 'El movimiento nacional inca', p. 22–23; Rowe, 'Colonial Portraits of Inca Nobles', in *The Civilizations of Ancient America: Selected Papers of the XXIXth International Congress of Americanists*, (ed. Sol Tax, New York: 1967, reprint of 1951 edn), pp. 258–268; Thomas B. F. Cummins, 'We are the Other: Peruvian Portraits of Colonial *Kurakakuna*', in *Transatlantic Encounters: Europeans and Andeans in the Sixteenth Century*, ed. Kenneth J. Andrien and Rolena Adorno (Berkeley and Oxford: California UP, 1991), pp. 203–231.

(especially the emperor Charles V). These did indeed incorporate predominantly Incan insignias and motifs; pre-conquest Incas had had, though, their own *divisas*, so that the coats of arms awarded noble families in the sixteenth century may have been based on pre-Columbian models. Yet another means of transmitting Incaic culture through plastic art was via the *kero*, the carved and painted wooden drinking vessels, though these, of relatively minor import, escaped Moscoso's jaundiced eye.

His attack on Inca culture encompassed also the crucial issue of the participation of the Incan nobility in the liturgical and ceremonial life of the region. It was through the religious pomp of the conquerors that the indigenous nobility was able to reaffirm and renew, at various junctures in the liturgical year, its own identity and its collective descent from the twelve Incaic 'houses' or *panacas*, and thereby perhaps command the fealty and respect of Native Andeans. 'In public festivities, soirées, processions, and other activities', Moscoso wrote, 'we observe that the Indians use no other adornment, than those that were esteemed in their Gentility'. At hand to illustrate his thesis was the principal religious festivity of the region: the feast of Corpus Christi and, in particular, the 'day and eve of Santiago'. Corpus in Cuzco was, as we know from contemporary canvases, a splendid occasion; it featured processions – one principal, preceded by several smaller *santo* marches – which celebrated indigenous religious devotions, and on the day of Santiago pride of place was given over to the surviving Incan nobility, decked out in Incan regalia and insignias, and led by the *alférez real* chosen by the electors representing the twelve 'houses' of the nobility. Fully in accord with contemporary artistic representations of colonial Corpus Christi, Moscoso's epistle recounted how, in the Santiago procession (25 July), nobles wore 'very rich' mantles of black velvet or taffeta (*yacollas*) with a black or dark-brown type of overshirt (the *uncu*). The undoubted centrepiece of this ensemble was, however, the *mascapaicha*, the decorative headband equivalent to a royal crown. This was embellished with plumes and precious stones and from it hung the symbol *par excellence* of the Inca, the famous *borla colorada* or tuft of coloured wool, the use of which was fiercely guarded and jealously circumscribed by the colonial Inca nobility.[27] An equally powerful reverberation of

---

[27] The 'royal crown' of the Inca was composed of three parts:

> El llautu, que es una parte de las tres que componían su real corona, ciñendo la cabeza a modo de guirnalda o laurel, iba toda tejida de gruesos hilos de perlas, sembradas grandes esmeraldas en él; el *mascapaycha*, que es una lámina o plumaje que se levanta del llautu encima de la frente, y es la segunda parte de la corona, era de finísimo oro con unos ramillos de esmeraldas; la *unancha*, que es la borla que cuelga del pie de la lámina o plumaje sobre la frente, y es la tercera parte que compone aquella corona ...

as described by Bartolomé Arzáns de Orsúa y Vela, *Historia de la Villa Imperial de Potosí* (ed. Lewis Hanke and Gunnar Mendoza, Providence: Brown UP, 1965), vol. I, p. 99. This account is a record of a 1555 procession in Potosí which featured representations of the Incas,

Tahuantinsuyu was the *champi* that was borne by the Incaic *alférez real* much as if he were a prelate wielding a crook, or, best to say, a monarch with sceptre.[28] Now, the *champi* is described by the chronicler Cobo as a halberd (*alabarda*), and represented by Guaman Poma as such, and appears to have evolved from a war-mace. Its colonial version may have metamorphosed into more of a broad staff or *vara*, to judge both from the variations mentioned by Cobo and the Bishop's account.[29] These *champis*, averred Moscoso, were embellished with either 'the image of the Inca' or that of the Sun, the principal deity of the quondam Inca 'emperors' – 'their adored deity'. This elaborate raiment was further adorned with decorations of gold and silver figurines (*mascarones*) at the extremities of the shoulders, on the knees and on the back of the legs; the fineness of these figurines was said to be an indicator of the respective 'qualities' of the wearers.[30] Quite what these symbols represented – erstwhile Inca rulers, Christian saints or autochthonous idols – is not made clear, but the general thrust of the nobility's imagery at Corpus was towards a commemoration and

and is subject to all the usual doubts concerning the verisimilitude of European perceptions of the ritual and material culture of the 'vanquished'. For some perceptive comments regarding Arzáns' account of the Potosí procession, see Manuel Burga, op. cit., p. 378–382. In spite of the above detail, the 'royal crown' of the Inca was conventionally described in colonial documents as the '*mascapaicha*' and/or '*borla colorada*'. Bravo, op. cit., p. 85, notes that the appearance of the *mascapaicha* approximated to 'a bloody martial and ceremonial axe'. For one of many examples of the fierceness with which 'kosher' colonial Inca nobles protected the right to wear the *mascapaicha*, see the documental appendix to J. Uriel García, 'El alferazgo real de indios en la época colonial', *Revista Universitaria* (Cuzco), vol. XXVI, 1937, pp. 189–208, esp. pp. 194–208.

[28] The *champi* is also present in the Loreto procession of 1692 (see anon), in which a ceremonial banner featured a painting of an Inca in traditional costume 'con su mascapaicha de la borla colorada y su champi, y valcanca en la mano ysquierda' (the *valcanca* being the Incaic shield or buckler featured in seventeenth-century pictorial representations of the Incas in the Corpus Christi procession and in the chronicle of Guaman Poma de Ayala), for which see, Archivo Departamental del Cuzco: Real Hacienda, Leg. 171, 'Instancia que han hecho Don Buenaventura Sicos: sus hijos y otros descienden [sic] de este Linage ...', 26 January, 1786, for a *traslado* of 22 August, 1692.

[29] Cobo, vol. II, book XIV, chap. IX: 'Tenían unas mazas de madera pesada y redondas, y otras, que eran propia arma de los Incas, con el remate de cobre, llamadas *champi*, y es una asta como de alabarda, puesto en el cabo un hierro de cobre de hechura de estrella con sus puntas o rayos alrededor muy puntiagudos. Destos *champis* unos eran cortos como bastones y otros tan largos como lanzas, y los más de mediano tamaño'. For woodcuts of the dress and insignias of successive Inca rulers, see Guaman Poma, vol. I, 85 [85] to117 [117], pp. 66–95.

[30] These *mascarones* are distinct from the *canipos* identified in the 1610 festivities held to celebrate the beatification of Ignatius de Loyola (discussed anon): 'canipos ... de plata, que son a figura de luna ...', for which see Carlos A. Romero (ed.), 'Festividades del tiempo heroico del Cuzco', *Inca*, vol. 1, no. 2, 1923, pp. 447–454, esp. p. 450. Cobo vol. 2, book 14, chap. 2, says of these, 'usaban traer al pecho y en la cabeza unas patenas de oro o plata, llamadas *canipos*, del tamaño y hechura de nuestros platos.'; Molina ('El Cuzqueño'), p. 67, simply defines it as a 'medalla de oro'.

perhaps even veneration of pre-conquest divinities, as indicated by the hand-held disc of the Sun borne by the *alférez real*.

The Bishop emphasised that the use of such insignia characterised all of the civil as well as ecclesiastical festivities of the city. Moreover, it is evident from discrete documentation that the Incaic content of the day of Santiago extended to the rural towns of the southern sierra.[31] While Moscoso did not single out the day of Santiago itself as being particularly reprehensible, there is little doubt that it was the surpassing feast of the colonial Inca nobility. The 'Twenty-four Electors of the Alférez Real' eagerly sought election for the honour of bearing the standard of Santiago in the Corpus procession, an honour that carried with it tacit recognition as *primus inter pares* of the colonial indigenous nobility. Why Santiago should have been so venerated within indigenous society is not made explicit in the documentation.[32] However, it has to do generally with the syncretic acceptance of the warrior-saint by Native Andeans. The Santiago *matamoros* and *matajudíos* of the peninsular *reconquista* and the Spanish conquest of the Americas became, during the latter event, Santiago *mataindios*, and there is evidence from several regions of colonial Peru that Santiago was equated with one or more pre-Columbian deities, above all with Illapa, the god of thunder. A Christian saint, then, became incorporated as a deity in the Andean pantheon, and Moscoso, observing that the Inca nobility carried their own banners 'with the sculpted images of their

[31] It is, though, unclear how widespread the discrete celebration of the feast of Santiago was in rural districts. Participation as *alférez real* was an important indicator of status and even nobility in a town. Evidence for rural celebrations is to be found in the applications for scholarships by sons of nobles, caciques and other *principales* for attendance at the Colegio de San Francisco de Borja. See Archivo Departamental del Cuzco: Colegio de Ciencias, 'Memoria y Calificación de los Indios Nobles, años 1763–1766' (Leg. 1). This indicates that the office of the indigenous *alferazgo real* was also available in each parish, complementary to that of the major Incan office for the day and eve of Santiago. The same documentation also makes clear that in the Marquesado de Oropesa, comprising the *doctrinas* of San Francisco de Maras, San Bernardo de Urubamba, San Benito de Alcántara (Huallabamba) and Santiago de Oropesa (Yucay) – all located in the Vilcanota Valley – a separate body of five Electors chose a noble *alférez real* for annual Santiago celebrations in Yucay; at least one of these Electors was also among the Twenty-four Electors for the main city festivities. The five appear to comprise one for each *doctrina*, plus one for Ollantaytambo in the Valley, which in the late eighteenth century formed part, with those four, of first the *corregimiento* and then (from 1784) the *subdelegación* of Urubamba. In the Yucay feast, the *alférez real* wore, like his counterpart in the city of Cuzco, the *mascapaicha*. There is also mention of a cognate *alferazgo real* for Santiago in the *doctrina* of Guarocondo, on the edge of the Valley of Jaquijahuana in the province of Abancay.

[32] A good account of the protean character of Santiago is Emilio Choy, 'De Santiago Matamoros a Santiago Mata-Indios', in idem, *Antropología y Historia* (Lima, 1979) vol. 1, pp. 333–437. See also Irene Silverblatt, 'Political Memories and Colonizing Symbols: Santiago and the Mountain Gods of Colonial Peru', in *Rethinking History and Myth: Indigenous Southern American Perspectives on the Past*, ed. Jonathon D. Hill (Urbana and Chicago: Illinois UP, 1988), pp. 174–329.

Gentile kings' on the day of Santiago,[33] recommended that in future only the royal standard (of the Spanish monarch) be permitted on such occasions.

Drawing on the experience of his visitation of the sprawling Cuzco diocese the previous year, the prelate also underscored the role of the rural churches in perpetuating a vivid memory of the Incas. There, indigenous congregations dressed statues of the infant Jesus in the *uncu, mascapaicha* and other such 'insignias', a usage paralleled in paintings hung in the churches. Alleging, with good reason, that indigenes regarded the former Inca 'emperors' as gods, the Bishop argued that this local cult was no superficial syncretism or banal folklore. He was on this point almost certainly correct, for traditional animistic beliefs had imbued religious art with real powers. The general point may be served by a single example: during the uprising of 1780–83, indigenous rebels systematically tied the hands of images of Santiago in rural churches so as to forestall the martial intervention of this fearsome warrior-saint on behalf of royalist forces.[34]

Finally, reinforcing the 'fantastic vaticinations that those Gentiles so venerate' were printed works whose prophetic content was allegedly diffused among Native Andeans. It now seems certain that José Gabriel Túpac Amaru had consulted the *Comentarios reales* of Garcilaso de la Vega, but Moscoso opined that other 'regicidal authors' had formed part of his staple reading matter. Of perhaps more importance in this context was the imprudence of unnamed persons who had fuelled the pretensions of Túpac Amaru to be recognised as the legitimate heir to the colonial Incaic succession. Here, among others, Moscoso doubtless had in mind the Creole cura, Antonio López de Sosa, who had helped raise the orphaned Túpac Amaru. Both the wife and son of the rebel *caudillo* were later to allege that it had been the cura who had incited the Inca to claim the succession. Moreover, in the aftermath of the uprising, López officiated at the funeral of an infant son of Diego Túpac Amaru, *primo hermano* of the rebel leader and his undisputed deputy on campaign, curiously arraying the child with Incaic as well as episcopal insignia.[35] On a wider canvas, it was indeed

[33] For a detailed description of just such a banner, see the account of the Loreto procession of 1692 (anon).

[34] See Archivo General de Indias, Audiencia del Cuzco, Leg. 15, 'Consejo Expediente sobre la ereccion en la Ciudad del Cuzco de una Cofradia de S[a]ntiago que se intenta establecer en una Parroquia de aquella Ciudad, y aprovacion de sus Constituciones', petition of José Agustín Chacón y Bezerra, 1 August, 1786, fol. 3r. During the Túpac Amaru rebellion, rebel troops claimed that they had seen Santiago among the royalist forces sent to suppress the rebellion: 'A cuya cauza en las Yglesias, y Capillas donde encontraron los simulacros de este nuestro portentoso Mesenas, llegaron al sacrilego arrojo de amarrarle las manos, y tenerlas como en prizion por que su ignorancia ô idolatria les preocupaba la razon para creer que assi no favorezeria a los fieles, y leales vazallos de un Monarca justo, y venigno cuyos Dominios Reales defendian.'

[35] On López de Sosa, see Cahill, *Crown, Clergy and Revolution*, pp. 205, 302. For the burial, Archivo General de Indias, Audiencia del Cuzco, Leg. 75, 'Copia de Cartas, y Otros

probable that street-corner *tertulias* and tavern talk were of more moment in diffusing such notions, while Native Andeans could of course draw on their strong oral and mythological traditions as well as a certain theatrical *cum* festive genre in which episodes of the Inca past were performed or acted out in Quechua.

Moscoso was, however, addressing his remarks to the influence of a wider literature which, if it did not itself presume to reinforce such longings for a return to a Golden Age, nevertheless was insidious in the immediate post-bellum context. Referring to unnamed works with prophetic, chiliastic or millenial tendencies, he singled out in particular the prologue by Gabriel de Cárdenas to the 1723 edition of Garcilaso's *Comentarios*. Cárdenas assured readers that a prophecy had been found in a religious sanctuary predicting the restoration of Peru to its natives, a return that was to be guaranteed by England (which, at the outbreak of the rebellion in 1780, was at war with Spain). It was precisely this Cárdenas edition that first Boleslao Lewin and then John Rowe suggested had been influential in the florescence of a 'national Inca movement'.[36] Further, the prologue of Cárdenas appears to have been regarded as a free-standing treatise in its own right: one of the Creole conspirators of 1805 named this dissertation of Cárdenas as one of the influences for his belief that the time had come for a restoration of the Incario.[37]

This disquisition of Bishop Moscoso y Peralta is seminal because it provides a contemporary confirmation of the hypotheses and concepts of

Docum[en]tos Comprovantes de haverse hallado en Casa de Dr. Anton[io] López de Sosa Cura de Pampamarca un retrato de Obispo de un hijo de Diego Christóval Túpac Amaru', n.d., but the baptism took place on 4 November 1782, the second anniversary of José Gabriel Túpac Amaru's capture of the corregidor Arriaga, the event that had precipitated the rebellion. The child died on 17 November, and was accorded a funeral befitting an heir to the Inca throne. A further, ironic twist was given by the fact that the godfather of the infant was Francisco Salcedo, the executed Arriaga's successor as corregidor of the province of Canas y Canchis (or Tinta); Salcedo arranged for the militia under his command to fire several volleys at the funeral in homage to the child.

[36] See note 10.

[37] The legal process relating to the Aguilar Ubalde conspiracy of 1805 is found in three parts, one each in the Biblioteca Nacional, Lima; the Archivo Departamental del Cuzco; and the Archivo General de Indias, Seville. The last has been transcribed by Carlos Ponce Sangines (ed.), *El conato revolucionario de 1805. El expediente referente al proceso seguido a Aguilar, Ubalde y otros* (La Paz: 1975); see pp. 56–58 ('4° Declaración de D. José Manuel Ubalde') for Ubalde's testimony that Cárdenas' preface to his edition of Garcilaso had influenced his views and actions, along with Raynal, Filangieri and 'many mystic books that he read as youth and adult'. Modern studies of the conspiracy are: John R. Fisher, 'La rebelión de Túpac Amaru y la conspiración de Aguilar y Ubalde en 1805', in *Actas del Coloquio Internacional: 'Túpac Amaru y su tiempo'* (Lima and Cuzco, Comisión Nacional del Bicentenario de la Rebelión Emancipadora de Túpac Amaru, 1982), pp. 261–270; idem, 'Regionalism and Rebellion in Late Colonial Peru: The Aguilar-Ubalde Conspiracy of 1805', *Bibliotheca Americana*, vol. I, no. I, 1982, pp. 45–59; Alberto Flores Galindo, 'In Search of an Inca', in Stern (ed.), op. cit., pp. 193–210.

several historians that there existed an underlying 'Inca Nationalism' or 'Andean Utopia' or 'colonial Andean Messianism' in colonial and even contemporary Peruvian society and politics, for all that many of the co-ordinates of Moscoso's own thesis were themselves hypothetical. Political movements and conspiracies were thus impregnated with Incaic concepts and symbolism in late colonial Peru. These were thoroughly grounded in colonial culture and religion, nowhere more so than in the religious extravaganzas and major processions that were such a familiar part of colonial culture. It is to an analysis of the Incaic symbolism of such festive phenomena that we now turn.

# CHAPTER TEN

# The Inca Motif in Colonial Fiestas – I

## The Beatification of Ignatius de Loyola, 1610

There was ample evidence to buttress Moscoso's critique of Incaic symbolism in religious fiestas, though his assertion that Incaic dress was *de rigueur* for the indigenous nobility on 'all' civic and ecclesiastical occasions remains problematic. Certainly, there is little support for this in contemporary descriptions of civic ceremonies; it might be supposed that such splendour on mundane occasions would have elicited some comment on the part of the authorities. In 1787 the Cuzqueño savant, Ignacio de Castro, in his ponderous yet erudite encomium to the King on the occasion of the ceremonies marking the foundation of the Real Audiencia in Cuzco, recorded (somewhat patronisingly) the appearance of the indigenous elites in procession thus: 'Los caciques y los Indios nobles de la Ciudad, de las Parroquias y de los contornos, eran los que aparecian al principio, vestidos no ya de sus antiguos trajes, sino del uniforme Español en caballos bellamente enjaezados que saben ya montar, manejar y adiestrar'.[1] There is, of course, a strong presumption that this circumstance was the direct result of the strictures of Moscoso and Areche on the deleterious effects of Incaic symbolism, and Castro certainly seems to imply that Incaic costume had been the norm but had been recently abandoned, yet this awaits further proof. However, it seems to have been more the result of a related 1785 representation to the Viceroy by the Intendant Mata Linares, in which he called urgently for the extirpation of Incaic costume on festive occasions, and with it abolition of the office of the indigenous *alférez real* and the bearing of dual standards or banners on such occasions.[2] This latter, he duly noted, was a custom singular in the entire Hispanic world, and the Viceroy, Teodoro de Croix, agreed to suspend such usages pending further advice. Nevertheless, it is abundantly clear that Incaic raiment was worn on major ecclesiastical occasions. For all that, descriptions of only six of these have come down to us, each an eloquent testimony to the Andean

---

[1] Ignacio de Castro, *Relación del Cuzco* (ed. Carlos Daniel Valcárcel Aranibar, Lima: San Marcos UP, 1978 repr. of 1795 Madrid edn), p. 81.

[2] Archivo General de Indias, Audiencia del Cuzco, Leg. 35, Mata Linares to Gálvez (No. 11), 6 August, 1785; Mata Linares to Gálvez (No. 28), 19 March, 1786.

'capacity for mimicry' and 'capacity for reinterpreting theatrical forms introduced by early evangelisation'.[3] First, there is Arzáns y Vela's account of the 1555 celebrations in Potosí, in acclamation of the patron saints of the city and of their success in delivering the viceroyalty from the revolt of Francisco Hernández Girón; Garcilaso de la Vega similarly recorded the 1555 inaugural Corpus Christi festivities in Cuzco, which also in part celebrated the crushing of that revolt; the detailed account of the 1610 Cuzqueño festivities consequent upon arrival of the news of the beatification of Ignatius de Loyola; an unpublished 1692 record of an Incaic procession connected with the Jesuit chapel of Loreto in Cuzco; and representations of the Incas in 1659 and 1725 festivities in Lima. For reasons of space, but also because the surviving colonial Inca nobility held centre-stage and because the festivities themselves appear to have shared a certain verisimilitude with pre-Columbian festivities, the remainder of this monograph will concentrate on the two Cuzqueño ceremonies of 1610 and 1692.

## Celebrating the beatification

The most complete record detailing participation of the colonial Inca nobility and the presence of colonial Incaic symbolism and raiment on festive occasions comes from a (now apparently lost) Jesuit account, the *Relación de las Fiestas*.[4] It records indigenous ceremonies in the city of Cuzco in 1610 in honour of the announcement of the beatification of Ignatius de Loyola, and followed close upon, and to a degree emulated, kindred celebrations of the *español* groups of the city of Cuzco. The indigenous festivities – consisting of three successive fiestas – ran from May 2 to May 26 inclusive, that is, 25 days of non-stop festivities. This feature of colonial festive or ceremonial life is not as singular as it may at first appear. Cuzco's Corpus Christi celebrations even today run for ten weeks, although work ceases for only a few days during that cycle. The 1555 celebrations in Potosí appear to have lasted for about a month; in late colonial Cuzco, the fiesta of San Roque was even extended from nine to fifteen days.[5] All

---

[3] Luis Millones, 'The Inka's Mask: Dramatisation of the Past in Indigenous Colonial Processions', in *Andean Art: Visual Expression and its Relation to Andean Beliefs and Values*, ed. Penny Dransart (Aldershot and Brookfield USA: Avebury, 1995), pp. 11–32. For Arzáns y Vela's account, see p. 109, n. 26; Garcilaso de la Vega, *Historia general del Perú (segunda parte de los 'Comentarios reales')* (Madrid: 1960; originally published 1617), book 8, chap. 1, pp. 84–88, 278–299, records the Corpus Christi of 1555; the 1659 and 1725 fiestas are related in Josephe and Francisco de Muguburu, *Diario de Lima (1640–1694)* (ed. Horacio Urteaga and Carlos A. Romero, Lima: 1917). For these Lima festivities, see Burga, op. cit., pp. 378–389.

[4] Carlos A. Romero (ed.), 'Festividades del tiempo heroico del Cuzco', *Inca*, vol. 1, no. 2, 1923, pp. 447–454, reproduced in Appendix 2. This is apparently the only fragment remaining from the larger work.

[5] Pablo José Oricaín, 'Compendio breve de discursos varios ... año 1790', in *Juicio de*

of these occasions involved drinking, dancing and associated revelry. In 1819, Martín de Mugica, a peninsular bureaucrat stationed in Cuzco on the eve of independence, calculated that such festivities in Cuzco totalled *seven months of the year*, i.e., more days of fiesta than days of work.[6] In all of this – even if we allow for considerable exaggeration in Mugica's arithmetic – colonial society appears to have been more generous to indigenes in apportioning leisure time than had been the Incas. Yet for all that, the 1610 celebrations appear to have been exceptional. In part, this stemmed from the special relationship that the colonial Inca nobility had with the Jesuit order, based on the late sixteenth-century marriage of Martín de Loyola, nephew (his father was Ignatius' elder brother) to the founder of the Jesuit order; oddly enough, Martín de Loyola had been responsible for the capture of the 'last' of the Inca rulers, Túpac Amaru I, who was beheaded soon after in the Plaza de Armas of Cuzco. Yet Loyola's marriage to a *Coya*, thereby uniting the Inca nobility with the house of Loyola, evidently entailed absolution for Don Martín's complicity in regicide.[7] This was perhaps especially so when a daughter of the union was born, Ana María Lorenza, uniting Jesuit order and Incas in *parentesco de sangre*. Thus was born the special relationship.

The first of the three fiestas consisted of daily (excepting Thursday) processions by the eight parishes of the city and *cercado*, apparently terminating at the door of the Jesuit church of La Compañia. The parish of Belén led off, 'all the Incas ... grandsons and descendants of the [H]Atuncuzcos' of the parish at the head of the procession. The description of the costumes and symbols in the procession is enormously detailed, but what follows is to some extent a distillation of its principal and most signal features. The first feature that strikes one's attention is the parish of Santiago 'receiving' the *cofradía* of Jesus, housed in La Compañia, 'taking out its child Jesus in Incan habit'. This identification of the child Jesus – probably to be equated with the 'Little King' familiar from universal Catholic iconography – is intriguing, because of its suggestion of an embryonic Incan messiah. It will be recalled that Moscoso alleged that statues of the child Jesus throughout his extensive diocese were customarily

*límites entre el Perú y Bolivia: Prueba presentada al Gobierno de la República Argentina por Víctor M. Maúrtua* (Barcelona: 1906), p. 338. For more discussion of the excessive duration of fiestas, David Cahill, 'Popular Religion and Appropriation: The Example of Corpus Christi in Eighteenth-Century Cuzco', *Latin American Research Review*, vol. 31, no. 2, 1996, pp. 67–110.

  [6] Archivo Arzobispal del Cuzco, Correspondencia xliii. 3.53, Martín Joseph de Mugica to Juan Munive y Mozo, Provisor and (at this time) 'gobernador y Vicario Capitular (sedevacante)', 5 August, 1819; Mugica's report on popular religion in late colonial Cuzco is further discussed in Cahill, 'Popular Religion and Appropriation', pp. 94–96.

  [7] The genealogy is discussed in considerable detail in Guillermo Lohmann Villena, 'El Señorío de los Marqueses de Santiago de Oropesa en el Perú', *Anuario de Historia del Derecho Español*, vol. XIX, 1948–49 pp. 347–458.

draped with Incaic costume. Certainly, this remarkable feature of South Andean Catholicism recurs in the last two centuries of colonial Cuzco. In the 1687–89 *visita* of the diocese of Cuzco by Bishop Manuel de Mollinedo y Angulo, statues of the infant Jesus located in the churches of San Jéronimo, Andahuaylillas and Caycay were identified as bearing the *mascapaicha*.[8] In 1774 the cura of Paucartambo (diocese of Cuzco) reported that 'El dia de S[a]ntiago colocaron en el Altar mayor y llevaron en procesion a la imagen del Salvador del Mundo vestido de Inga con todas las insignias de la Gentilidad . . .'.[9] In 1781, the cura of the Cuzqueño *doctrina* of Pampamarca (province of Canas y Canchis/Tinta) interred the dead infant of rebel leader Diego Túpac Amaru, the child clothed both in the vestments of a Bishop and the *mascapaicha*.[10] There may be present, too, some echo or evocation of Garcilaso's assertion that the heir to the Incan throne 'wore a yellow [mascapaycha] smaller than that of his father', suggestive of the possibility that colonial indigenes may have drawn a connexion between the young heir with his yellow *mascapaycha* and the Christchild, who was always depicted with a golden halo.[11] Clearly, there was a strong identification of the Inca (past, present, future?) with the Christchild, though the identification is wider, more complex. For example, the Paucartambo document suggests an identification with the 'adult' Christ the Saviour, while the conflation of Incan and episcopal dress in the case of Diego's infant is obviously a related phenomenon, if somewhat of a puzzle – a benediction or imprimatur of the idea of a redeeming Inca?

Yet the ritual nexus between Christchild and a putative Incan messiah is susceptible to explanation in terms of Incan ritual iconology in the pre-1532 imperial capital. Here, in dealing with the imperial religious framework 'we find ourselves on what can be the most treacherous ground

---

[8] Archivo General de Indias, Audiencia de Lima, Leg. 306, 'Resumen de la Visita Eclesiastica que se hizo de los beneficios curados que ay en las provincias de Quispicancha [*sic*] Paucartambo, Calca y Lares Marquesado de Oropesa y las de la de Abancay = Pertenecientes al Obispado del Cuzco Año de 1687'. The Bishop ordered that in the *doctrina* of Andahuaylillas (Quispicanchis), 'al Niño Jhs. que esta en un altar de la yglesia se le quite la mascapaycha, y se le pongan ô rayos ô corona imperial'; in the *doctrina* of Caycay (Paucartambo), he similarly ordered, 'Que se quite la mascapacha al Niño Jhs, que esta en la yglesia, y se le pongan ô rayos ô corona imperial'. In the *doctrina* of San Jerónimo, one of the two principal foci of the colonial Inca nobility, the Bishop ordered, 'Que se quite al niño Jhs que esta en un Altar del cuerpo de la yglesia la masacapaicha y el sol, que tiene en el pecho, y se le dexen los rayos solamente que estan en la cabeca', indicating an existing relationship between Inca and Sun, while the 'rayos' or halo might represent Santiago/Illapa and/or Incan solar worship.

[9] Archivo Arzobispal del Cuzco, Pleitos xiv. 5.87, 'Querella criminal seguido p[o]r Juan Gonzales, cura Paucartambo, contra el corregidor Tiburcio de Landa, sus criados y comensales, p[o]r injurias graves levantadas', 1774.

[10] See p. 112, n. 35.

[11] Garcilaso de la Vega, *Comentarios reales*, book I, chap. XXIII.

of all'.[12] The fluidity of cults and deities confounded the early chroniclers, who struggled to impose an order on the 'overlapping and interlocking ideas' that characterised Incan religion. Researchers have focused their attention on three principal deities and their cults: Viracocha, the solar cult of Inti, and Illapa, the god of thunder and lightning, all of which had several manifestations and gradations; to these should be added Huanacari, of particular importance to the *Sapay Inca* himself. In their original Incaic formulation, these divinities 'were far less sharply differentiated than they eventually came to be'.[13] For all that, the chroniclers recorded sufficient evidence for a divine child in the imperial cult(s) for us to suspect that colonial – both rural and urban – representations of the Christchild as Inca were echoes or remembrances, explicit or implicit, of Incaic cultic praxis connected above all with memories of Inti.

The earliest mention of a child as divinity comes in the 1551 chronicle of Betanzos.[14] In his renovation of the imperial cult, Pachacuti Tupa Yupanqui, following a dream and a vision in which first a shining child and then an unidentified shining figure appeared to him, ordered that an 'idol' be cast in gold; this was the Punchao Inca, henceforth to be seated in Coricanchi.[15] This representation was the height and size of a child of one year of age, naked, which was then richly dressed; this was set off by the *llauta* ('atadura') and *mascapaycha* ('borla'). There is a further Incaic dimension to this statue. Betanzos tells us that it was at once solidly cast and apparently 'hollow' ('vaciadizo'). It is Cobo (1653) who clarifies for us the meaning of this hollowness: he informs us that the statue was of gold except for the stomach, 'which was full of a paste made of milled gold mixed with the ashes or dust of the hearts of the Inca kings'.[16] Betanzos also notes that Pachacuti ordered the idol to be carried in procession in the city on a litter or sedan chair or float (*andas*), borne by the three most important *principales* of the city ('his three friends') and the mayordomo of the cult. The similarity of this to the Corpus Christi procession and especially that of 1610 will be obvious. Cristóbal de Molina 'El Cuzqueño' (c. 1573) records a pre-Columbian May ceremony in which the priests of Coricancha pray to the Viracocha, Inti and Illapa that they remain eternally young, never to grow old.[17] Youth is here explicitly

[12] Geoffrey W. Conrad and Arthur A. Demarest, *Religion and Empire: The Dynamics of Aztec and Inca Expansionism* (Cambridge and New York: Cambridge UP, 1984), p. 100.

[13] Ibid., pp. 100–101.

[14] Juan de Betanzos, *Suma y narración de los Incas* (ed. María del Carmen Martín Rubio, Madrid: 1987 [1551]), chap. 11.

[15] The connexion between the colonial representation of the Christchild adorned with the *mascapaicha* and the Punchao was suggested to me by Lilian Yackeline Cáceres Gómez, an archaeology student of the Universidad de San Antonio Abad, Cuzco.

[16] P. Bernabé Cobo, *Historia del Nuevo Mundo* (ed. Francisco Mateos, Madrid: 1964 [1653]) vol. II, book 13, chap. 5.

[17] Cristóbal de Molina, *Relación de las fábulas i ritos de los ingas* in *Fábulas y mitos de los incas*, ed. Henrique Urbano and Pierre Duviols (Madrid: Historia 16, 1988 [1573]).

associated with strength and vigour. When, in 1572, Martín de Loyola captured Túpac Amaru I, he was brought to Cuzco with his two idols of Huanacari and Punchao. This Sun Godchild is portrayed by Guaman Poma already in the hands of a Spanish captor, symbolic of ultimate conquest.[18]

One of the remarkable features of this first fiesta is the space allotted in the festivities to the Incas' erstwhile underlings: the *yanaconas* and the ethnic groups of the Cañaris and Canas. The *yanaconas* had been the retainer and (to some extent) administrative class of the Incario,[19] while both the Cañaris from the Quito region and the Canas of the altiplano south of Cuzco had been conquered by the Inca, thence to become allies. The Cañaris had played a central role in the Inca war of succession, and then moved seamlessly to become allies of the Spanish conquistadores; for their service they were awarded privileges in the colonial period, free from tribute, labour service and (with the Chachapoyas, another 'immigrant' (*etnía*) the monopoly of the postillion or courier positions (*chasquis*) within the postal service. Relations between the colonial Inca nobles and the somewhat parvenu Cañaris were poisonous in the seventeenth century, and appear to have remained so throughout the colonial era. The *yanaconas*, generally regarded as having disintegrated as a distinct social group or retainer 'class' soon after the conquest,[20] are nevertheless here in full strength:

[18] Felipe Guaman Poma de Ayala, *El primer corónica y buen gobierno* (ed. John V. Murra, Rolena Adorno and Jorge L. Urioste, Lima: Instituto de Estudios Peruanos, 1980), vol. II, 449–450 [451–452], pp. 416–417.

[19] On the pre-conquest *yanaconas*, see especially Sócrates Villar Córdova, *La institución del Yanacona en el Incanato* (Lima: San Marcos UP, 1966). Also David Cahill, 'Inca Retainer Groups and Destructuration: The *yanaconas* of Cuzco's Cathedral Quarter under Colonial Rule', *Tawantinsuyu: Una Revista Internacional de Estudios Inkas/An International Journal of Inca Studies*, vol. I, 1995, pp. 97–103. For both *yanaconas* and Cañaris, Ken Heffernan, 'Paullo, Tocto Usica and Chilche in the royal lands of Limatambo and Quispiguanca', *Tawantinsuyu*, vol. I, no. I, 1995, pp. 66–85. An eighteenth-century account of the post-conquest role of the Cañaris in relation to the postal service is by the 'Administrador sub-principal de la Real Renta de Correos' of the city of Cuzco, in Archivo Departamental del Cuzco, Intendencia: Real Hacienda, '2no. Q° sobre provision de Cañaris pa. la Adminon. y Rta. de Correos', 1801; See also, Udo Oberem, 'Los cañaris y la conquista española de la sierra ecuatoriana. Otro capítulo de las relaciones interétnicas en el siglo XVI', *Cultura* (Quito), vol. III, núm. 7, 1980, pp. 137–151; Oberem and Roswith Hartmann, 'Indios Cañaris de la sierra sur del Ecuador en el Cuzco del siglo XVI', *Revista de Antropología* (Cuenca), vol. 7, 1981, pp. 114–136. The classic account of a journey connected with a review (visita) of the postal service is Concolorcorvo, *El lazarillo de ciegos caminantes desde Buenos Aires hasta Lima con sus itinerarios* (ed. José J. Real Díaz and Juan Pérez de Tudela, Biblioteca de Autores Españoles, vol. 122, Madrid: 1956 [1773]). 'Concolorcorvo' was the pseudonym of the peninsular Alonso Carrió de la Vandera, *Visitador* of the postal service and something of an *arbitrista*: see his *Reforma del Perú* (ed. Pablo Macera, Lima: San Marcos UP, 1966).

[20] The widespread use of the term 'yanacona', in the colonial period and beyond, to describe hacienda peons is a corruption of the original context, which referred to a retainer

vn lucido alarde de los oficiales indios que llaman yanaconas, en numero de
mas de mil bien aderezados y vestidos, en hileras de quatro en quatro con
su capitan alferez y sargento, y con muchas cadenas de oro, perlas, bordados
y pedreria, con diversos generos de armas ... dieron vuelta a la plaza.[21]

There is evidence that there was stratification within this group during
the Incario, and this passage provides further corroboration. Of more
interest, though, is that they bore arms, a notable feature of major fiestas
that in the eighteenth century would be a source of real worry to the
crown. Even more extraordinary is the following description of two groups
(of 400 and 200 respectively) of Cañaris, the second accompanied by a
group of Canas:

> salieron ... quatrocientos indios Cañares ... muy bien aderezados en forma
> de esquadron con sus capitanes, muy vizarros, con turbantes, chipanas, ajorcas
> de plata, canipos tambien de plata, que son a figura de luna con las armas
> que ellos vsauan, y las que nosotros vsamos, espadas, picas, arcabuzes, &,
> hizieron su entrada con gran aparato de guerra ... entraron tras ellos otros
> dozientos indios tambien Cañares, y los Canas de Acocana ... turbantes
> adornados con hilos de plata, y canipos, resplandores o rayos de oro, llamados
> purapura, que es encomienda o diuisa de nobleza que solia dar el Inga por
> servicios de la guerra.[22]

The obvious suspicion that these impressive armaments were *ersatz* –
theatrical props, as it were – is indicated, first, by the prevailing law that
only *hidalgos* might bear arms, and second, by the fact that the second
group of Cañaris and Canas then proceeded to engage in a ritual battle
to commemorate events of the Incario. Quite simply, royal officials would
never have permitted a ritual battle with real arms to take place in a square
filled with ten thousand spectators, half of them *españoles*, and would never
have allowed re-armament of the indigenous population on such a scale
at any time, much less so soon after the conquest.

Once these and other processions and displays were over, there followed
a further fiesta in which the eleven Inca emperors (up to and including
Huayna Capac) appeared, all of them represented by 'the nearest of their
descendants'; they were carried in litters borne on the shoulders of 'indios',
much as present-day Corpus saints are carried, or the *pasos* of Semana
Santa in Sevilla are carried by *cofrades*. The chronicler of these events
noted that a full account of this fiesta would be excessively long were it
to detail the many and various 'insignias and emblems (*divisas*) according
to the conquests and deeds of each King'.[23] It is worth recalling in passing

---

*cum* administrative class. However, some of these original yanaconas appear to have lasted
beyond the colonial period as a distinct category: see David Cahill, 'Inca Retainer Groups
and Destructuration'.

21 Romero (ed.), 'Festividades'.

22 Ibid.

23 These emblems etc. appear to be similar to those in the 1692 banner of the 'desendientes

Guaman Poma's representation of the respective details of each Inca's individualised dress and heraldry. The chronicler of 1610, however, gave the general thrust of the Incas' livery:

> venian vestidos al trage inca de cumbis, ricos, que es su brocado dellos, con cetros reales en las manos, y vn principal al lado con un quitasol, lleuaua cada uno sus insignias reales gente de guarda lucida, y vestida a su trage, y estos eran los descendientes de aquel Rey.[24]

This procession of representations of former Inca emperors was headed by the 'Captain of all' Don Alonso Topatauchi, the uncle of Melchor Inca who at the time lived in a kind of velvet captivity at the Spanish court (then in Valladolid).[25] The Topa Atauchi family was among the most prestigious of the colonial Inca nobility, its immediate descent stemming from the Topa Atauchi who had deputised for Huayna Capac when he departed Cuzco to conquer the Quito region; Huayna Capac stayed years in Quito, during which time Topa Atauchi was one of the diarchy which ruled Cuzco in the *Sapay Inca*'s absence. He also became the *segunda persona* of Huayna Capac's successor Huascar. Don Alonso Topa Atauchi was the illegitimate son of Paullu Inca, himself the son of Huayna Capac and puppet ruler after the conquest. For all that the 1610 festivities were in certain measure theatrical events – colonial constructions – they lacked neither verisimilitude with pre-Columbian traditions, rituals and iconography, nor the requisite social cachet, afforded in this case by the turnout of the descendants of the erstwhile Inca emperors: the 'first families' of colonial indigenous society.

The third of these fiestas was celebrated entirely by San Jerónimo, a *cercado* town some two leagues from the city. This was, on the face of it,

del Gran Tocay Capac Inga' (see anon) and with those 'with the sculpted images of their Gentile kings' to which Bishop Moscoso referred – see n. 31. The *chipanas*, according to Cobo, vol. II, book 14, chap. 2, were the bracelets: 'Adornaban los brazos y muñecas con manillas y aljorcas de oro, que llamaban *chipana*. Garcilaso de la Vega, *Comentarios reales*, vol. II, book VI, chap. XXII, noted the ritual importance of one version of the *chipana*, in recording the sacrifice to the Sun at Inti Rayme: 'El fuego para aquel sacrificio había de ser nuevo, dado de mano del Sol, como ellos decían. Para el cual tomaban un brazelete grande, que llaman *chipana* (a semejanza de otros que comúnmente traían los Incas en la muñeca izquierda), el cual tenía el Sumo Sacerdote; era grande, más que los comunes ...'.

[24] Romero, op. cit.

[25] There is an important body of work on the early colonial descent of the house of Huayna Capac. On Tito Atauchi, see Rostworowski, *Estructuras*, pp. 167–169; and Ella Dunbar Temple, 'Un linaje incaico durante la dominación española: Los Sahuaraura', *Revista Histórica*, vol. XVIII, no. 1, 1949, 45–77. On Melchor Inca, see Temple, 'Azarosa existencia de un mestizo de sangre imperial incaica', *Documenta*, vol. 1, no. 1, 1948, pp. 112–156. Closely related works are: Temple, 'La descendencia de Huayna Capac', *Revista Histórica*, vol. XI, nos 1–2, 1937, pp. 93–165; 'La descendencia de Huayna Capac: Paullu Inca', *Revista Histórica*, vol. XI, no. 3, pp. 284–333; vol. XII, 1939, pp. 204–245; vol. XIII, 1940, pp. 31–77; 'Don Carlos Inca', *Revista Histórica*, vol. XVII, 1948, pp. 135–179. See also, Lohmann, op. cit.

somewhat odd. San Jerónimo and San Sebastián (a half league from the city) were the two main post-conquest locations of the colonial Inca nobles, following Toledo's resettlement of most of the surviving nobility attendant upon the re-organisation of the city from twelve (Incaic) *barrios* into (6–8) parishes.[26] In the late eighteenth century, at any rate, the two towns together housed 169 male nobles out of a total of 212 in Cuzco, i.e., *c.* 80 per cent; of these, however, precisely 146 were located in San Sebastián (86 per cent), and only 23 (14 per cent) in San Jerónimo.[27] It might be thought that the former would have been a more appropriate celebrant. Either the chronicler is in error or, more likely, the nobles of San Sebastián had borne the brunt of the first two fiestas of this 'Jesuit' cycle. One further possibility is that these also represented the upper moiety, Hatun Cuzco, while those of the previous two days were of Hurin Cuzco, its counterpart. Reference is made to 'la Magestad que se dixo de los de arriba',[28] with particular allusion to figures representing two 'Inca Kings' from whom the others had descended. At any rate, with some 20,000 people packing the main plaza – twice that of the first fiesta – 400 'indios' of the town were led in squadrons, with the *cacique principal* of San Jerónimo as their 'captain'. At the head of the procession, even before the 'captain', another *principal* announced grandly that the 'Lords Incas' were coming 'to display their greatness'. Another 'soldier' carried a war helmet[29] of 'the Inca King' that had been inherited by his descendants. At the close, the last Inca declaimed ('with great effect') that they were greatly in the debt of the Blessed Ignatius and the Jesuit fathers. That this was no mere rhetorical flourish will be evident from the following account of the fiesta of the Virgin of Loreto: the links between Inca nobles and Jesuits were abiding.

[26] On the Toledan reorganisation of the parishes, Antonio Vásquez de Espinosa, *Compendio y descripción de las Indias Occidentales* (Biblioteca de Autores Españoles vol. 231, Madrid. 1969 [1637]), chaps LXXXIV, CVIII, pp. 369–371, 395–396. The city and *cercado* of Cuzco comprised the parishes of San Cristóbal, San Blas, Hospital de Naturales (or San Pedro), Santiago, Santa Ana, and Belén, and the two towns of San Jerónimo and San Sebastián. However, this conventional definition excludes the Cathedral parish with its two *curatos de españoles* and one *curato de piezas* or 'Indian' parish, each of which was often referred to as a 'parish' in colonial usage.

[27] Archivo Departamental del Cuzco, Intendencia: Real Audiencia, Leg. 175, 'Expediente relativo a los tributos del Cuzco, matrícula hecha en el año de 1786 ...'. Note, though, the comments and caveats at note 7 of previous chapter.

[28] Romero, op. cit. On the moieties Hanan/Hurin, see especially, Zuidema, *The Ceque System*, passim; Zuidema, 'The Moieties of Cuzco', in David Maybury-Lewis and Uri Almagor (eds), *The Attraction of Opposites: Thought and Society in the Dualistic Mode* (Ann Arbor: Michigan UP, 1989), pp. 255–275; Rostworowski, *Estructuras*, passim, but especially pp. 107–179.

[29] This was probably the *uma chuco* or 'casco' in the representations of the Incas in Guaman Poma de Ayala, 98 [98] to 115 [115], pp. 79–94.

# CHAPTER ELEVEN

# The Inca Motif in Colonial Fiestas – II

## The Feast-day of Nuestra Señora de Loreto, 1692

On 22 August 1692 a remarkable ceremony took place in and from the Chapel of Our Lady of Loreto. It was the occasion of the customary annual fiesta and procession of the Virgin, whose *cofradía* was located in the chapel, adjacent to La Compañía on Cuzco's Plaza de Armas. There was nothing extraordinary about a religious procession wending its way through the old Inca capital. Apart from the great religious festivals such as Corpus Christi and Semana Santa, such processions were a regular feature of daily life in colonial times. A glance through Diego Esquivel y Navia's *Noticias crono-lógicas de la gran ciudad del Cuzco* (c. 1749) indicates that such processions – whether confraternity *santo* celebrations, rosaries, friars' devotions, good news from the court, earthquakes, inclement weather, and so forth – were abundant in colonial life. What was most singular about the Loreto fiesta and procession is that it appears to have been celebrated principally by the Inca nobles of Cuzco. The apparent reason why a description of this ceremony has come down to us is that the father of the *'alcalde mayor ... de los Ingas nobles'*, one Don Juan Sicos Inga, arranged for a notary to record the proceedings. This bureaucratic twist relates to the perennial need for noble families to possess legal documentation of their noble status, the better to guard against sporadic official attempts to classify such families as non-noble, thereby rendering them liable for tribute and labour service. Of perhaps even more moment, any such re-classification as a tributary would have devastating ramifications for social status in a society in which inherited status and honour often overrode wealth in calibrating an indi-vidual's place and prestige in the social order. It is due entirely to such prosaic circumstances that we have an account of this ceremony, which provides a unique window on to colonial Incaic ritual praxis and the construction of a distinct colonial Incaic identity.[1]

[1] Archivo Departamental del Cuzco, Intendencia: Real Hacienda, Leg. 171, 'Ynstancia que han hecho Don Buenabentura Sicos: sus hijos y otros descendien. de este Linaje para se les excima de la contribucion de su tasa', 26 January, 1786, fols 2–3, reproduced in Appendix 2; see also the related 'Ynstrumto e Ynformacn. producida pr. Dn. Antonio Sicos, como Cazique Pral. y Governador de la Parrochia de Sn. Sebastian de los Aillos de Pumamarca y Aiarmaca sobre la Noblesa de los Yndios de los 6. Aillos comprehendidos en los dos referidos',

The procession commenced with the removal of the standard of 'Nuestra Señora de Loreto' from the chapel, in which the the the Virgin's *cofradía* 'is founded'.[2] Here we note an echo of the 1610 ceremonies, which began with the removal of the statue of the Little King from La Compañía itself; it is possible that these two saints were paired within the overarching Native Andean system of oppositions and complementarity, much in the way that Santiago and Santa Barbara were twinned during Corpus Christi. The Virgin's standard was carried by Juan Sicos Inga, and preceded her float (*andas*). Sicos Inga wore the *mascapaicha*, which was 'adorned with many strings of pearls (*perlarias*) and very precious jewels'. To round off this ensemble, Sicos Inga was decked out with 'two chains of gold ... the one hung from his neck and the other crossed his highly adorned right shoulder'. These golden chains call to mind Garcilaso's account (citing a passage in Zárate) of the golden rope (*maroma, soga*, Quechua *huasca*) that Huayna Capac ordered to be made on the birth of his first-born Huascar, 'so thick ... that more than two hundred *orejones* could hardly lift it'.[3] Yet the other half of Sicos' outfit also compels attention: 'su espada y daga a la sinta y todo el traje de español de gala muy lucida y costosa ...'.[4] Here, then, Sicos Inga juxtaposed an Incaic ceremonial costume with a Spanish ceremonial or festive ('de gala') outfit. What did this mean? It referred to Sicos' *hidalgo* status, which had been granted to him during a ceremony of *caballerosidad* in the same Chapel of Loreto in 1689. The report of the ceremony in which Sicos Inga 'se siñio espada y daga' during the saying of a mass goes on to record that 'acavada la ddha misa vestido como estava el contenido de Español y con la insignia de la mascapaicha en la cavesa como havia benido'.[5] This grant of *hidalguía* had followed his request 'de consederle lisencia para que pueden ttraer espada y armas ofensivas y defensivas para el adorno y defenssa de sus personas y que pueden andar en el ttraxe que andan los cavalleros hijos dalgo como descendientes de dhos ingas ... '.[6]

Thus the wearing of this type of Castilian dress was in itself a symbol of indigenous or Incan nobility. The nexus of Incaic status and *caballero-*

1786; also, Archivo Departamental del Cuzco, Intendencia: Real Hacienda, Leg. 176, 'Expediente formado por el Casique Don Rafael Amau sobre que se declare a su Comun por libre de la contribucion de su tasa', 18 January, 1786 (Amau was the cacique of the ayllus of Pumamarca and Ayarmaca, to which the Sicos belonged).

[2] For another *cofradía* with Incaic resonances, see Archivo Departamental del Cuzco, Cabildo: Ordinarias-Civiles, Leg. 34, 'Testamento de Dn. Andres Navarro Cacxhagualpa Inga', 13 June, 1767, for mention of the 'Cofradía de Nuestra Señora del Rosario de Ñustas' also known as the 'Cofradía de la Ñusta', founded in the Convent of Santo Domingo (the erstwhile Coricancha, or Inca Temple of the Sun). A 'ñusta' was a female noble rank, usually translated as 'princess'.

[3] Garcilaso, book 6, chap. II.

[4] Ibid., 'Ynstancia que han hecho Don Buenbentura Sicos: sus hijos ... '.

[5] Ibid.; fols 8–16, esp. fol. 16.

[6] Ibid., fol. 7.

*sidad* or hidalguía is patent, and this, rather than merely being evidence of acculturation, is the principal meaning of the above description. Sicos' part-Castilian, part-Incaic costume was, therefore, all of a piece – literally and figuratively. This symbiotic 'crossover' dressing was the logical livery for the Inciac nobility in the colonial context. Incaic status and *hidalgo* status reinforced and complemented one another: to be the one was to be the other. As if to buttress the symbolic symmetry, Sicos Inga was flanked in procession by the *españoles* Don Juan Niño Casimiro de Guzmán, 'Jues de Naturales', and Don Jerónimo de Alegría de Carvajal, Protector de Naturales, who thereby 'honoured him as such principal Inca noble'. He was similarly 'honoured' by the 'many known principal Incas of the eight parishes of [the] city'.

If the above is an impressive confirmation of the extent of syncretism in colonial ritual, and especially of the leading role of the colonial Incas in amending standard liturgical practice, it is nevertheless quite what we would expect in the light of both Moscoso's jeremiad against the 'Gentile' rites and from the well-known pictorial representations of Cuzco's Corpus Christi celebrations. Rather more remarkable in the Loreto procession was the notary's recording of the details of a second standard that complemented that of the *cofradía*. The standard was carried by three 'indios' dressed in the 'ancient' style or usage, also preceded by an Antisuyu or *selva* Indian (*indio chuncho*) who, like a pirate, bore a 'royal parrot' on his shoulder. The details of the standard borne by the indigenes merits citation in full:

> En un palo grande delgado y plateado un lienso pintado a dos ases, que en el uno estava pintado un Inga en su traje antiguo con su mascapaicha de la borla colorada y su chambi, y valcanca en la mano ysquierda, y en la derecha un baso de oro al pareser que ofrecia al sol que estava pintado en dho lienso y al pie de dho Inga unos cinco carneros de la tierra los dos colorados y los otros dos amarillos y el uno color sani = y a la buelta estava pintado un arco de verde amarillo y colorado y en medio una corona de oro dorado del Rey Nuestro Señor y mas abajo la ynsignia de la mascapaicha que le detienen dos papagaios R[eale]s y mas abajo una lista pintada de tocapos yacnopos y al ultimo un letrero en que decia armas de los desendientes de Gran Tocay Capac Inga Rey Señor natural que fue de estos reinos del peru = y a los dos lados de este los dhos dos yndios llevaron dos llacachuquis en otros dos palos guarnecidos de Plata con plumajes de diferentes colores bien adornados a la usanza antigua, que es la ynsignia que en semejantes actos publicos sacan los que son alfereses R[eale]s el dia del glorioso Apostol Santiago en cada año ...[7]

[7] Ibid., fols 2–3. Some of the symbols mentioned in this passage require clarification. The *mascapaycha*, the *chambi/chanbi/champi* and *valcanca* (shield or buckler) have already been mentioned; the first two, at least, had undergone some colonial changes, such that, e.g., the *chambi* appears to have evolved from a kind of mace or warclub to a staff of office or a sceptre. But note the definition of Murúa, book I, chap. XXII, p. 84, and book II, chap.

The two-sided standard or banner thus is entirely Incaic, with the sole exception of the reference to the 'gilded golden crown of our lord the King [of Spain]'. Here it is worth recalling Moscoso's observation that the Inca nobility carried their own banners 'with the sculpted images of their Gentile kings'.[8] The Spanish crown is sandwiched between two symbols of Incan sovereignty — the *mascapaicha* and the representation of the rainbow (*cuchi* or *cuichu* or *cuychi*). Quite what this precise juxtaposition or triad signifies is not clear, but assuredly was meant to convey some message about the specific relationship between crown and Inca nobility and the nature of the allegiance of the one to the other.

The Incaic symbolism in this description appears to replicate the heraldry of either Incaic and/or Spanish coats-of-arms. Each of the Incas appears to have had his own escutcheon, which seems to have been guarded by the corresponding *panaca*; there are drawings of these in Guaman Poma de Ayala's *Nueva corónica y buen gobierno* of 1615.[9] The extent to which these were colonial constructions and how far they reproduced 'authentic' pre-colonial Incaic heraldry are questions that would merit

III, p. 350, wherein he refers to another 'cetro' of gold called *tupa yauri*. There may thus have been some colonial conflation of *chambi* and *tupa yauri*. The 'arco' described refers to the rainbow (*cuchi*, *cuichi*), feared and venerated by the Incas, and which was represented in Coricancha. The *tocapos*, the squared patterns on the Inca tunics (*uncus*), are discussed anon. The *llacachuquis* are identified as weapons of war, apparently a form of mace or club, by Juan de Santa Cruz Pachacuti Yamque, *Relación de antigüedades deste Reyno del Perú*, in *Crónicas peruanas de interés indígena*, ed. Francisco Esteve Barba (Biblioteca de Autores Españoles, vol. 209, Madrid: 1968), p. 299. Murúa, book II, chap. XXXIII, p. 436, refers to Illapa ('trueno') as *Chuquii Llaquees*, and there is probably a lexical connexion between the two usages. It is worthy of remark that neither the description of the costume of the Inca here, nor for that matter in the 1610 fiestas, mentioned the elaborate head ornament called the *suntur paucar*, observed in pictorial representations of Corpus Christi. This, like the colonial *mascapaicha*, tended to become more elaborate: See the comments of Caroline Dean: 'According to numerous depictions of viceregal period headgear, the *suntur paucar* became a complex forest of icons. In the Corpus Christi canvases, these elaborate assemblages rise what must have been one or two feet above the head of the wearer. Each forehead assemblage is unique, but they share a number of the same items'. See Caroline Sue Dean, *Painted Images of Cuzco's Corpus Christi: Social Conflict and Cultural Strategy in Viceregal Peru* (unpublished Ph.D. dissertation, UCLA, 1990), p. 238. As to the 'royal parrots', the precise meaning is unclear, though the depiction of birds is usually a reference to Incan conquest of the Antis (cf. 1610 fiestas), and occasionally appears also to be a symbol of nobility. For some comments on avian symbolism in colonial 'Incaic' fiestas in Lima, see Luis Millones, 'The Inka's Mask: Dramatisation of the Past in Indigenous Colonial Processions', in *Andean Art: Visual Expression and its Relation to Andean Beliefs and Values*, ed. Penny Dransart (Aldershot: Avebury, 1995), pp. 11–32.

8 Archivo General de Indias, Audiencia del Cuzco, Leg. 29, Moscoso to Areche, 13 April, 1781.

9 Felipe Guaman Poma de Ayala, *El primer nueva corónica y buen gobierno*, ed. John V. Murra and Rolena Adorno (trans. Jorge L. Urioste, 3 vols., Lima and Madrid: Siglo Veintiuno & Instituto de Estudios Peruanos, 1980 ), vol. 1, pp. 62, 65, for examples of this heraldry.

further investigation, not least because the array of these encoded symbols and their alignment in relation to one another conveyed, conveys, distinct meanings to those capable of decoding them. In the Loreto document, the armorial bearings are strikingly Incaic, with the Spanish crown seemingly, at least at first glance, an afterthought. On one side of the banner there was a painted image of an Inca in 'ancient costume' donning a *masacapaicha* with the 'chambi, y valcanca' (sceptre and buckler, respectively), to which Moscoso's description also referred, in his left hand, and with his right 'apparently offered a vessel of gold to the Sun', a painted image of which was included on the banner; this was probably the *tupa cusi napa* mentioned by Murúa and/or the *aquilla* mentioned by Garcilaso.[10] On the obverse were the aforementioned triad of rainbow (*Cuchi*), Spanish crown and (again) the *mascapaicha*.

The depiction of the five Andean cameloids ('carneros de la tierra') similarly bore cultic resonances. These had been integral to pre-conquest Incaic sacrifices, especially to the Sun, and their respective colours were of ritual significance, though the precise ritual content of each colour is unclear. It is worthy of note that, of the five represented on the banner, two were red ('colorado'), two yellow and one 'color sani' – presumably white.[11] Cobo tells us that, after human sacrifice, 'the principal and most acceptable was that of cameloids', noting that in their sacrifice there was 'much order and observance, as much in the number [of animals] as in their colour and other features, according to the divinity ('dios') to whom they were offered, and to the [particular] fiesta, and to the reason for which the sacrifice was made. Because distinct colours and differences of this breed were stipulated for each one of the divinities'. In a long disquisition on the ceremonial importance of cameloids, Cobo specifies that the dark ones ('pardos de color de *guanacos*') were offered to Wiracocha, while each day in the city a red ('rojo') animal, dressed in a 'red vest' was burnt – 'and this they called the offering of the sun'.[12] A dappled ('pintado')

[10] Murúa, book I, chap. XXII; Garcilaso, book VI, chap. XXII, the latter an exposition of the ritual function and significance of these 'golden cups'.

[11] I have sought to track down this word in Spanish as well as Quechua dictionaries, Early Modern as well as modern. I can find no reference to it, but assume that it derives from the Latin 'sanus', i.e., 'sano', referring to health and purity, which I interpret to correspond with 'white'.

[12] Cobo, book 13, chaps XXII, XXV, vol. II, pp. 202, 209. Cobo's lucid and well-organised account, here as elsewhere, largely follows Molina, esp. pp. 66–71, who provides (p. 67) more information on the colours and types: 'Sacrificavan en [mayo] al Sol gran cantidad de carneros de todos los colores llamados los unos *huarcarpata*, que eran blancos y lanudos y otros carneros llamados *huanacos*, y otros *pacos* blancos lanudos llamados *cuyllor*, y otros *pacos* llamados *paucarpaco*, que eran hembras, bermejos y lanudos y otros *pacos* llamados *oquipaco*, y otros carneros grandes llamados *chumpi*, que eran negros y lanudos. Y asimismo sacrificauan en este tiempo corderos de los mismos colores ...'. Indispensable para understanding the multiple classifications of Andean cameloids and their ritual significance is: Jorge Flores Ochoa (ed.), *Pastores de puna: Uywamichiq punarunakuna* (Lima: Instituto de Estudios Peruanos, 1977).

animal corresponded to sacrifices made to Illapa. These were only a few of the specifications for *carnero* sacrifices. More to the point, Cobo also informs us that in the principal fiesta of Capac Raimi, at the head of the procession 'were borne the royal insignias, which were a white cameloid and the royal standard or banner, called *Sunturpaucar*. This cameloid was similar to the sun offering, in that it was 'very white, dressed in a red vest and with golden ear decorations … and they said that it represented the first of its species that has emerged after the Flood, and they [therefore] assumed it [had] to be white'.[13] Murúa's account is broadly in accord with Cobo's disquisition, noting also that the white, dressed cameloid was called *pillco llama*.[14] To the fiery sacrifice during Capac Raimi were added golden and silver figurines of cameloids – presumably *conopas*[15] – that Molina tells us were called *corinapa* and *colquinapa* respectively.[16]

There then follow the two most remarkable elements of this unique description. The first is the inclusion on the banner of 'a painted list of tocapos yacnopos'. These *tocapos* were small, square ideograms (probably presented as raised embroidery) arrayed in lines and columns, familiar both from colonial portraiture and from the famous wood-cuts in the *Nueva corónica* in which they are represented on the tunics (*uncus*) of successive Inca emperors.[17] What is most singular about these is that it has recently been controversially argued, on the basis of allegedly new evidence, that contrary to all that has been taught about Inca civilisation, these *tocapos* in fact constituted a form of writing; thus, for example, the 'tunics' on Guaman Poma's woodcut images of the Incas might perhaps now be read in accordance with this hypothesised Inca 'alphabet'.[18] The banner, then, may well have carried a written message apparently

---

[13] Ibid., see also n. 7. The *sunturpaucar* was a somewhat protean conflation of symbols worn as part of the ceremonial headdress by the Inca figure (*alférez real*) in the colonial Corpus Christi and other processions, and which might be considered as approximating a standard or banner. See the excellent discussion in Carolyn Sue Dean, *Painted Images of Cuzco's Corpus Christi*, chap. IX.

[14] Murúa, book II, chap. XV, pp. 385.

[15] On *conopas*, see especially Penny Dransart, *Elemental Meanings: Symbolic Expression in Inka Miniature Figurines* (University of London, Institute of Latin American Studies Research Paper No. 40, London: 1995). For the colonial period: Kenneth Mills, *Idolatry and its Enemies: Colonial Andean Religion and Extirpation, 1640–1750* (Princeton: Princeton UP, 1997), esp. 93–100, chap. 3 passim, for discussion of both *conopas* and the related *chancas*.

[16] Murúa, book II, chap. XXXVII, p. 450; Molina, p. 70.

[17] Ibid., vol. 1, pp. 84–96. On the *tocapos*, see esp. R. Tom Zuidema, 'Guaman Poma and the Art of Empire: Toward an Iconography of Inca Royal Dress', in *Transatlantic Encounters: Europeans and Andeans in the Sixteenth Century*, ed. Kenneth J. Andrien and Rolena Adorno (Berkeley and Oxford: California UP, 1991), pp. 151–202. The *tocapos* are well-known from their appearance on pre-colonial and colonial tunics (*uncus*) in museums and collections, and their depiction in colonial portraits.

[18] First reactions to this 'discovery' are summarised in Viviano Domenici and Davide Domenici, 'Talking Knots of the Inka', *Archaeology*, vol. 49, no. 6, Nov/Dec. 1996, pp. 50–56.

decipherable only to the indigenous elites. Yet this was matter-of-factly identified by the *español* witness as *tocapos*, so that presumably these were still in use – and presumably in common use, given the laconic account of the notary – at the end of thé seventeenth century. Were that the case, it would be convincing evidence of the continuing integrity and even vitality of Incaic culture thoughout the colonial period: i.e., not merely were the Inca nobles able to retain their ancient regalia and costume in tandem with the received Catholic rites and liturgy, but perhaps even to maintain the hypothesised 'lost' Incaic writing system.

The other extraordinary feature of the banner is probably related to the *tocapos*, and may even have been a Spanish translation of these, at least were it to be demonstrated that the 'lost' alphabet indeed existed. It is the mention of the 'desendientes of Gran Tocay Capac Inga Rey Señor natural que fue de estos reinos del peru'.[19] Such a description of the 'descendants' of a particular erstwhile Inca ruler was common enough in the petitions and *probanzas de nobleza* of the colonial Inca nobles, and is probably *ipso facto* proof of the survival of the *panacas* thoughout the colonial period, in contradistinction to the widely-held view that they were totally eradicated by Viceroy Toledo in the 1570s. Yet what is most singular here is that no Gran Tocay Capac Inga appears in any of the 'king-lists' of Inca rulers in either the numerous chronicles or extant colonial documents. The name of this obviously mythical Tocay Capac was, according to Guaman Poma, one of the first generation of 'Incas' ('Primer Inga') who ruled in an earlier age, before those Incas from Manco Capac onwards began to govern; as such, they don't appear in the usual 'king lists'. Garcilaso's version is that a great lord of Tiahuanaco divided the world into four parts, granting the third, or eastern part, to Tocay.[20] The ethnohistorian María Rostworowski concurs: Tocay Capac was one of the two 'generic names of the chiefs of the Ayarmacas', who had ruled the Antisuyu quarter of the known world or Tahuantinsuyu ('four quarters'), prior to their conquest by the Incas in an earlier expansionary phase.[21] Following this conquest, the Incas and the Ayarmacas exchanged brides, with the Inca Yahuar Huacac marrying the daughter of Tocay Capac. Two reigns later, Inca Pachacuti crushed an Ayarmaca revolt led by yet another Tocay Capac, who died in imprisonment. The colonial Ayarmaca variously described their ancestral descent thus:[22]

[19] 'Ynstancia que ha hecho Don Buenabentura Sicos: sus hijos ... ', op. cit.

[20] Garcilaso, book 1, chap. VIII.

[21] María Rostworowsky (sic), *Los Ayarmacas* (Valladolid: Casa Museo de Colón, 1975), is an outstanding and pioneering evaluation of most of the surviving evidence on the Ayarmaca.

[22] Archivo Departamental del Cuzco, Intendencia: Real Hacienda, Leg. 176, 'Expediente formado por el Casique Don Rafael Amau sobre que se declare a su comun por libre de la contribucion de su tasa', 18 January, 1786, fols 12–13, 16; Archivo Departamental del Cuzco, Intendencia: Real Hacienda, Leg. 171, 'Ynstrumto. e Ymformacn. producida pr. Dn. Antonio

que los d[ic]hos yndios nobles eran descendientes de los Señores Reyes Yngas de Tocay Capac Chiuan Capac Cusi Ynga y de Apollamac Chauca Amaro y Aposicos y Aposuna y deudos y parientes muy propinquios de Vira Cocha Ynga Señor Natural ...

ser nobles y desendientes de ingas de Tocai Capac Chivan Capac y Cussi Inga Señores Naturales ...

sus Asendientes, y Desendientes desde el tiempo del Gran Ynga Toccay Ccapac Yntimanya Sinchi Chiguanguay, Señor que fue de esta tierra ...'.

The protean description of Tocay Capac's name is puzzling: it may have resulted from a confused oral tradition of the colonial Ayarmaca themselves, or through a misunderstanding of one or more of the *español* notaries who recorded the original testimony and later transcriptions (*traslados*). Perhaps more likely, it may represent some customary conflation of founding and prominent heads of lineage, as well as celebrated matrimonial alliances. Indeed, there are still other 'Ayarmaca Inca' progenitors who do not figure in any 'king-list', e.g., the Nancay family claimed descent not only from 'Gran Tupa Yupanqui Inga' but also from one 'Gran Guaypartupa Ancio Inga, asimismo Señor Natural que fue de estos Reynos'.[23] The first two notations indicate that a list of founders was intended, though the third was possibly the definitive version of Tocay Capac's name. Given the ritual homage paid to Tocay Capac both by his descendants and, at least after 1687, the extant Inca nobility of the eight parishes, it is hardly likely that the colonial Ayarmaca were confused about their founder's identity and name. It is, however, probable that this ceremony represents a conflation of several mythic accounts of (perhaps several) Tocay Capacs. In any case, it is clear that he is the common ancestor of all Incas, such that the participation of all the royal ayllus and/or *panacas* in the 1692 procession should occasion little surprise. It is nonetheless the case that it was led by an Ayarmaca who had recently been locked in dispute with these other colonial *panacas*.

A further possibility is suggested by an intriguing hypothesis presented by R. T. Zuidema concerning the (pre-1532) Incaic construction of their history.[24] Zuidema reminds us that some chroniclers (Polo de Ondegardo, Acosta, Gutiérrez de Santa Clara) aver that the dynasties of Hurin and Hanan Cuzco were contemporaneous, rather than comprising a list of ten sequential rulers. Linking this premise to the position of the Incan

Sicos ...', 1786, fols 20–22; Archivo Departamental del Cuzco, 'Ynstancia que ha hecho Don Buenabentura Sicos: sus hijos ...', op. cit., fol. 9v.

[23] Archivo Departamental del Cuzco, Colegio de Ciencias, 'Memoria y Certificación de los Indios Nobles años 1763–1766', Leg. 1, Petition of Don Eusevio Nancay *et alii* of Ayllo Ayarmaca y Tamboconga of San Salvador de Pucyura, s. f. There is also mention of a further lineage ancestor, Pinahua Cápac: see Rostworowski, *Los Ayarmacas*, pp. 39–41.

[24] R. Tom Zuidema, 'El origen del imperio inca', in idem, *Reyes y guerreros: Ensayos de cultura andina* (Lima: Fomciencias, 1989), pp. 198–201.

mummies in Coricancha, Zuidema noted that these were arrayed around the image of the Sun, the five Hanan rulers to the right, the five Hurin to the left, with the mummy of Huayna Capac, representing the actual Sapa Inca (Huascar), seated facing the Sun image: 'the mummies closest to the Sun image occupied the highest positions in the hierarchy and the furthest [positions] were occupied by those lowest [in the hierarchy]'. This arrangement symbolically represented 'the four ranks within the tribe of the Incas'. Reading this as a cipher for the Incas' construction of their history, Zuidema suggests that the Incas projected their social organisation towards the past, effectively reconstruing the past so as to calibrate it with the present organisation at any point in time; this he contrasts with Western historical thinking, which departs from a fixed point in the past towards the present. Now, extrapolating from this, Zuidema's hypothesis is that with each succession, the mummy placed in front of the Sun image moves next to the image, that is, in the case of Huayna Capac on the right befitting a Hanan ruler, while his Hurin counterpart takes a corresponding place on the immediate left of the Sun idol. Given that the Coricancha alignment of *momias* is a reflection of existing social organisation at any given point in time, it perforce follows that the Hanan and Hurin rulers farthest from the Sun image drop off, effectively disappearing from the Incan account of Incan history. Were this the case, then a long list of Inca rulers prior to those on the conventional king-list, many of whom would have been little more than provincial kurakas and sinchis, would effectively have been erased from official Inca history by the time Pizarro's hordes arrived in Cuzco, notwithstanding that a few of these Incan ghost-kings emerge sporadically in legendary or mythical accounts, above all those recorded in Guaman Poma. If we accept Zuidema's suggestion as a working hypotheis, the possibility arises that the collection or conflation of names with that of Tocay Capac may in part represent some Ayarmaca and/or Incan group memory of some of those 'lost' Inca rulers. If this is something of a remote contingency, it nevertheless has the virtue of being commensurate with the most plausible thesis of the Incas' construction of their own history. For all that, it appears impossible to assess the degree to which such an Incan account may be harmonised with any putative Ayarmaca ideological history. To the extent that the latter existed as an ordering of the past separate from that of the Inca rulers, some sort of *modus vivendi* would manifestly have been reached by the late seventeenth century.

In the post-conquest period, the Ayarmaca were still settled in the districts around Pucyura and Chinchero to the east of the city and San Sebastián just half-a-league to the west; at least one Ayarmaca *ayllu* was formally registered by the Peruvian government as late as 1956.[25] Related to the Incas, they are perhaps best classed among the associated group of

25 Rostworowski, *Los Ayarmacas*, pp. 38.

honorary Incas: 'incas de privilegio' of long standing, to all appearances.[26] They were nobles, but of a lower caste. Quite why the Ayarmaca (and the related Pumamarca) led the Loreto procession is something of a mystery that would merit further investigation, given that representatives from a dozen Incan 'houses' were available for that undoubted honour. The mystery deepens when we recall that Don Juan Sicos Inga was 'accompanied by many known principal Incas of the eight parishes of the city who similarly honoured [Sicos Inga]'.[27] It is clear, then, that the Loreto procession was not merely a matter for the descendants of the Ayarmaca and Pumamarca etnías, who overwhelmingly resided in the town of San Sebastián. It was a more broad-based noble rite in which, to all appearances, Inca nobles either paid court to these long-related 'incas de privilegio' or signified their acceptance of the Ayarmaca into their ranks as equals. This surmise is further underscored by the notation that, juxtaposed with the banner of the descendants of Tocay Capac, were the decorated silver staffs that were traditionally borne by the alféreces reales on the feast of Santiago, the centrepiece of the Corpus Christi procession and the feast par excellence of the colonial Inca nobility.

Yet colonial identity is never quite so clear-cut, much less when racial categories intersect with ethnic identities and introduced Hispanic notions of estate (estamento). The Inca nobles who had 'honoured' Juan Sicos Inga in 1692 had been locked in litigation (pleito) with him and his entire ayllu of Pumamarcas y Ayarmacas in the 1680s over the very question of whether the latter were indeed true descendants of the Incas; that is to say, as to whether they shared the jealously-guarded right to wear the mascapaicha. In 1687 judgement in the affirmative was awarded the latter, a decision which the nobles appear to have accepted without demur.[28] For on 23 September, 1689 the full body of the Twenty-four Electors of the Alférez Real voted Sicos Inga unanimously as Alcalde Mayor de los Ingas Nobles. On 6 June 1689, the incoming Viceroy, the Conde de Monclova, referred to the 'enhorabuena ' ('in the name of the principal Incas of the eight city parishes') that Sicos Inga had accorded him upon his arrival in Peru.[29]

[26] The class of 'Incas de privilegio' is poorly understood. There was a hierarchy of elites who bore the suffix 'Inca': 'auquicuna' who were the close relations of the reigning Inca ('Sapay Inca'); the 'Incacuna', all the remaining members of the nobility; the 'no-Incas' of Cuzco were the 'Uaccha Inca' (poor Incas), whose curacas/caciques were 'Huau Inca' (literally, 'incas nietos'). Beyond these, there was a further provincial and regional nobility. It is not clear to which group the Ayarmaca belonged, but it was probably the 'Uaccha Inca', with their most prestigious leaders therefore 'Haua Inca'. See the convenient summary by Bravo, op. cit., pp. 97–98, which relies in large part on R. Tom Zuidema, 'The Inca Kinship System: A New Theoretical View', in Andean Kinship and Marriage, ed. Enrique Mayer and Ralph Bolton (Washington D.C.: American Anthropological Association, 1977), pp. 240–292, esp. pp. 276–279.

[27] 'Ynstancia que ha hecho Don Buenabentura Sicos: sus hijos ... ', op. cit.

[28] Ibid., passim.

[29] Ibid., fols 17–18.

This abrupt turnaround in Sicos Inga's relations with the corps of the city's Inca nobles is bewildering, and testimony to the fluidity, instability and ambiguity of social relationships in the colonial period, above all with respect to the anachronistic group of Incas – victims of 'destructuration', as Nathan Wachtel has put it.[30]

In the late eighteenth century a prophetic charlatan, Juan Quispe Inca, announced the imminent coming of an Inca, remarking that none of the Inca nobles of the eight parishes was worthy of consideration as a candidate for messiah, because they 'buy their nobility for money'.[31] The falsification of *probanzas de nobleza* was certainly not unknown in Cuzco, yet there seems little doubt that the Ayarmacas and Pumamarcas had a strong claim to be considered Inca nobles. This would seem to be indicated by the extant nobility's post-1689 change of attitude towards Sicos Inga. More-over, in the mid-sixteenth century the then two caciques of the *ayllu* – also called 'Ayllo Pomamarca Anancuzco y Urincuzco' – were recognised by the crown as *Ingas Orejones*.[32] Still more interesting is the 1664 descrip-tion of the *ayllu* as comprising 'six ayllus':[33]

|   |   |
|---|---|
| Hanancosco Collana | Orincosco Collana |
| Hanancosco Payan | Orincosco Paian |
| Hanancosco Caiau | Orincosco Caiau |

These three categories of 'collana', 'payán', and 'cayao' represent the tripartite social organisation of the Incario: the first was the group of 'pure Incan descent', the *cayao* were the subject population – considered of inferior status – while the *payán* were the product of unions between *collanas* and *cayaos*.[34] Given the divergent social status of these groups, it is somewhat

---

[30] Nathan Wachtel, *The Vision of the Vanquished: The Spanish Conquest of Peru through Indian Eyes* (trans. Ben and Siân Reynolds, Trowbridge: Harvester Press, 1977), esp. p. 85, for its definition: 'the term "destructuration" is here used to signify the survival of ancient structures, or parts of them, no longer contained within the relatively coherent context in which they had previously existed', which appears to be much the same as 'anachronistic' structures or institutions.

[31] See p. 102, n. 11. This recalls some passages in Garcilaso, *Comentarios reales*: (referring to the use of a royal insignia), 'they say that now, in these times, many Indians wear them calling themselves descendants of the royal blood of the Incas; most make fun of them, because that blood has been almost completely extinguished' (book 6, chap. XXVIII); (on the results of Atahualpa's massacre of Huascar's kinsmen and kinswomen) 'in such manner the entire royal blood of the Incas was extinguished and eradicated within the space of two and one half years' (book 9, chap. XXXVII). Garcilaso soon resiled from this view by adding a coda to his manuscript noting that in 1603 there remained no less than 567 heirs to the Inca 'throne' by the male line. It is perhaps worth noting that, in eighteenth-century Cuzco, Garcilaso was widely read, not least among the upper tiers of indigenous society.

[32] Archivo Departamental del Cuzco, Intendencia: Real Hacienda, Leg. 176, 'Expediente formado por el Casique Don Rafael Amau ...', op. cit., fol. 8r.

[33] Ibid., fol. 12r.

[34] Zuidema, 'Inca Kinship', loc. cit., passim.

surprising that they should be linked in the one *ayllu* in this fashion, for all that many *ayllus* in the region had a mixture of nobles and 'commoners' (*hatun runa*). This impression is reinforced when one takes into account a 1664 claim that the *ayllu* 'doesn't admit [a] mixture of Indians other than their descendants ... in which they are most observant and do not suffer the introduction as Incan descendant of one who is not ...'.[35]

The terms 'Hanan' and 'Oran [*Hurin*]' refer to the upper/lower moiety division of the city which had corresponded in part to a division of functions in the Incario. Prior to the Spanish conquest, the Ayarmaca *etnía* and especially the 'descendants of Tocay Capac' had been associated with the Antisuyu quarter of both the city and Tahuantinsuyu generally, and indeed there is an oblique reference to sixteenth-century litigation between the Ayarmacas and 'The Indians of Collasuyu'.[36] Of the four quarters of the empire, Antisuyu was the inferior half of Hanan and Cuntisuyu the inferior half of Hurin; by extension, Chinchaysuyu was the superior half of Hanan and Collasuyu the superior half of Hurin. In later tribute lists (*matrículas de tributarios/contribuyentes*) of 1801, 1836 and 1845,[37] the *ayllu* Pumamarcas y Ayarmacas does not appear at all, despite a record of its survival as late as 1956. A separate listing of nobles of 1786 resolves this paradox: not one of the 80 members of the *ayllu* paid tribute, and for this reason did not feature in any of the tribute *revisitas*.[38] There was a certain irony here, given the 1680s' legal challenge to their 'Incan' status, in that the *ayllu* Pumamarcas and Ayarmacas was only one of two *ayllus* (the other being the Sahuarauras) to have maintained or been formally granted such a privilege. The Loreto ceremony is remarkable in highlighting the ambivalent and fragile identity of the colonial indigenous nobility. It points up the importance of ritual life as both a battleground for social status and as a venue for harmonising contradications and settling the most rancorous disputes, tensions that in some cases were effectively the continuation of arguments or claims – at any rate, some kind of jostle for status – begun well before the Spanish conquest. The extraordinary appearance of the Ayarmaca descendants of Tocay Capac in a colonial context is sufficient demonstration of the importance of public ritual for asserting a group's

---

[35] 'Expediente formado por ... Don Rafael Amau', fol. 12r; similar sentiments are expressed at fol. 16r.

[36] Ibid., fol. 8r.

[37] Archivo General de la Nación, Sección Tributos-Matrículas, Leg. 5, Cuad. 115, 'Extracto de la Matrícula actuada en esta ciudad y sus 8 parroquias en 1801', (Cuzco) 1801; Archivo Departamental del Cuzco, Tesorería Fiscal, 'Extracto de la Matrícula de Indígenas de la provincia del Cercado', 1836; idem, Tesorería Fiscal, 'Extracto de la Matrícula de Indígenas de la Provincia del Cercado', 1845.

[38] Archivo Departamental del Cuzco, Intendencia: Real Hacienda, Leg. 175, 'Expte. relativo a los tributos del Cuzco, matrícula hecha en el año de 1786 y demas incidencias', 'semester' of San Juan, 1786; idem, 'Nota de los yndibiduos qe. han quedado libres de contribuzn. de tasa por haber calificado ser Nobles en las ocho Parroquias y Gremios de esta ciudad', s.f.

separate identity and its claims for precedence or at least equality with other elites. The Loreto documentation, in particular, underscores the intersection of Native Andean and Hispanic elite status: for indigenous elites, to be Incan was to be *hidalgo*, and to be *hidalgo* was proof of Incan status. On that tenuous nexus hung the honour, status and social place of noble families, and should one condition be called into question, so too perforce would the other. The status and welfare of families and their succeeding generations were in large part built upon such flimsy foundations. Ritual involvement by indigenous nobles was not just a psychological comfort or sop to their self-esteem, but rather one of the principal markers of their place in a world turned upside down.

The question remains as to how the Inca nobility's affinity for, and devotion to, the Virgin of Loreto slotted into the larger narratives of colonial accommodation and cultural appropriation, of why in other words the nobles felt themselves impelled to honour this particular representation of Our Lady. Was she accepted on her own terms or did her acceptance and veneration involve some kind of shuffling within the now highly syncretic Andean pantheon, with all that this might imply for her insertion into the traditional system of oppositions and complementarity? For according to the internal logic that, structuralists insist, lies at the core of native Andean belief system(s), Nuestra Señora de Loreto had to have her complement or twin in that otherworld, and, by the same token, that twin had to be male. Of course, it remains possible that the Virgin of Loreto was, effectively, allocated her own pedestal in the colonial pantheon without a corresponding male saint *cum* deity. Yet to imbricate syncretic Catholic devotion to the saints in such a system of oppositions and complementarities immediately calls into question the way in which Andean Catholicism has been written. While, to take but one example, the representations of the saints in Cuzco's Corpus Christi procession have been studied ethnologically, and while some saints are 'paired', few clues are available as to their putative 'logical' counterparts in pre-Columbian ritual; it may be that these do not exist, in which case such questions would be superfluous. However, there is one case, again within the context of the *pasos* of the saints during Corpus Christi, which points to some insertion of received saints into autochthonous dualistic categories: the day of Santiago (25 July), the feast par excellence of the colonial Inca nobility, is shared with Santa Barbara, whose nominal feast-day is 4 December.[39] Why

[39] Carol Ann Fiedler, *Corpus Christi in Cuzco: Festival and Ethnic Identity in the Peruvian Andes* (Ph.D. dissertation, Tulane University, 1985), p. 139. Note that Fiedler records 27 July as the shared Corpus day, whereas 25 July was the colonial 'day of Santiago', although 27 July was used in the early seventeenth century. This colonial change may perhaps have been due to the switch from the Julian to the Gregorian calendar, but there is no obvious explanation for the leap from 25 to 27 July in the modern period, given that 25 July remains the feast-day of Santiago generally. Note too that Santa Barbara is also 'twinned' with San Isidro in the village of Poroy on 15 May, the latter saint's feast-day: see Fiedler, p. 314.

this discrepancy? The answer seems to be that the two saints have been twinned because of their identification with thunder and lightning, as well as with warfare in Christian tradition. In one Cuzqueño community, Santiago is the patron saint of llamas, while Santa Barbara is the patron of alpacas. Recalling that Santiago is identified with Illapa, the 'thunder god', it is of interest that in another community, the feast of Santa Barbara is dedicated to Apu Qhaqha, the 'Lord of the place struck by lightning'. The 'logic' of the twinning of Santiago with Santa Barbara is manifest.[40]

The geographic location of the chapel of Nuestra Señora de Loreto is adjacent to the Jesuit Church of La Compañía, both occupying the erstwhile Amaru Cancha, site of Huayna Capac's palace. It is juxtaposed to the site of the Acllahuasi, the former 'cloister' of the so-called Virgins of the Sun, from which it is separated only by a laneway now known as the Calle Loreto. Such topographical commonplaces find an intriguing echo amongst the lands belonging to the *cofradía* of Our Lady of Loreto which, like several other colonial Jesuit confraternities, were located in the eponymous chapel. In colonial Peru, such confraternity lands were nearly always small parcels of a few *topos*, the produce of which was directed towards the upkeep of a particular saint's cult. Now, when in 1767 the Jesuit order was expelled from the empire, all its possessions and records were sequestered at the crack of dawn coeval with the seizure and transportation of the friars themselves, thereby obviating the possibility of the order's dispatching, hiding or otherwise disposing of its holdings. To this circumstance is due an apparently complete set of colonial documentation concerning the chapel and confraternities of Nuestra Señora de Loreto.[41] Less fortunately, these records tell us little about the Incaic connexion of the cult, though there are a few tantalising hints. Most notably, much in the way in which the site of the chapel abutted the erstwhile Acllahuasi, so too the *cofradía* held at least two houses in Calle Ahuacpinta, which abuts the cloister of Santo Domingo, formerly Coricancha, the Incan temple of the Sun. One of these appears to have been a 1653 donation from a devotee, the other purchased in 1673 by the mayor-

---

[40] For these associations, Michael J. Sallnow, *Pilgrims of the Andes: Regional Cults in Cusco* (Washington, D.C. and London, Smithsonian Institution Press, 1987), p. 131; Catherine J. Allen, *The Hold Life Has: Coca and Cultural Identity in an Andean Community* (Washington, D.C. and London: Smithsonian Institution Press, 1988), pp. 53, 242 n. 17.

[41] The principal Jesuit papers and subsequent administration of Jesuit properties and holdings in respect of the Cuzco area are held in several archives: The Archivo Departamental del Cuzco, the Archivo General de la Nación (Lima), the Biblioteca Nacional (Lima), the Archivo Histórico Nacional (Madrid), and the Biblioteca Nacional (Madrid). The ADC papers referring specifically to the Chapel of Loreto and its confraternities are scattered throughout the Colegio de Ciencias section; see also, Biblioteca Nacional (Madrid), MS No. 17614, 'Inventario de los papeles, títulos de haciendas, capellanías y libros del Archivo del Colegio del Noviciado de la Compañía en el Cuzco' (1767), fols 68–79, which includes accounts and a list of ornaments (none apparently Incaic) of the Chapel and image of Nuestra Señora de Loreto.

domos of the 'Cofradía de Loreto de los Mactas'.[42] The donor and both mayordomos bore Quechua surnames, but there were at other times priostes and mayordomos with Spanish surnames: e.g., in 1694 the prioste was Miguel José Gutiérrez, and the mayordomos Juan Tito Yupanqui, Juan Pilco Topa, and Juan Flórez, the *alcalde* of the guild of barbers of the city which had a formal corporative devotion to the Virgin of Loreto. There are some probable indications of noble Incan involvement: Tito Yupanqui and Pilco Topa are probably noble names, another donor bore the noble name of Cusi Rimachi. Furthermore, from at least 1595 the cofradía held lands in the nearby town of San Jerónimo, one of the two main settlements of the colonial Inca nobility, and these lands may have been a donation from the royal ayllus of Sucso and Aucaylli.[43]

However, such associations may well be no more than serendipitous. In the small city of colonial Cuzco there were Incaic resonances in almost every street and every parish. Yet the *cofradía* dimension is the key to understanding the origin of the obvious link between the Virgin of Loreto and the colonial Incas. It is revealed in a prosaic 1783 application by José Chacón y Becerra, mayordomo of the cofradía of Santiago in the city parish of Santiago, for formal 'canonical foundation' of this existing *cofradía*.[44] The connexion between Santiago and Nuestra Señora de Loreto is

---

[42] See ADC, Colegio de Ciencias, Leg. 10 (16?), cuaderno 26, 'Títulos de la Casa de Nra. Sra. de Lorteo, ubicada en Ahuacpinta, pertenece a la Cofradía de Mactas', 1660; idem, Leg. 11 (18?), cuad. 14, 'Testimonio de donación de un solar en Ahuacpinta a Nra. Sra. de Loreto, q. hace Doña Juana Payco', 1653; idem, Leg. 8 (13?), cuad. 4, 'Ahuacpinta – testimonio de Títulos de la Casa de Nra. Sra. de Loreto que tiene sus aposentos bajos en dicho barrio', 1673–1810. Note that new and old *legajo* numbers refer to a reorganisation of ADC section of the Colegio de Ciencias, which involved both division and conflation of containers (*legajos*). Unfortunately, some confusion exists as to the relation between archive catalogue and containers, and the subsequent filing of many documents; some inventoried documents are, moreover, missing. Citation of new *legajos* is therefore provisional.

[43] Ibid. Also: ADC, Colegio de Ciencias, Leg. 12 (21?), cuad. 6, 'Libro ... de las cuentas de esta Cofradía del Glorioso San Cosme y San Damian, nuevamente fundada en esta Capilla de Nra. Sra. Virgen María de Loreto ... siendo Prioste y Mayordomos don Miguel José Gutiérrez, don Juan Tito Yupanqui y don Pilco Topa, y Alcalde de los Barberos de esta dha. Cofradía don Juan Flórez ... ', 1694; idem, Leg. 11 (18?), cuad. 8, 'Testimonios y actuados relativos a la donación qe. Juan Cusirimachi hace de su casa de San Cristóbal, a favor de la Cofradía de Nra. Sra. de la Consolación, que es la de Loreto', 1640; ADC, Corregimiento, Leg. 26, cuad. 8, 'Autos ordinarios seguidos por los indios Parra. Sn. Jerónimo con Dn. Guillermo Balladeres sre. propd. 18 topos trras Oscollopampa y otros ... ', 1691. Note that this last document, and others referring to the Oscollopampa lands are at the time of writing missing from their *legajos*, possibly due to current litigation over these very lands.

[44] Archivo General de Indias, Audiencia del Cuzco, Leg. 15, 'Consejo Expediente sobre la ereccion en la Ciudad del Cuzco de una cofradía de S[a]ntiago que se intenta establecer en una Parroquia de aquella Ciudad, y aprovación de sus Constituciones', petition of José Agustín Chacón y Becerra, 1 August, 1786. ADC, Notariales: José Agustín Chacón y Becerra, Libro No. 73, 1786–87, 'Fundación de la Hermandad y Cofradia de Sor. Santiago', 20 March, 1786.

revealed in the confraternity's articles of foundation and association. The mayordomo noted that the *cofradía* would devote itself to the cult of Santiago, but also set aside several days each month for the cult of Nuestra Señora de Loreto. The simple reason for including veneration of the Virgin within the remit of the *cofradía* of Santiago stemmed, he made clear, from the mundane circumstance that the effigies of Santiago and the Virgin of Loreto were juxtaposed in a diptych held within the parish church of Santiago in the city of Cuzco. In this prosaic context, then, we find the apparent genesis of the cultic and Incaic dimensions of the simultaneous religious veneration of Santiago and the Virgin of Loreto, above all for the veneration of the Virgin by the Inca nobles, whose premier feast-day was the day of Santiago. There remains, of course, the obvious but unanswerable conundrum of which came first: did a pre-existing Incaic linking of pre-conquest counterparts of Santiago (i.e., Illapa) and the Virgin of Loreto find expression in the diptych, or was the diptych itself the origin of the cult of the Incaic Virgin? It is worth recalling here that Santiago and Santa Barbara share, shared, the former's feast-day (25 July) during the ten-week Corpus Christi celebrations in Cuzco, but that Santa Barbara's own feast-day is and was 4 December; the feast-day of Nuestra Señora de Loreto was 10 December.[45] The putative link here between Santa Barbara and the Virgin of Loreto appears to be that both had their respective feast-days in December, such that there may have been an identification of the two female saints.

Why, finally, should the Incas have celebrated precisely under the aegis of the Virgin of Loreto, and why in August? Manifestly, there is some correspondence to the pre-conquest feast of Coya Raimi, literally, the feast of the Queen. Such an identification is, of course, largely circumstantial, but to the extent that it is valid — and most of the evidence points in that direction it would provide yet further evidence of the astonishing creativity of native Andean structuralist thinking. The pre-Columbian feast of Coya Raimi is placed by Molina in August, yet according to Cobo and Guaman Poma it took place in September, while Garcilaso has Citua itself

---

[45] The feast-day of the Virgin of Loreto does not appear in either of the two colonial liturgical calendars known to me, but is mentioned in ADC, Notariales: José Agustín Chacón y Becerra, Libro No. 73, 1786 87 (see previous note). Note also (idem) that Santa Barbara shares her feast-day of 4 December with San Pedro Chrisolongo. Thus not every opposition or twinning within Andean Catholicism was necessarily inspired by Native Andean dualism. Note in this context that, in Spain, the Virgin of Loreto was specifically twinned with San Lorenzo. In Huesca, an Agustine ('calzados') 'sanctuary and convent' was built on the site of the martyr San Lorenzo's birthplace, into which was built the chapel of Nuestra Señora de Loreto: see *Diccionario de historia eclesiástica de España*, ed. Quintín Aldea Vaquero, Tomás Marín Martínez, and José Vives Gatell (Madrid: 1978), vol. IV, p. 2284.

[46] Molina, pp. 73–96 is the principal account, replete with the orations (in Quechua); Cobo, book 13, chap . XXIX, pp. 217-219; Guaman Poma, 1155 [1165]-1157 [1167]; Garcilaso, book VII, chap. VI.

commencing on 'the first day of the September moon following the equinox'.[46] This disparity, however, may be harmonised, at least ostensibly. It has to do with the correlation of the Incaic calendar with its introduced European counterpart, and, indeed, with the relationship between the latter's ecclesiastical or liturgical calendar to its agricultural counterpart. Molina, in outlining the ritual year, adverts that the Incas 'commenced to count the year in the middle of May',[47] which, extrapolating, would seem to imply that Coya Raimi commenced from approximately the middle of August to the middle of September. Were this the case, there would exist no fundamental conflict between the account of Molina and those of Cobo and Guaman Poma. The Loreto celebration of 22 August would thus fall within the Incaic parameters of Coya Raimi. The matter is of more than ephemeral interest, inasmuch as there are certain parallels between the Incaic feast of Coya Raimi and the late seventeenth century Loreto celebration, resemblances which may help explain why the latter – indeed, that specific representation of the Virgin above all others – was apparently of particular significance to the entire community of colonial Inca nobles.

First of all, however, it will be necessary to consider some alternative Catholic liturgical explanations that might have induced colonial Cuzqueños to lend particular importance to the Loreto celebrations. For colonial fiestas, however much they echoed the Incario, were not merely matters for the colonial Inca nobility, as indeed their syncretic or hybrid characteristics would seem to imply. It follows that in evaluating the significance of colonial fiestas and processions in which exotically stylised Incas appeared, these were also susceptible of explanation in terms of Hispanic Catholicism and its prevailing liturgical calendar. Two versions of the colonial liturgical calendar are available: a late colonial (1788) one which was formally ratified by the Real Audiencia of Cuzco, and that provided by Guaman Poma, which he juxtaposes month by month with its Incan homologue.[48] For September, there are only two major feasts of the Virgin (8, 24 September), neither of which appear to have any Coya Raimi resonances. By contrast, August offers the premier feast-day of the Virgin Mary in the entire Catholic world: that of her Assumption into heaven, celebrated on 15 August. Now, the octave of a feast was in colonial times of equal or greater importance to that day itself, and the octave of the Assumption fell on 22 August, precisely the day of the Incaic procession from the chapel of Loreto in Cuzco. In the light of this, then, the Virgin of Loreto becomes merely circumstantial – it is the Virgin Mary *per se* who is being venerated in this instance, not any particular representation.

[47] Molina, p. 66.

[48] 'Fiestas coloniales (Lista comprensiva de todos los días feriados y de guarda, formulado por el Secretario de Cámara, de acuerdo con lo dispuesto por el Regente y Oidores de la Real Audiencia ...)', *Revista del Archivo Histórico del Cuzco*, no. 4, 1953, pp. 169–173. Guaman Poma, 1130 [1140]–1166 [1176].

Moreover, if we accept the premise that calibration of the Incaic ritual calendar with its Catholic, European counterpart does not provide an exact fit, and also that the Incan ritual month commences at the middle of each (European) calendar month, then 22 August falls within the timespan of the celebration of Coya Raimi. Here, it is suggested, the Virgin is being equated with the Coya, an appropriation by the Inca nobles of the Catholic icon while simultaneously reworking their own heritage of Incaic ritual, memory and identity. What appears to be being celebrated is a harmonised, syncretic version of Coya Raimi and the Virgin Mary's feast *par excellence*, her Assumption into heaven.

What, then, might a celebration of a colonial version of Coya Raimi bring to devotees, apart from the way participation in the liturgy carried with it plenary or temporal indulgences for any practising Catholic. For whether saints or *apus* were being venerated, devotion paid dividends to Andean Catholics. Yet attempting to divine the practical outcomes anticipated by participants from their immersion in pre-conquest or colonial ritual is vitiated not only by the fragmentary nature of the sources but also of the innate confusion of those sources. The Incan ritual months, each embracing major and often numerous minor ritual events, are sketched only in broad by the chroniclers, who noted but a small selection of the individual ritual practices that must have inhered in the ritual cycle; as Cobo noted, 'were all these to be told, one would never finish'.[49] The chroniclers' accounts of ritual praxis, then, effectively collapse each ritual month into a few days. Such descriptions are thus little more than epitomes, in which what is left out is of as much moment as what remains. This makes it doubly difficult to compare descriptions of colonial and pre-conquest ritual life: what seem colonial novelties may be no more than pre-Columbian praxis that has been just missed or otherwise elided from the chronicles; both accounts, of course, are themselves colonial constructions, with all their attendant problems of interpretation. Moreover, residual post-conquest Incaic praxis probably did not consciously aim at recreating an entirely accurate reprise of pre-1532 ritual. Echoes, coincidences and symmetries can be unpacked, but the significance which participants and observers attached to these is the crux of the matter, and in the absence of explicit testimony it can only remain elusive.

Nevertheless, the principal *raison d'être* of Coya Raimi was the Citua ceremony, the major of two such directed towards the ritual cleansing of Cuzco, at which all *forasteros* (strangers or foreigners), the halt and the lame, those otherwise impaired, and even dogs were banished from Cuzco until such time as illness and 'pestilence' had been ritually driven and transported from the (ritually defined) city precincts. The moment marked the cyclical coming of the rains, considered as ushering in a seasonal cycle of illness, so that the ritual was directed to an eminently practical purpose.

---

[49] Cobo, book 13, chap. XXX, p. 220.

The need for such amelioration can hardly have vanished with the conquest, not least because that event brought in its train epidemics on a scale never hitherto witnessed in the Andes. Some colonial religious ceremony, syncretic or not, might have been expected at this time. The confluence of Coya Raimi, the rains, and the pre-eminent feast of the Assumption perhaps preordained that this ceremony should exhibit both a resplendent Virgin and pronounced Incaic features. Citua was a ceremony in which the entire community of Cuzco was involved, a community that extended to the ancestors, with each lineage bringing out the mummies of their 'lords and ladies' for ritual baths and ritual meals. The role of the postconquest *panacas* in the Loreto procession springs to mind here, with the oddity of their dancing attendance on the Ayarmaca *alcalde mayor de los ingas* – with whom they had for years been locked in litigation – perhaps partly due to the mandatory inclusiveness of the pre-conquest Coya Raimi. Whatever their dispute with the colonial Ayarmaca descendants, the necessity for *all* the community to participate may have militated against their withdrawl or possible holding of an alternative ceremony. In any case, all the *panacas* were present on both occasions, and the emphasis placed on the magnificence of Sicos Inga's costume ('de gala muy lucida y costoso') recalls a similar emphasis on dress in the chroniclers' descriptions of Coya Raimi: 'the Inca as well as the priests, caballeros and ordinary folk came out wearing the best ('las mejores galas') they had'; 'the entire populace of Cuzco came out by ayllu and *parcialidad,* which came the most richly dressed that it could'.[50]

Coya Raimi had been more than a communal purification rite. It was a gathering of the gods. It also featured the sacrifice of a woman to the Sun, and the appearance of two female dieties described as 'the women/wives of the Sun'. The Inca with his wife and 'courtiers of his Council' – again, 'the most richly dressed they could be' – entered the main plaza. Then, the image of the Sun, *Apinpunchao,* was simultaneously brought to the plaza, together with the Sun priests bearing 'the two images of gold, [the Sun]'s women/wives called *Yncacollo* and *Palpacollo*'. Then, a most singular moment occurred, when 'the woman named Coyapacssa, who was sacrificed as a woman of the Sun' entered the plaza. Molina's description tells us nothing more of her other than the cryptic remark that she was 'sister, daughter of he who governed'. Neither Guaman Poma nor Cobo, who follows Molina, records this sacrifice, but there is a strong presumption that it was not merely symbolic. A female sacrifice to the Sun in the main plaza, however, was a vivid vignette that can hardly have been forgotten until long after the conquest; its ritual function presumably related to Citua and the commencement of a new phase in the agricultural cycle.[51]

---

[50] Molina, p. 78; Cobo, book 13, chap. XXIX, p. 218.
[51] Molina, pp. 76–78.

The next phase of this surpassing ritual was devoted to a communal feast of the gods, in which the principal deities, the Sun, Wiracocha, Chiquiylla (Illapa), and Huanacauri sat on their golden benches in the plaza. Then came the mummies of the former Inca rulers and their Coyas, and they too were placed on golden seats ('as if they were alive') in chronological order. These were brought out by their respective *panacas*. Finally, the rest of the city population came and they too were seated according to moiety: *Hanancuzcos* and *Hurincuzcos*. The priests of the four deities drank with one another, and the mummies themselves 'drank' with one another, those of one moiety with the other. The eating and drinking, all of it ritually significant, involved the entire urban congregation. Coyaraimi embraced, then, the Sapa Inca with all of the principal gods, all of the *panacas* or noble descendants, and all who belonged to the two great moieties. It was remarkable for the presence of the two 'wives' of the Sun, and especially for the sacrifice of the Coyapacssa to the Sun.

Transcending the relevance of Coya Raimi and Citua for the Cuzco community was its extension to the entire subject population of the empire and its local and imposed Incan governing cadres. Coya Raimi ritually integrated the four quarters of Tahuantinsuyu with Cuzco, and vice versa; not only Cuzco but the entire empire also was ritually cleansed. As Molina put it, 'in all provincial capitals, all the Inca governors observed the feast', and notwithstanding that such provincial rituals were on a much reduced scale, they did not 'exclude any of the ceremonies'.[52] Participation by imperial subjects came in two forms. The first was the massing of (according to Molina's informants) 100,000 sacrificial cameloids 'of every type', all of which were to be free from blemish, gathered from the four *suyus*. This extraordinary scene, however, was rather an overture to a more spectacular participation by imperial subjects. First, the female deities of Moon ('Luna') and Pachamama ('Tierra') took their place alongside the male gods – the Sun, Illapa, Viracocha, and Huanacauri – such that, with the presence of the 'wives of the Sun', Incaocclo and Palpaocclo, there was established a prefect gender symmetry of four male to four female deities. Once that had been set in place, there came 'all the nations that the Inca had subjugated, which came with their deities (*huacas*) and their customary costumes, as fine as they could be; and their priests brought their deities in litters'.[53] There, they paid homage to the four principal deities and then to the Inca. Finally, those who had been exiled from Cuzco prior to the commencement of Citua, the halt and the lame, were admitted to the Cuzqueño and imperial communities once more. Thus was the circle closed.

The Loreto procession was remarkable not merely for its Incan insignia, raiment and symbolism. Quite as striking is the apparent appropriation by

[52] Ibid., p. 96.
[53] Ibid., p. 94.

the colonial Inca nobility of the *cofradía* 'format' to celebrate what appears to be a symbolic gesture towards the quondam feast of Coya Raimi and the all-important Citua rites. There is certainly no re-enactment as such of Coya Raimi, and indeed such an identification must remain hypothetical given the lack of precise testimony on this point. There is, though, a strong presumption that this was the case. The massed descendants of the former Inca rulers (and perhaps Incas-by-privilege) had their own ceremonial framework in the Twenty-four Electors, yet they still needed a meaningful occasion in which to marshall their numbers for ritual praxis. Clearly, the octave of the surpassing Marian feast of the Assumption is one such occasion, and its contiguity with that of Coya Raimi can hardly have been overlooked by the colonial Incas who, we know from other sources, had a keen sense of their Incan past expressed as a group memory: Coricancha, the Plaza de Armas itself, the site of the Chapel of Loreto, indeed the city itself, were all *lieux de mémoire* of this anachronistic and slowly-disappearing nobility. There are of course other associations to be made, quite apart from comparisons of the notarial description of the Loreto procession with the chroniclers' renderings of Inca Cuzco and its religious calendar, of Coya Raimi and the Assumption. There are numerous puzzles to disentrail and decipher: Incan and Spanish elements and meanings of the armorial bearings; the posited dualisms between Santiago and the Virgin of Loreto, between Santiago and Santa Barbara, and between the latter and the Virgin of Loreto; the mythical and historical (in the Western sense) dimensions of the figure(s) of Gran Tocay Capac Inga Rey Señor; the comparison between pre-1532 *panacas* and their ostensible colonial homologues; and so forth. Yet the very existence of these problems, this problematic, points once again to the validity of colonial Inca culture. To judge from the asseverations of Bishop Moscoso, Ignacio de Castro and other colonial pundits, there were many occasions on which the Inca nobles sallied forth in full finery. The Loreto procession is merely one of these, but descriptions of such *res gestae* combined with the numerous colonial testimonies of the nobles themselves are likely to cast a great deal of new light on pre-conquest Inca society and culture, and not least remind us once again that the defeated Inca elites retained a great deal of their group, individual and cultural integrity until long after the Spanish conquest.

# CHAPTER TWELVE

# Conclusion

Yet it might be argued that the paradoxes, ironies, exemptions and privileges which Inca nobles had to negotiate were innate to the colonial condition, wherein the identities and status of colonised indigenous elites were rendered at best contingent and at worst anachronistic, and which might even disappear overnight should a colonial official high-handedly decide not to accept documentary proof of noble status. A descendant of Inca emperors might, as a result of such a stroke of the quill, be consigned to the ranks of the tributaries, and neither he nor his descendants might ever be able to climb back to noble ranks. Such social death was contingent upon the vagaries of State census categories and fiscal imperatives, but even so, downward mobility often took place by degrees, through an inter-generational erosion of family fortunes, which were usually meagre in the case of the colonial Inca noblility. This could hardly apply to elites who were an integral part of a ruling class. Indeed, there was clearly a disjunction between the colonial Inca nobility's very lack of power, and the status and prestige to which it laid claim. If on one level they sought to present, in the institution of the Twenty-four Electors of the *Alférez Real*, a united front to the world, the existence of countervailing claims to noble privilege by elite groups such as the Ayarmaca can only have diluted the Electors' claim to represent the indigenous nobility. Clearly, there were multiple indigenous nobilities, *de facto* and *de jure*: besides the Ayarmaca, there were the inveterate post-conquest enemies of the Incas, the Cañaris, and even the numerous erstwhile 'incas de privilegio' in provinces such as Paruro. Beyond these lay a regional network of many hundreds of caciques who often outstripped the Inca nobles in wealth, authority and power, for all that there was some overlap between the two groups.[1]

---

[1] Their numbers and distribution are best seen in the viceregal census of 1754: Manuel A. Fuentes (ed.), *Memorias de los virreyes que han gobernado el Perú* (6 vols, Lima: 1859), vol. IV, anexo pp. 2–15. See also Alfredo Moreno Cebrián (ed.), *Relación y documentos de gobierno del virrey del Perú, José A. Manso de Velasco, Conde de Superunda (1745–1761)* (Madrid: Instituto 'Gonzalo Fernández de Oviedo', CSIC, 1983), pp. 241–247. In the fourteen provinces corresponding to the Diocese of Cuzco (including three of the five provinces in the Puno region), there were 639 'caciques y principales'; of these, only 29 are registered for the Cercado of

The fault-lines in this uppermost stratum of indigenous society are most manifest in the ceremonial context, for it is there that annual decisions had to be made concerning precedence and protocol, above all in the election of the indigenous *alférez real*. Such concerns were of much moment in both native Andean society and Early Modern Hispanic society generally, for they were significant pointers and determinants of honour; and honour was quite as important as wealth – at least in the short run – in calibrating one's place in the colonial social order.[2] Throughout the colonial period, the descendants of the twelve Incan 'houses' fought to retain the exclusive right to wear the *mascapaicha*, talisman of 'Incanhood', and the frantic tone, almost panic, in which they did so was a distillation of this crucial struggle to maintain the integrity of colonial Incan ranks. It was probably more: the passion with which the colonial Inca denounced attempts by other indigenous elites to don the 'borla colorada' may also point to a concern with ritual purity, with a concern to avoid ritual defilement or pollution. For we can only guess at the meaning of the colonial Inca figure in ceremonial mode. Processions, as a trawl through Esquivel y Navia's Annals of Colonial Cuzco will indicate, were almost quotidian features of colonial life, and each bore its own particular meaning. There is good reason to think, in the light of cultural, religious and lexical identifications between the Inca, Santiago, Illapa, the Sun and other symbolism on display during the great processions, that such rituals amounted to much more than folklore in the minds of native Andean participants and onlookers, whatever other social and racial groups might have thought they were witnessing. The phenomenology of these processions, taken together with the organisation of the twelve Incaic 'houses' for the express purpose of choosing the standard bearer for the 'day and eve of Santiago', and their fierce rejection of interlopers, would indicate that the colonial Inca nobility read a deep meaning into the involvement of one of their number as *alférez real* at Corpus. It is possible, if not provable on present evidence, that the Incan representative was regarded as having entered into some intermediate, liminal state for the duration

Cuzco, indicating that nobles were, for all intents and purposes, largely excluded *as nobles* from that category in the 1754 census.

[2] The crucial question of honour in relation to social stratification is central to the argument in Patricia Seed, *To Love, Honor, and Obey in Colonial Mexico: Conflicts over Marriage Choice, 1574–1821* (Stanford: Stanford UP, 1988); See also José Antonio Maravall, *Poder, honor y elites en el siglo XVII* (Madrid: Siglo Veintiuno, 1979); Elena Postigo Castellanos, *Honor y privilegio en la corona de Castilla. El Consejo de las Ordenes y los Caballeros de Hábito en el siglo XVII* (Almazán (Soria), Junta de Castilla y León, 1988). A rise or decline in wealth might not be reflected in an individual's calibration in the colonial social order for one or more generations – pungently expressed in the *refrán*, '*padre comerciante, hijo caballero, nieto pordiosero*' – for which see, Magnus Mörner, 'Economic Factors and Stratification in Colonial Spanish America with Special Regard to Elites', *Hispanic American Historical Review*, vol. 63, no. 2, 1983, pp. 335–369.

of the Corpus procession.[3] During that moment, at any rate, the Incan *alférez real* achieved parity with the *alférez real de los españoles*.

The political meaning and ramifications of ritual involvement and Incaic symbolism, again, may only be guessed at. On one level it may be read as acceptance of the colonial regime, yet on another it may be seen as a seed-bed of subversion, a platform for the emergence of radical political movements, whether of millenial, nativist or merely secular tendency. It was probably subversive *ipso facto*, in that it kept alive not only the memory, but also the possibility of some future, alternative and Inca-based order, one that could only have been seen as fairer than the existing colonial order. It was the politics of *l'imaginaire*.[4] Such, indeed, was the thrust of the concerns of Bishop Moscoso and Visitor-General Joseph Antonio de Areche. The Incan ritual dimension was also a font from which Creole malcontents drew inspiration for their own separatist dreams and agendas. Even at the most banal level of local law and order, it was a worry for officialdom, which was only too aware that during such festivals 'there might be a "switching of codes", from the language of ritual to the language of rebellion'.[5] A great festive occasion such as Corpus Christi, much like carnival in early Modern Europe, could 'evolve so that it can act both to reinforce order and to suggest alternatives to the existing order'.[6]

---

[3] A theoretical discussion of liminality would exceed the bounds of this study. It was coined by Arnold Van Gennep, *The Rites of Passage* (trans. Monika B. Vizedom and Gabrielle L. Caffee, London: Routledge and Keegan Paul, 1960 [1908]). The notion was especially taken up by Victor Turner, *The Ritual Process: Structure and Anti-Structure* (London: Routledge and Kegan Paul, 1969), notably in connexion with Turner's own controversial concept of 'comunitas', for which see pp. 94–165. See also idem, 'Variations on a Theme of Liminality', in Sally F. Moore and Barbara G. Myerhoff, *Secular Ritual* (Assen/Amsterdam: Van Gorcum, 1977), pp. 36–52; idem, *The Forest of Symbols: Aspects of Ndembu Ritual* (Ithaca and London: Cornell UP, 1967), pp. 93–111. A useful summary of liminality is Michael D. Bristol. *Carnival and Theater: Plebeian Culture and the Structure of Authority in Renaissance England* (New York and London: Routledge, 1985), pp. 29–39. More generally, see Edward Muir, *Ritual in Early Modern Europe* (Cambridge, Cambridge UP, 1997).

[4] The allusion here is to Benedict Anderson, *Imagined Communities: Reflections on the Origin and Spread of Nationalism* (London and New York: Verso, rev. edn, 1991); Serge Gruzinski, *La colonisation de l'imaginaire. Sociétés indigènes et occidentalisation dans le Mexique espagnol XVI-XVIII siècle* (Paris: Gallimard, 1988). For discussion in the Peruvian context, see: Cecilia Méndez, 'República sin indios: La comunidad imaginada del Perú', in *Tradición y modernidad en los Andes*, ed. Henrique Urbano (Cuzco: Centro de Estudios Regionales Andinos 'Bartolomé de Las Casas', 1997), pp. 15–41; Mark Thurner, *From Two Republics to One Divided: Contradictions of Postcolonial Nationmaking in Andean Peru* (Durham and London: Duke UP, 1997), esp. chap. 2 ('Unimagined Communities').

[5] Peter Burke, *Popular Culture in Early Modern Europe* (London: Temple Smith, 1978), p. 203.

[6] Natalie Zemon Davis, 'The Reasons of Misrule', in idem, *Society and Culture in Early Modern Europe* (Oxford: Polity Press, 1987 [1965]), p. 123. See also the formulation of Robert Muchembled, *Popular Culture and Elite Culture in France 1400-1750*, trans. Lydia Cochrane (Baton Rouge and London: Louisiana State UP, 1985 [1978]), pp. 126–127, that fiestas 'might

Yet whatever the political import of such ritual parity, it is clear that these grand religious and cultural occasions were the principal public conduit for the retention, maintenance and reaffirmation – in a word, 'reivindicación' – of colonial Incaic culture and identity. The symbolism, extraordinarily 'pagan' at first sight, was nevertheless reproduced under the aegis of the Jesuits, at least in the case of the 1610 and 1692 festivities. The kinship links between the colonial Incas and St. Ignatius helps explain ecclesiastical imprimatur in those two cases, but that the context was far broader will be obvious from the Church's indulgence of the same kind of out-and-out Incaic symbolism during the Corpus cycle. Yet to remark the 'pagan' elements of these processions is not necessarily to imply that the overarching liturgical form was merely cover for a celebration of atavistic, pre-conquest religion. Tristan Platt has argued that the syncretic popular religion in present-day Bolivia is more or less the finished product, rather than representing an early stage in the conversion process and that it is no less Christian for all the 'pagan' elements that it so unequivocally contains; he contends that the native Andean elements of Corpus Christi in highland Bolivia are indispensable to the fiesta's Christian character, rather than subversive of it.[7] It is worth noting in this context that it was crown officials, and not the clergy, who, in the wake of the Túpac Amaru rebellion, first voiced concern at the deleterious effects of Incaic imagery. Moscoso's broadside against such symbolism was made only in response to Areche's request, and was partly a product of Moscoso's attempt to defend himself against charges that he had knowingly or unwittingly provoked the rebellion; it was in his interest to portray the rebellion as the inevitable outcome of the persistence of Inca culture. Yet, in the final analysis, examination of such festivals does add weight to the view, first expressed by John Rowe, that colonial Inca culture, while it exhibited syncretic features, was nevertheless 'genuine' Inca culture rather than just folkloric colour; it was a post-conquest continuation of Incaic belief, custom and praxis.[8] As such, it was pregnant with potential for subversion – the Incan past as future.

The 1692 procession of Nuestra Señora de Loreto was not so much syncretic as anachronistic in its central Incan symbolism and Inca noble participation, which all but occluded its Christian dimension to a degree never attained by the colonial Corpus Christi processions. Casual observers may have viewed it as a kind of moving tableau or diorama, folklorically instructive. For the Incan nobles, it obviously held a deeper significance, at the very least a mixture of history, collective memory and myth that

easily end in a challenge to established values that took place in a dream time and unfenced space'.

[7] Tristan Platt, 'The Andean Soldiers of Christ: Confraternity Organisation, the Mass of the Sun, and Regenerative Warfare in Rural Potosí (18th–20th Centuries)', *Journal de la Société des Américanistes*, vol. 73, 1987, pp. 139–192.

[8] Rowe, 'El movimiento inca nacional'.

underlay their special plea for their interpolation and calibration in the
ranks of the colonial elites, rather than as the downwardly mobile social
curiosities they were sometimes considered to be by their contemporaries
(and, following them, by some modern scholars). Here it is worth noting,
also parenthetically, the increasing scholarly interest in rescuing the colonial Inca nobles from the enormous condescension of posterity, in
E. P. Thompson's useful phrase. Their struggle throughout three centuries
of colonial rule to maintain the respect they felt to be their due, was
necessarily grounded in their pre-Columbian past and its reiterated re-
membrance in popular culture and popular religious display, but the
nobility perforce had also to stake a claim in Hispanic terms. Thus their
need – though there is no real reason to judge it cynical – for their
integration in Catholic, public religious celebrations; to align their erstwhile
*panaca* structures to Spanish corporatist institutions such *cabildo* and confraternity; to insert themselves in a Western historical framework; and,
finally, to identify themselves with the classical tradition in which ideological structures of the Spanish state were steeped. If Spanish and Creole
elites sometimes looked askance at the Incas' boast of nobility, then the
imprimatur of ecclesiastical authority could lend weight to their social
pretensions. As the case of Sicos Inga demonstrates, ritual affirmation in
the context of the celebration of a mass buttressed the link between Incan
nobility and *hidalguía*, indispensable for their claim to special status, and
which they insisted was a cipher of the colonial pact from at least the time
of the Emperor Charles V.

Arguing for the existence of this cipher and defending it against doubting
officials, peninsular and Creole, was a surpassing passion of the colonial
Inca nobles of Cuzco. Much of the relevance of their parading in Incaic
regalia and costume turned on this point, as they ceremonially mingled
with non-indigenous, civil and ecclesiastical office-holders, aristocrats and
other *hombres de bien*. Above all, their claim to elite status was publicly
highlighted when their representative, the *alférez real de los ingas*, paced
the Corpus Christi route side by side with his Hispanic homologue. This,
if perhaps merely a dash of folkloric colour for non-indigenous participants
and observers, was an accurate reflection of what might be called a group
*imaginaire*: it was a metaphor of the prestige to which the Inca nobles laid
claim, a level of equality of status which pointed to a fervently desired
harmonisation and reconciliation of Incaic and Hispanic elites. This wish
for a reconciliation of the colonial condition is expressed not only in ritual
context but also in the *probanzas de nobleza* and sundry protestations of
noble status. The case they made rested on a mixture of myth, memory
and (comparative) history through which they hoped to buttress their
claims, a mixture crucial to their individual and group identity. Logically,
however, reconciliation could only be fully realised via an end to the
colonial condition, to the colonial master and servant relationship. It was
precisely this alternative 'imagining' that, in the late colonial period, would

draw the attention of disaffected Creoles to the possibility of a post-colonial polity featuring an Incan head of State, a cultural veneer for an imagined community firmly under the heel of a Creole elite that had displaced its peninsular counterpart. It was in the notion of an Incaic future that Creole and Incaic 'imaginings' neatly dovetailed, for all that they anticipated different outcomes. In the seventeenth century, however, after the failure of the Vilcabamba resistance and the nativist Taqui Onqoy and Mori Onqoy movements, an Incaic 'future past' was neither feasible nor rational. Then, the Inca nobility's own 'imagining' was directed solely to the survival of its group identity, and their pretensions were best expressed in the public domain through their continued use of the raiments and regalia of the past in the colonial present.

APPENDIX I


## List of works and documents in English relating to Peru*

George Abbot, *A Briefe Description of the Whole Worlde* (London: 1599, *1608).

Acarete du Biscay, *Relation des voyages du sieur ... dans la rivière de la Plate, et de là par terre au Pérou* (Paris: 1696).

*An Account of a Voyage up the River de la Plata, and thence over Land to Peru*, in *Voyages and Discoveries in South America* (London: 1698).

José de Acosta, *Historia natural y moral de las Indias* (Barcelona: 1591).

——, *The Naturall and Morall History of the East and West Indies* (London: 1604).

Cristóbal de Acuña, *Nuevo descubrimiento del gran río de las Amazonas* (Madrid: 1641).

——, *An Historical and Geographical Description of the Great Country and River of the Amazones in America* (London: 1661), and in *Voyages and Discoveries in South America* (London: 1698).

Philip Ayres, *The Voyages and Adventures of Capt. Bartholomew Sharp* (London: 1684).

Alvaro Alonso Barba, *Arte de los metales* (Madrid: 1640).

——, *The First Book of the Art of Mettals, The Second Book of the Art of Mettals* (London: 1669).

Roger Barlow, *A Briefe Summe of Geographie*, ed. Eva G. R. Taylor (Hakluyt Society, 2nd series, vol. 69, London: 1932).

Willem Janszoon Blaeu, *Theatrum orbis terrarum sive Atlas novus* (Amsterdam: 1635–55).

Richard Blome, *A Geographical Description of the Four Parts of the World* (London: 1670).

Edmund Bohun, *A Geographical Dictionary ... of all the Countries, Provinces ... of the Whole World* (London: 1688).

Giovanni Botero, *Le relationi universali* (Rome: 1591).

——, *The Travellers Breviat, or an Historical Description of the Most Famous Kingdomes in the World* (London: 1601).

Pedro Cieza de León, *Parte primera de la chrónica del Perú* (Seville: 1553).

——, *The 17 Years Travels of Peter de Cieza through the Mighty Kingdom of Peru*, in *A New Collection of Voyages and Travels*, ed. John Stevens (London: 1708–10).

Samuel Clarke, *A Geographical Description of all the Countries in the Knowne World* (London: 1657).

William Dampier, *A New Voyage round the World* (London: 1697).

——, *Dampier's Voyages*, ed. John Masefield (2 vols, London: 1906), vol. 1.

William Davenant, *The Cruelty of the Spaniards in Peru* (London: 1658).

* Indicates the edition cited in Part I where more than one appears in the Appendix.

John Dryden, *The Indian Queen* (London: 1665).

Pierre Duval, *Le monde, ou la Géographie universelle* (Paris: 1670).

———, *Geographia Universalis. The Present State of the Whole World* (London: 1685).

Richard Eden, *The Decades of the Newe Worlde or West India* (London: 1555).

———, *The History of Travayle in the West and East Indies*, ed. Richard Willes (London: 1577).

———, *A Treatyse of the Newe India ... after the Descripcion of Sebastian Münster* (London: 1553).

Alexander O. Exquemelin, *De Americaensche Zee-rovers* (Amsterdam: 1678).

———, *Bucaniers of America* (London: 1684, *1685).

Robert Fage, *Cosmography, or a Description of the Whole World* (London: 1658).

Martín Fernández de Enciso, *Suma de geographia* (Seville: 1519).

———, *A Briefe Description of the Portes, Creekes, Bayes, and Havens, of the Weast India* (London: 1578).

Francis Fletcher, *The World Encompassed by Sir Francis Drake* (London: 1628); *ed. W. S. W. Vaux (Hakluyt Society, 1st series, vol. 16, London: 1854).

François Froger, *Relation d'un voyage fait en 1695, 1696 et 1697 aux côtes d'Afrique, détroit de Magellan, Brésil, Cayenne et îles Antilles* (Paris: 1698).

———, *A Relation of a Voyage to the Coasts of Africa, Streights of Magellan, Brasil, Cayenna, and the Antilles* (London: 1698).

Garcilaso de la Vega, *Historia general del Perú* (Córdoba: 1617).

———, *Primera parte de los comentarios reales* (Lisbon: 1609).

———, *The Royal Commentaries of Peru* (London: 1688).

George Gardyner, *Description of the New World, or America Islands and Continent* (London: 1650).

Humphrey Gilbert, *A Discourse of a Discoverie for a New Passage to Cataia* (London: 1576).

Ferdinando Gorges, *America Painted to the Life* (London: 1659).

William Hacke, *A Collection of Original Voyages* (London: 1699).

Richard Hakluyt, *A Discourse of the Commodity of the taking of the Straight of Magellanus* (London: 1579–80)

———, 'Discourse of Western Planting' [1584], and various 'Notes', in *The Original Writings and Correspondence of the two Richard Hakluyts*, ed. Eva G. R. Taylor (Hakluyt Society, 2nd series, vols 76 and 77, London: 1935).

———, *Divers Voyages touching the Discoverie of America, and the Islands adjacent to the same* (London: 1582).

———, *The Principall Navigations, Voiages and Discoveries of the English Nation* (London: 1589).

———, *The Principal Navigations, Voyages, Traffiques, and Discoveries of the English Nation* (London: 1598–1600, and *London: Dent, 1927–28).

Richard Hawkins, *The Observations of Sir Richard Hawkins Knight, in his Voiage into the South Sea, 1593* (London: 1622), in *The Hawkins' Voyages*, ed. Clements R. Markham (Hakluyt Society, 1st series, vol. 57, London: 1877).

Johannes de Laet, *Nieuwe Wereldt ofte beschrijvinghe van West Indien* (Leiden: 1625).

Bartolomé de las Casas, *Brevísima relación de la destrucción de las Indias* (Seville: 1552).

——, *The Spanish Colonie, or Briefe Chronicle of the Acts and Gestes of the Spaniardes in the West Indies* (London: 1583).

Jacques l'Hermite, *A True Relation of the Fleete which went under the Admirall Jaquis Le Hermite through the Straight of Magellane* (London: 1625).

Jan H. van Linschoten, *Itinerario, voyage ofte schipvaert, van J. H. van Linschoten, naer Oost ofte Portugaels Indien* (Amsterdam: 1596).

——, *John Huighen van Linschoten, His Discours of Voyages into ye East and West Indies* (London: 1598).

Francisco López de Gómara, *La historia de las Indias y conquista de México* (Saragossa: 1552).

——, *The Pleasant Historie of the Conquest of Weast India, now called New Spayne* (London: 1578).

Cristóbal de Mena, *La conquista del Perú* (Seville: 1534).

Gerard Mercator, *Atlas, sive cosmographicae meditationes de fabrica mundi* (3 parts, Duisberg: 1585, 1589, 1595).

——, *Historia Mundi: or Mercator's Atlas*, ed. Jodocus Hondius (London: 1635).

Robert Morden, *Geography Rectified: Or, a Description of the World* (London: 1688).

Sebastian Münster, *Cosmographei oder beschreibung aller Lander* (Basle: 1544).

——, *A Treatyse of the Newe India*, ed. Richard Eden (London: 1553).

N. N., *America: or an Exact Description of the West Indies* (London: 1655).

John Narborough, *An Account of Several Late Voyages and Discoveries. A Journal kept by Sir John Narborough* (London: 1694).

John Ogilby, *America: Being the Latest and Most Accurate Description of the New World* (London: 1671).

Pedro Ordóñez de Cevallos, *Viage del mundo* (Madrid: 1614).

Abraham Ortelius, *Theatrum orbis terrarum* (Antwerp: 1570).

——, *The Theatre of the Whole World* (London: 1606).

Alonso de Ovalle, *Histórica relación del reyno de Chile* (Rome: 1646).

——, *An Historical Relation of the Kingdom of Chile*, in *A Collection of Voyages and Travels*, ed. Awnsham and John Churchill (4 vols, London: 1706), vol. III, pp. 1–154.

Gonzalo F. de Oviedo y Valdés, *La historia general de las Indias* (Seville: 1535).

Samuel Purchas, *Hakluytus Posthumus or Purchas his Pilgrimes* (London: 1625).

Raveneau de Lussan, *Journal du voyage fait à la Mer du Sud* (Paris: 1689).

——, *Journal of a Voyage to the South Sea* (London: 1699).

Willem Schouten, *Journal ofte beschrijvinghe van der wonderlicke reyse* (Amsterdam: 1618).

——, *The Relation of a Wonderful Voiage* (London: 1619).

Robert Stafforde, *A Geographical and Anthologicall Description of all the Empires and Kingdomes ... of this Terrestrial Globe* (London: 1618).

André Thevet, *Les singularitez de la France Antarctique* (Paris: 1557).

——, *The New Found Worlde, or Antarctike* (London: 1568).

Lionel Wafer, *A New Voyage and Description of the Isthmus of America* (London: 1699), *ed. L. E. Elliot Joyce (Hakluyt Society, 2nd series, vol. 73, Oxford: 1934).

William Waller, *An Essay on the Value of Mines* (London: 1698).

Cornelis Wytfliet, *Descriptionis Ptolemaicae augmentum* (Louvain: 1597).

Francisco de Xerez, *Verdadera relación de la conquista del Perú y provincia del Cusco* (Seville: 1534).

Agustín de Zárate, *Historia del descubrimiento y conquista del Perú* (Antwerp: 1555).

——, *The Strange and Delectable History of the Discoverie and Conquest of the Provinces of Peru* (London: 1581).

## Standard bibliographical sources relevant to the period

Antony F. Allison, *English Translations from the Spanish and Portuguese to 1700* (Folkestone: Dawsons, 1974).

Antony F. Allison and Valentine F. Goldsmith, *Titles of English Books (and of Foreign Books Printed in English): An Alphabetical Finding List* (Folkestone: Dawsons, 1976–77).

Frederick N. W. Bateson, (ed.). *The Cambridge Bibliography of English Literature* (Cambridge: Cambridge UP, 1940 and 1957), vols. 1, 2 and 5.

Henry S. Bennett, *English Books and Readers 1475–1557, being a Study in the History of the Book Trade* (Cambridge: Cambridge UP, 1952), also *1558–1603* and *1603–1640* (1965 and 1970).

George W. Cole, *A Catalogue of Books relating to the Discovery and Early History of North and South America forming a Part of the Library of E. D. Church* (5 vols, New York: 1907).

Edward G. Cox, *A Reference Guide to the Literature of Travel* (Seattle: Washington UP, 1935–38), vols 1 and 2.

Valentine F. Goldsmith, (ed). *A Short Title Catalogue of Spanish and Portuguese Books (1601–1700) in the Library of the British Museum* (London: Dawsons, 1974).

Remigio Ugo Pane, *English Translations from the Spanish (1484–1943): A Bibliography* (New Brunswick: Rutgers UP, 1944).

John Parker, *Books to Build an Empire: A Bibliographical History of English Overseas Interests to 1620* (Amsterdam: N. Israel, 1965).

Alfred W. Pollard and G. R. Redgrave, *A Short Title Catalogue of Books printed in England, Scotland and Ireland ... 1475–1640* (London: Bibliographical Society, 1926).

Joseph Sabin, *A Dictionary of Books relating to America* (29 vols, New York: Bibliographical Society of America, 1868–92).

Colin Steele, *English Interpreters of the Iberian New World (1603–1726)* (Oxford: Dolphin, 1975).

Henry Stevens, *Catalogue of the American Books in the Library of the British Museum at Xmas MDCCCLVI* (London: Whittingham, 1866).

Henry Thomas, *Short-Title Catalogue of Books printed in Spain and of Spanish Books printed elsewhere in Europe before 1601 now in the British Museum* (London: Oxford UP, 1921).

——, *Short-Title Catalogue of Spanish American Books printed before 1601 now in the British Museum* (London: British Museum, 1944).

George Watson, (ed.), *The New Cambridge Bibliography of English Literature* (Cambridge: Cambridge UP, 1974), vols 1 and 2.

Alva Curtis Wilgus, *The Historiography of Latin America* (Metuchen: Scarecrow, 1975).

Donald Wing, *A Short-Title Catalogue of Books printed in England, Scotland, Ireland, Wales and British America . . . 1641–1700* (3 vols, New York: Index Society, 1945–51 and 1972).

## Relación de la Fiesta, 1610 [1]

Animados los naturales desta ciudad con lo que auian visto en los Españoles, y desseosos de acudir a pagar en algo la voluntad conque los padres de la Compañia les acuden y tambien desseosos de cumplir la del Corregidor, hizieron vnas soleníssimas fiestas, y dexando, (por ser sabido) el numero destos indios, que es de treinta mil sin niños y mujeres, y la mas calificada gente de todo este Reyno, por ser este el asiento de los Ingas, en quienes ha quedado la memoria de las cosas mas memorables, &. Comenzaré las fiestas por las espirituales a que dieron principio el lunes del quarto Domingo de Pascua.

Concertaronse las seis parochias desta ciudad y dos de fuera della para venir por su antigüedad cada una a la Iglesia de la Compañia de Jesus en procesion, y tener en ella Missa cantada, y sermon, con lo demas que se dira, lo comun en estas procesiones fue venir por medio de la ciudad con muchas Cruzes, pendones, danzas, musica, y muy galanes los Indios principales, y al fin de la procesion el cura de la parochia, y el cacique principal trahian differentes inuenciones, con que se tirauan la gentes, celebrauase la Missa a las diez a canto de organo, con diversos instrumentos de musica, y se les predicaua en su lengua.

Lo particular fue que el Lunes dicho uino la parochia de Bethlen, illustrando la procesion todos los Ingas della nietos y descendientes de los Atuncuzcos muy galanes, recibiose en la Compañia con repiques de campanas y musica. El Martes vino la parochia de Sanctiago cantando el golpe de la gente canciones en loor del Sancto, venian muy vistosos a su vsanza, y cantauan vnas chanzonetas de cierta ave negra, llamada Curiquenque preciada entre ellos ... [original torn] ... color y propiedades buenas al Sancto y habito de su Religion. Entró el Miercoles la Parochia del Hospital, de los naturales con grande estruendo de danzas y musica &. haziendo un recozijo que se vsaua en tiempos del Inga Huaynacapac, mudado a lo diuino en loor del Sancto, esta precesion reciuió la cofradia de Jesus, que esta en la Compañia sacando su niño Jesus en habito de Inga, uiuamente aderezado, y con muchas luces. Viernes acudio la Parochia de San Christoual, a donde estan reducidas dos casas ilustres de Ingas, vinieron con gran magestad, y vltra de la musica y demas aparato; llevaron algunas danzas muy vistosas. Sabado entro la parochia de San Blas en que uenian

[1] Source: Carlos A. Romero (ed.), 'Festividades del tiempo heroico del Cuzco', *Inca*, vol. I, no. 2, 1923, pp. 447–454.

dos Reyes Ingas, llevauan cierta inuencion que significava vna vitoria que
sus antepasados ganaron en vna insigne batalla, aplicando el canto al Sancto
las aclamaciones que hizieron al capitan general que consiguio aquella
vitoria, acompañando esto caxas, clarines y otros instrumentos belicos. El
Domingo, que fue el dia de la fiesta de los Vizcaynos vino la parochia de
Santa Anna poco antes de la Missa mayor, entro la procession por la plaza
que estaua llena de Españoles, metio delante trezientos soldados cañares,
armados de picas, alabardas y muchos arcabuzes, y muy bien vestidos,
sitiaron en la placa vn castillo que trahian, combatieronlo haziendo sus
escaramuzas al son de las caxas, no entro la procession en la Iglesia, por
estar llena de Españoles, y ser estos mas de cinco mil Indios, y assi se les
predico en la plaza. El lunes vinieron los del pueblo de San Sebastian,
que esta media legua desta ciudad, y esforzaronse a hazer vna solene fiesta
por la competencia comun, hizieron vna muy buena procesion llena de
bultos de sanctos en sus andas, pendones, &. y al fin della sus dos caciques
principales descendientes de Ingas, lleuauan delante quatro hombres de
armas vestidos de colorado con vnas hastas de plumeria en que yuan las
armas de los dos caciques, que eran la borla del Inga, y dos culebras con
vn castillo, vuo mucho que ver en esta procession por la diuersidad de
danzas e inuenciones, rematose con su Missa y sermon que se acauó a la
vna de la tarde, entreteniendo el resto della a toda la ciudad con sus danzas
y cantares, &. La vltima procession fue del pueblo de San Geronimo, que
esta legua y media del Cuzco, y fue buen remate de todas las passadas
por la. mucha gente principal que trahia de Ingas con las insignias de
aguilas y coronas del Inga, venian representado la uictoria que sus passados
alcanzaron siendo pocos de los chancas que eran veintemil aplicando el
canto de la uictoria al Beato Ignacio. Esto es lo tocante a las fiestas
espirituales, dexando las muchas confessiones y comuniones que en ellas
vuo, por uenir a las que los Indios hizieron en la plaza de la Compañia.

Fueron estas fiestas tales que no se sabra hazer relacion de modo que
se forme el deuido concepto dellas, por no hauerse hecho otras semejantes
en el Cuzco. El dia de la Ascension por la tarde asistiendo a este regozijo
el Corregidor y caualleros de la ciudad, y mas de diez mil almas entre
Españoles e indios que en la plaza auia, entro por ello vn lucido alarde
de los officiales indios que llaman yanaconas, en numero de mas de mil
bien aderezados y vestidos, en hileras de quatro en quatro con su capitan
alferez y sargento, y con muchas cadenas de oro, perlas, bordados y
pedreria, con diuersos generos de armas, dauan su rociadas a trechos,
dieron buelta a la plaza, en la qual se hizo vn esquadron, uiose un indio
muy costosamente uestido con vna pica arbolada en el extremo della un
estandarte con las armas de España, y tocandose las caxas hizieron vna
escaramuza que dio grandissimo gusto por no esperarse tanto orden de
gente en cosa que no auian exercitado; siguiendose a esto vnos alcanciazos
a manera de juego de cañas que dio mucho que uer y entretuuo toda la
tarde junto con la musica de chirimias, &.

Las fiestas que el Domingo siguiente despues de la Ascension se hizieron se auentajaron a estas, salieron en primer lugar quatrocientos indios Cañares (que como se dixo arriba era la guarda del Inga) muy bien aderezados en forma de esquadron con sus capitanes, muy vizarros, con turbantes, chipanas, ajorcas de plata, canipos tambien de plata, que son a figura de luna con las armas que ellos vsauan, y las que nosotros vsamos, espadas; picas, arcabuzes, &, hizieron su entrada con grande aparato de guerra, como los passados que diximos, entraron tras ellos otros dozientos indios tambien Cañares, a los Canas de Ancocana vestidos a su trage antiguo con ondas en las manos, haziendo demostracion de que tirauan con ellas, turbantes adornados con hilos de plata, y canipos, resplandores o rayos de oro, llamados purapura, que es encomienda o diuisa de nobleza que solía dar el Inga por seruicios de la guerra, dieron estos tambien buelta por la plaza, representauan estos dos campos las batallas que antiguamente tuvieron entre si los Cañares a los Canas, comenzaron la Batalla, que duro buen rato, tocando los instrumentos belicos y al fin uenzidos los canas, fueron presos y traydos al Corregidor cantando uictora, y porque reducidos los Canas a la corona del Inga le ayudaron en sus conquistas ualerosamente sacaron este dia las insignias que se ha dicho se dauan a los soldados ualerosos.

Siguiose a esta otra fiesta que dio mas gusto a los Españoles por auerse introducido en ella onze Ingas deste Reyno; y ser toda la demostracion que se podia hazer de regozijo, Reyes del Peru Ingas fueron Onze. 1 Topacinchiroca, 2 Mangocapac, 3 Capaclloquiupangui, 4 Ingarocac, 5 Maitacapac, 6 Apusitinca, 7 Yarariuacal, 8 Biracochainca, 9 Pachacuti, 10 Topainca, 11 Vainacapac salieron representando estos Reyes los mas cercanos de su descendientes, uenían en su literas, las mas cubiertas de plumas de diuersas colores, y las lleuauan en hombros de Indios yuan assentados con mucho magestad (que fue lo que mas se advirtio en este acto) y al passar hazian su cortesia al Corregidor y demas caualleros inclinando solo algun tanto la cabeza, a que respondian el Corregidor y demas caualleros quitando las gorras que parecio muy bien, uenian vestidos al trage inca de cumbis, ricos, que es su brocado dellos, con cetros reales en las manos, y vn principal al lado con vn quitasol de pluma, lleuaua cada uno sus insignias reales gente de guarda lucida, y uestida a su trage, y estos eran los descendientes de aquel Rey, yuan entre la infanteria (que seria de mas de mil indios) dando la buelta a la plaza; y por capitan de todos Don Alonso Topoatauchi tio de Melchor Inca, que agora esta en la corte, y fue el que se auentajo en yr mas galan u uizarro, yua muy acompañado y lleuaua a su lado quatro capitanes, y los Ingas dichos uenian en sus tronos a trechos y por su orden, siendo el vltimo el primero Rey Inca que vuo en este Reyno, y el primero del Cuzco el Inca Vaynacapac a quien alcanzaron los primeros conquistadores, seria alargar mucho esta relacion si se vuiessen de poner en particular las insignias y diuisas conforme a las conquistas y proezas de cada Rey, pero con todo esso el primero lleuaua por adorno de su gente de guarda, vnos mazos de plumages redondos que ellos nombran purupuru representando al globo del mundo, y que este primero Inca lo auia conquistado, y a este modo yuan los demas Reyes con sus blasones harto arrogantes. Iunta toda esta infanteria en mitad de la plaza comenzaron a ganar vn castillo que estaua en ella cercado de vna laguna llamada Yahuarcocha, esto es laguna de sangre en memoria de la gran mortandad que el Inca Vaynacapac hizo en la conquista de los Cañares de Quito, que fue tal que se lleno de sangre vna laguna ya por los muertos, ya por haber lauado las armas en ellas los soldados del Inca, que fueron cinquenta mil, y se detuuieron en salir desta ciudad saliendo cada dia tres compañias tres meses, uencieron el castillo, traxeron a los castellanos pressos al Corregidor, y algunos con cadenas de oro en lugar de hierros, salieron con orden de la plaza, y assi se acabo este dia la fiesta, y antes de uenir a la vltima en que se dio fin a estos regozijos, es bien dezir que el que en gran parte los solicito a pedimiento de los indios fue el juez de los naturales, que es vn cauallero uezino encomendero del Cusco, que mostro su grande affecto a las cosas del Sancto y su Religion, y se hallo en todas las fiestas tan galan cauallero que pudiera parecer en la corte, mudando galas mochilas y cauallos cada dia, y saco dos jaezes de chaperia de plata costossisimos, y uistosos.

El Miercoles siguiente fue el vltimo de las fiestas, y celebraronle los Indios de San Geronymo, hallaronse en la plaza ueinte mil almas, y las uentanas con grande adorno, y en ellas las señoras del lugar, y muchos caualleros en la plaza, el corregidor con su cabildo en la puerta de la Compañia. Estaua en vn cerrillo que esta a vn lado de la plaza vn bosque, y en el vna gran sierpe llamada Llactayoc, que fue en siglos passados dañossisima a los Ingas, porque mato muchos dellos en la conquista de los Andes, a otro lado de la plaza se hizo vn castillo para lo que despues se dira, entraron a las dos de la tarde estos Ingas de San Geronymo en esquadron formado con sus caxas, clarines, y otros instrumentos ricamente vestidos, y con muchas armas, trahian por capitan estos que eran quatrocientos soldados al cacique principal del dicho pueblo lleuaua en la rodela vn leon por diuisa con otras que hazian alusion a las armas de sus passados, delante del qual yua vn principal con su honda, diziendo en voz alta, aqui vienen los señores Ingas de tal parte a mostrar su grandeza: yua tambien casi en aquel paraje otro soldado que lleuaua vn yelmo, con que el Inga Rey entraua en las batallas, y por sucession le heredauan sus descendientes uenia por alferez la segunda persona del cacique principal uestido de seda de colores, y en los hombros dos leones de plata, y en el calzado otros dos, venian en la retaguarda dos Incas Reyes, de donde estos descendian con la Magestad que se dixo de los de arriba particularizandose estos en dos collares ricos, y por orla el vno mucho numero de dientes que por memoria auia quitado a los capitanes de aquellas naciones que sus passados auian conquistado, y el otro varios dientes de leones, ossos, tigres, y otros animales fieros que tambien sus antepasados auian desquijarado y muerto, siendo en realidad de uerdad los mismos dientes de los indios y fieras venzidos, llegando pues a emparejar con el Correxidor y los demas que estauan con el, el vltimo Inca paró con su acompañamiento, y dixo en breves palabras, aunque con grande afecto, el que el y los suyos tenian al beato padre Ignacio, y a los padres de la Compañia, y como esta fiesta le hazian en reuerencia del Sancto Padre, a quien los Incas en particular eran en obligacion. Acauado el passo, y entrada de los quatrocientos Incas salieron de traves como ciento y cinquenta de los mismos representando la gente belicosa de Chile armados como de punta en blanco de cierta uestidura que parecia corazas llegauales hasta las espinillas, y fue cosa tan peregrina, que admiro, y dio notable contento porque significaba grande fiereza, y salieron vniformes todos, lleuauan vnas grandes mazas en las manos casi del genero que la piel o vestidura hizieron dos campos representando la batalla, el Mapocho Chileno que es hasta adonde llegó el Inca, esto es hasta Santiago de Chile sin poderlos conquistar mas, representada pues la batalla acometieron los vnos a los otros con mucho orden y concierto escaramuzando sin hazerse ventaja en gran tiempo, al fin los Chilenos hizieron demostracion de verse apurados, assi retiraron su escuadron al cerrillo que se dixo, defendiendose valerosamente, y acometiendoles mas se hallaron apurados y obligados a retirarse al castillo, combatiolo el Inga, y rindiolo, y aprendio a los cercados y aprisionolos entregandolos a sus capitanes, que se passeauan con ellos por toda la plaza, quemaronles las casserias del cerrillo, cuyo incendio represento al viuo lo que suele suceder en semejantes ocasiones, duro esta fiesta hasta las quatro, siguieronse vnos toros, muchos caualleros en la plaza, y grandissimos numero de Indios que como era la fiesta suya se quisieron mostrar mas animosos en hazer lances de que escaparon sin daño. Entre algunas cosas que passaron de gusto es digna de saber vna, que fue auerse atreuido vn Indio a dar vna lanzada, salio a la gineta bien vestido pusose en sitio comodo con gran denuedo y admiracion, no le acometio el toro, retirole el juez de los naturales pareciendole que hauia hecho harto, mas despues incitado con la braueza de vn toro que salio y hizo lanzes en algunos, torno a salir el a hazerle en el toro, aguardole sin turbarse, acometiole, dio su lanzada, y metiole dos varas de lanza en el cuerpo, donde se quebro, el toro auia entrado muy apriessa, y assi matto al cauallo, y echo al cauallero en tierra, acudieronle los Españoles a tiempo, y acauaron de matar el toro, tomo otro cauallo el Indio y passeo la plaza, recibiendo mil parabienes que se le dauan con gusto, por auer sido este hecho raro y vnico en esta gente, con lo cual se acauaron las fiestas auiendo durado veinte y cinco días, que se quentan desde dos de Mayo, hasta veinte y seis del confirmandose con ellas, la deuocion al bienauenturado padre Ignacio, al qual trato la ciudad tomar por abogado del tabardillo que en aquella ciudad es muy grande, y con voto se obligo el Cabildo caualleros y todos los Indios de acudir cada año a su casa y celebrar su fiesta con la solenidad possible, y su deuocion es tanta que con auer sido estas fiestas tan complicadas, les

parece auer quedado cortos en celebrar al patron de Religion que tanto
bien haze a la republica, los padres de la Compañía reconocidos a lo que
se auia hecho dieron las gracias al Corregidor, como al principal autor de
todo esto, y al Cauildo y otros caualleros.

## Procession de Nuestra Señora de Loreto, 1692 [2]

*Testimonio*: Yo Joseph Gomez de Lequena scrivano del Rey Nuestro Señor
vezino y natural que soi de esta gran ciudad del Cuzco caveza de estos
reinos y provincias del peru = doy fe y verdadero testimonio como ...
[*unclear*] ... dia viernes veinte y dos ... [*unclear*] ... de este presente mes
de Agosto y año corriente de mill y seiscientos y nobenta y dos estando
en la Plaza maior de las de esta Ciudad como aora de las quatro de la
tarde vi a Don Juan Sicos Inga alcalde maior q fue de los Ingas nobles de
las ocho Parroquias de esta Ciudad que con ocacion de celebrarse la fiesta
y procesion que esta en costumbre en la Capilla de Nuestra Señora de
Loreto en cada año cuia cofradia esta fundada en dha Capilla, pegada a
la Yglesia de la Compañia de Jhs. sacar el Gion de Nuestra Señora de
Loreto el qual fue por delante de las andas de la dha Ymagen por el ledor
de la dha procesion por toda la plaza maior puesta en su caveza la
Mascapaicha de la borla colorada, la qual estava, bien aderesada de muchas
perlerias y joias muy preciosas. Y el cuerpo de dho Dn Juan Sicos Inga
con dos cadenas de oro al pareser, el uno colgado al cuello y el otro
atravesado al ombro derecho muy adornado y su espada y daga a la sinta
y todo el traje de español de gala muy lucida y costosa. Y a sus lados Dn
Juan Niño Casimiro de Guzman vezino y Jues de naturales de esta ciudad
y Dn Geronimo de Alegria y Carvajal Protector de los naturales de ella
que le llevavan en medio acompañandole, y onrrandole como a tal Inga
noble principal y por delante muchos Ingas Principales conocidos de las
ocho Parroquias de esta Ciudad q asimismo le honrraron y por delante
de estos dhos Ingas Principales, fue un Yndio chuncho vestido al uso
antiguo llevando en el hombro un papagaio grande Rl y mas adelante
fueron tres yndios asimismo vestidos de traje antiguo y en sus cavezas con
unas ynsignias que llaman Mamaypacras y el de en medio llevava en un
palo grande delgado y plateado un lienso pintado a dos ases, que en el
uno estava pintado un Inga en su traje antiguo con su mascapaicha de la
borla colorada y su chambi, y valcanca en la mano ysquierda, y en la
derecha un baso de oro al pareser que ofrecia al sol que estava pintado
en dho lienso y al pie de dho Inga unos cinco carneros de la tierra los dos
colorados y los otros dos amarillos y el uno color sani = y a la buelta
estava pintado un arco de verde amarillo y colorado y en medio una corona

---

2 Source: Archivo Departamental del Cuzco, Intendencia: Real Hacienda, Leg. 171,
'Instancia que han hecho Don Buenabentura Sicos: su hijos y otros descendien. de este
Linage para que se les excima de la contribucion de su tasa', Cuzco, 26 de enero de 1786.

de oro dorado del Rey Nuestro Señor y mas abajo la ynsignia de la mascapaicha que le detienen dos papagaios Rs y mas abajo una lista pintada de tocapos yacnopos y al ultimo un letrero en que decia armas de los desendientes del Gran Tocay Capac Inga Rey Señor natural que fue de estos reinos del peru = y a los lados de este los dhos dos yndios llevaron dos llacachuquis en otros dos palos guarnecidos de Plata con plumajes de diferentes colores bien adornados a la usanza antigua, que es la ynsignia que en semejantes actos publicos sacan los que son alfereses Rs el dia del glorioso Apostol Santiago en cada año = y asimismo doi fee que en el lienso de ariva mencionado estavan dos cavezas colgadas hechas a mano el uno de chanca que llaman, y el otro de chuncho ambas ensangrentadas que se significa las cavezas de los traidores que fueron en tiempo de la Gentilidad lo qual a sido publico y notorio en toda esta Ciudad a que en todo me refiero y para que de ello conste de pedimiento de Don Diego Sicos Ynga padre lexitimo de Don Juan Sicos Inga doi el presente en la dha Ciudad del Cuzco en el dho dia veinte y dos de Agosto de mill y seiscientos y nobenta y dos años siendo testigos el Br. Alonso de Espinosa y el Lizdo. Dn. Manuel Mogrovejo de la Cerda clerigos presviteros y el Padre Domingo Gonzales perfecto de la Compañia de Jhs de esta Ciudad y Don Juan Bautista Palomino de Villavisencio asimismo clerigo presbitero y el Rdo Pe. Geronimo de Herrera Viserector del Colegio de la dha Compañia de Jhs y el Padre Domingo de Torres perfecto de la Congregacion de San Phelipe Neri y sacristan maior de la Santa Yglesia Cathedral de esta Ciudad y otras muchas personas que concurrieron a la dha procesion presentes = y en fee de ello fize mi signo en testimonio de verdad = Joseph de Requena scrivano de su Magestad.

# Index

Note: page numbers in **bold** refer to main entries